HOW TO REGULATE

Markets sometimes fail. But so do regulatory efforts to correct market failures. Sometimes regulations reach too far, condemning good activities as well as bad. Sometimes they do not reach far enough, allowing bad behavior to persist. In this highly instructive book, Thomas Lambert explains the pitfalls of both extremes and offers readers a manual of effective regulation, showing how the best regulation maximizes social welfare and minimizes social costs. Working like a physician, Lambert demonstrates how regulators should diagnose the underlying disease and identify its symptoms, potential remedies for it, and their side effects before selecting the regulation that offers the greatest net benefit. This book should be read by policymakers, students, and anyone else interested in understanding how the best regulations are crafted and why they work.

Thomas A. Lambert holds the Wall Family Chair in Corporate Law and Governance at the University of Missouri Law School. He is the author of more than twenty legal articles, mostly focused on regulation, and is co-author of a leading antitrust casebook.

How to Regulate

A GUIDE FOR POLICYMAKERS

THOMAS A. LAMBERT
University of Missouri Law School

CAMBRIDGE
UNIVERSITY PRESS

CAMBRIDGE
UNIVERSITY PRESS

University Printing House, Cambridge CB2 8BS, United Kingdom

One Liberty Plaza, 20th Floor, New York, NY 10006, USA

477 Williamstown Road, Port Melbourne, VIC 3207, Australia

4843/24, 2nd Floor, Ansari Road, Daryaganj, Delhi – 110002, India

79 Anson Road, #06–04/06, Singapore 079906

Cambridge University Press is part of the University of Cambridge.

It furthers the University's mission by disseminating knowledge in the pursuit of education, learning, and research at the highest international levels of excellence.

www.cambridge.org
Information on this title: www.cambridge.org/9781107144880
DOI: 10.1017/9781316534885

First published 2017

Printed in the United States of America by Sheridan Books, Inc.

A catalogue record for this publication is available from the British Library.

Library of Congress Cataloging-in-Publication Data
NAMES: Lambert, Thomas A. (Law teacher), author.
TITLE: How to regulate : a guide for policymakers / Thomas A. Lambert
(Wall Family Chair in Corporate Law and Governance, University of Missouri Law School).
DESCRIPTION: New York, NY : Cambridge University Press, 2017. | Includes bibliographical references.
IDENTIFIERS: LCCN 2017026026 | ISBN 9781107144880
SUBJECTS: LCSH: Administrative regulation drafting.
CLASSIFICATION: LCC K3403 .L36 2017 | DDC 342/.066–dc23
LC record available at https://lccn.loc.gov/2017026026

ISBN 978-1-107-14488-0 Hardback
ISBN 978-1-316-50800-8 Paperback

For Bob and Footy Lambert, who taught me to optimize.

Contents

Preface

It seems a bad marketing strategy to give one's book a title that suggests a limited audience. For that reason, I have some trepidation about this book's subtitle: *A Guide for Policymakers*. Isn't that a pretty small group? Sure, it includes legislators, regulators, advisers to government officials, analysts at think tanks – maybe even lobbyists. But who else?

As it turns out, the class of people who are policymakers is enormous. Many people are policymakers and don't even know it. As used in this book's subtitle, the term "policymaker" refers to anyone who helps shape government "policy" – that is, the principles that guide government action. The people mentioned above are certainly policymakers, but so are plenty of other folks.

If you work for any branch of any level of government, you have occasional opportunities to influence your employer's position on various matters. When you take them, you are shaping policy. You are a policymaker.

If you are a lawyer or law student, you will likely at some point seek to persuade a court or government agency to make some decision or take some action as the government. When you do that, you are shaping policy.

If you are a teacher of any course that ever examines the propriety of government action, you are in a position to influence your students' thinking on what government should and should not do. When you shape the views of students who, in the future, will exercise government authority or seek to influence government action, you are a policymaker. The same goes for students who are taking courses in which the appropriateness of some government position or conduct is a topic of discussion. When your comments influence the views of classmates who will affect future government stances, you are shaping policy.

If you're out of school but continue to discuss and debate the merits of government decisions with your friends and family, you affect what others think about how government should and should not act. Some of those people will likely, at some point, make choices that influence government action. When you say things that shape their thinking, and thus their decisions, you are helping to make policy.

If you are an utter loner who has no job and never speaks to anyone, *but you vote*, you help to select the people whose views will determine the course of government conduct. Your voting shapes policy.

So, the class of people for whom this guide on how to regulate is written – policymakers – doesn't consist merely of legislators, regulators, government advisers, lobbyists, and think-tank wonks. If you're one of those folks *or if* you're a government employee, a lawyer or law student, a teacher or student of any course examining government action, a person who likes to discuss government decisions, or a voter, then this book is for you. Its goal is to help you think more clearly about one particular set of government decisions: those involving regulation (which we'll soon define). I hope, and I believe, that the book will enable you to make persuasive arguments in favor of better regulatory decisions that produce greater human welfare.

Before we begin, allow me a brief word on the motivation for the book, its structure, and the nature of the contribution it makes. For the past fourteen years, I have taught law at a major state university. Over the years, I've been surprised at the number of my students who have become legislators or who have very quickly risen to high-level positions in regulatory agencies. When I run into a former student who tells me he or she now holds one of these positions of power, my first thought (unspoken, of course) is, "Did we teach you how to make the decisions you now have to make?" I am not confident about the answer to that question. One motivation for this book, then, is that there are lots of people who really need to know how to regulate and probably aren't getting that training in their formal education.

Another thing that has surprised me as a law teacher is the large number of my students who want to know more about regulatory theory. I begin each of my courses with an extended consideration of whatever problem the body of law we're studying is seeking to address. In antitrust, we examine market power. In business organizations, agency costs. In environmental law, externalities. Soon after we've finished that discussion, I usually get a few emails or after-class questions asking "What should I read to learn more about that?" I've always recommended excellent books and articles – there are many – on each of the distinct subject areas. But I've never been able to suggest a single source that, in a readable fashion, covers all the major bases for regulating (at least, for purposes of enhancing social welfare) and locates everything within a unified theory of regulation. That is what this book aims to provide.

As you will see, the bulk of this nine-chapter book – Chapters 4 through 9 – addresses the classic market failures (externalities, public goods, market power, and information asymmetry), a problem that is closely related to a couple of those market failures (agency costs), and a prominent non-market failure-based justification for regulation (the cognitive and volitional limitations observed by behavioral economists). Before getting into all that, three short chapters define regulation (at least, for purposes of the book) and set forth a general model for how to regulate. Those first three chapters should probably be read in order and at the outset, but one could easily pick and choose among Chapters 4 through 9, each of which follows a common format and generally stands on its own. Although the book is not intended to be a reference book, readers could use it as such.

The major contribution this book makes is to bring together insights of legal theorists and economists of various stripes – neoclassical, Austrian, public choice, behavioral – and systematize their ideas into a unified, practical approach to regulating. While the ideas are put together in a novel and, I believe, useful fashion, I break little new ground in legal theory or economics. At times during the drafting, I have wondered whether this book is "original" enough. And in those times, I have taken comfort in the words of C.S. Lewis, whose *Mere Christianity* systematized the ideas of scores of philosophers and theologians, spoke plainly, and became a classic. On the closing page of that book, Lewis writes,

> Even in literature and art, no man who bothers about originality will ever be original: whereas if you simply try to tell the truth (without caring twopence how often it has been told before) you will, nine times out of ten, become original without ever having noticed it.[1]

That is what I have endeavored to do here.

Many people contributed to this book, either by helping to hone the ideas presented, providing feedback on drafts, or assisting with research. As a teacher myself, I must at the outset thank two outstanding professors who started me down the path that led to this book. At Wheaton College, P.J. Hill altered the course of my life by introducing me to "the economic way of thinking." Cass Sunstein, then at the University of Chicago Law School, taught me how to think about law and inspired in me a love for regulation (the study of it, at least).

Joshua Wright and Geoffrey Manne contributed far more than they likely know. Collaborating with Josh and Geoff through the years has helped me

---

[1] C.S. Lewis, *Mere Christianity* (New York: Macmillan Publishing Co., 1960), 190.

grasp the power of this book's organizing principle – i.e., that regulation of "mixed bag" behavior should minimize the sum of error and decision costs.

Numerous other friends and colleagues provided helpful feedback on the project. Among them are Jonathan Adler, Martha Dragich, Virginia Harper Ho, Todd Henderson, John Howe, Peter Kingma, Paul Litton, Uma Outka, Ajit Pai, Jordan Pandolfo, Michael Sykuta, and Stephen Ware. Alex Thrasher provided excellent research assistance, and Chuck and Nancy Wall have consistently offered support and encouragement. I am most grateful.

1

Defining Our Subject

Regulation is a hot topic of conversation these days. The financial crisis of the last decade and the subsequent economic downturn have sparked all sorts of categorical statements on "regulation" generally. Progressives often blame the financial crisis on a lack of regulation; conservatives complain that excessive regulation has held back the economic recovery. All this talk suggests that one must be either "pro" or "anti" regulation.

Regulation, though, is no monolith. Some regulations are good. Some are bad. Governments overregulate in some areas, underregulate in others, and many times "misregulate" by imposing rules that do not really fit the problems they are ostensibly aimed at correcting. Surely we can do better.

Part of the problem is that the two groups most involved in crafting the substance of regulations – lawyers and economists – have blind spots. Lawyers, who typically write the rules governing private conduct, receive precious little training in policy analysis. Most lawyers study administrative law, the body of law governing the administrative agencies that set forth most complex regulations. But administrative law courses tend to focus almost exclusively on the process of regulating, not the substance of the rules being adopted. Accordingly, the lawyers tasked with writing rules are often in a poor position to assess the substantive merits of the rules they are writing and to consider alternative regulatory approaches.

Economists, who are trained in policy analysis, often augment the work of the lawyers drafting the rules. They regularly provide testimony and analysis to legislatures and regulatory bodies, and interest groups lobbying for or against rules frequently enlist them to provide intellectual support for a favored policy position. Academic economists, though, tend to have little exposure to regulatory, enforcement, and litigation processes. They do not have a good sense of how their textbook models may become corrupted in the regulatory process or for how imperfect (over- or under-) enforcement of a rule may occur, thwarting the rule's effectiveness.

1

This book aims to improve regulatory performance by providing some relevant economic education to the lawyers (and law students) who write (or will write) rules, and an understanding of the "limits of law" to the economists and other policy wonks who advise on the substance of regulations. Of course, anyone with an interest in regulation – and, given the prominent role regulation plays in all our lives, that should be a great many people – may benefit from the ideas set forth herein.

At the outset, we need to define our subject. It's easy to tick off examples of regulations – emission limits for coal-fired power plants, registration requirements for companies selling stock to the public, workplace safety rules – but what exactly *is* regulation? We know that it involves some sort of rule or order coupled with an "or else" – a sanction for noncompliance. But that is too broad a definition. We're constantly being subjected to threat-backed commands in contexts that don't seem to involve "regulation." Examples of a directive plus a threat of sanction for noncompliance would include:

1) your spouse telling you to pick up your dirty laundry or else he won't make the morning coffee;
2) your boss telling you to finish a report by Monday or else you'll get a bad review that will reduce your bonus;
3) your favorite ski mountain telling you not to ski too fast or else you'll lose your lift ticket;
4) the Securities and Exchange Commission (SEC) telling you not to share your spouse's confidential work information with your stock broker or else you'll be penalized for insider trading;
5) your state legislature telling you to buckle your seatbelt when driving or else you'll have to pay a ticket;
6) the Internal Revenue Service (IRS) telling you to pay your federal taxes or else you'll face fines and eventually jail time;
7) a court in your state telling you not to operate a smelly pig farm on your property or else you'll have to pay damages to your neighbors;
8) a federal court telling you not to agree with your business rivals on the prices you will charge for your products or else you'll have to pay three times the amount of the overcharge.

Each of these eight directives sets forth a behavioral norm and is backed by a threat of sanctions, but they don't all comport with our intuitive understanding of regulation. The first three, in particular, don't seem regulation-like. For one thing, they're not imposed upon you without your consent. You assent to be in a spousal relationship with certain norms of reciprocity, to obey your boss's orders in exchange for a paycheck, and to follow the rules of a ski resort in exchange for the right to ride its lifts and ski down its slopes. Regulation, by contrast, tends to be imposed from the "top down," even absent the assent of the regulated. We might therefore think that imposition *regardless of assent* is an essential aspect of regulation.

But what about government-imposed rules governing professionals? Physicians, for example, choose to become doctors knowing that their right to practice medicine is conditioned on their compliance with certain state-imposed rules. They have in some sense "assented" to be governed by those rules and to suffer punishment for noncompliance, just as you assent to refrain from reckless skiing (and to suffer a punishment for noncompliance) when you purchase a lift ticket at your favorite ski mountain. Yet our intuitions, as well as common parlance, tell us that physicians are "regulated." An absence of assent, then, does not seem to be part of the essence of regulation.

Examples 1–3 above also share another feature: Your failure to comply with the directive cannot legitimately result in your being physically locked up. While your noncompliance may cause you to lose your morning coffee, annual bonus, or skiing privileges, the command-giver could not legitimately confine you because of your noncompliance with the directive or the assented-to penalty.[1] By contrast, you may legitimately be thrown in jail for insider trading (4); for repeated refusal to pay driving citations, taxes, or nuisance damages (5–7); or for price-fixing (8). This is because directives 4–8, unlike directives 1–3, are government imposed rules, and the government is the only institution in society that may legitimately use physical coercion to enforce its directives. It possesses, as Max Weber famously put it, "a monopoly of the legitimate use of physical force within a given territory."[2] Our intuitions tell us, then, that for a directive to count as regulation, it must be government-imposed – i.e., it must ultimately be backed by a threat of legitimate physical force if the one being regulated flat-out refuses to comply.

The fact that force is a legitimate penalty for noncompliance is not sufficient, however, to turn a directive into a regulation – at least as defined for purposes of this book. Every governmental directive involves an explicit or implicit threat of legitimate physical coercion for noncompliance, but not

---

[1] With respect to example 3, one might respond that a speeding skier who loses his lift ticket and refuses to leave the ski area may legitimately be confined. But that is because remaining on the property after having been legitimately ordered to leave is itself a tort – trespass – not unlike the tort in example 6 (nuisance). It is failure to comply with a state-imposed tort duty that would create the right to confine the violator.

[2] Max Weber, *Politics as a Vocation*, in *From Max Weber: Essays in Sociology* 77, (eds. & trans. H. H. Gerth and C. Wright Mills, New York: Oxford University Press, 1958), 78.

every law or governmental command is a "regulation." To segregate those that qualify as regulations, we could focus on the source of the directive. Expert agencies such as the SEC, Environmental Protection Agency (EPA), and Federal Communications Commission (FCC) promulgate many regulations, so we might think that a regulation must come from an expert agency with an acronym. That would cover example 4 (the SEC's command not to misappropriate your spouse's confidential information in connection with a stock trade), but it would not cover example 5 (a state legislature's command to buckle your seatbelt when driving). Surely, though, the legislature is "regulating" citizens' driving behavior when it mandates seatbelt usage. It seems, then, that a regulation need not arise from within the alphabet soup of administrative agencies; some legislative directives should count.

Some, but not all. Legislatures pass laws to cover all sorts of matters. They may seek to police the conduct of individuals or businesses, to redistribute wealth from rich to poor or from disfavored to favored groups, to raise money for public goals (defense, a social safety net, etc.), to express official support or condemnation for a cause or behavior, or to accomplish some combination of these or other ends. Legislation need not be regulatory in nature.

A workable definition of regulation would be any threat-backed governmental directive aimed at fixing a defect in "private ordering" – the world that would exist if people did their own thing without government intervention beyond enforcing common law rights to person, property, and contract[3] – where the defect causes total social welfare (i.e., the aggregate welfare of all citizens) to be lower than it otherwise would be. Such a definition would count as regulation of the seatbelt mandate in example 5, but would exclude statutes aimed solely at raising revenue for the government (example 6), redistributing wealth, or expressing official favor or disfavor. It would include some judicial directives, such as the court ruling not to engage in naked price-fixing (example 8), but it would deem the traditional common law of torts, property, and contracts to be part of the scheme of private ordering and would therefore exclude judicial directives, such as example 7, that simply state the long-recognized background rules on rights to person, property, and contract.

---

[3] These "common law" rights are those that do not arise from statute, an express vote of a legislature, but have instead arisen as judges throughout the centuries have decided discrete disputes among individuals and have created a body of precedent that sets forth rights and duties. The common law rights that appear in the law of torts, property, and contract are so well established that they may well be deemed part of the private order. Indeed, many of the rights first appeared when judges were not public officials but were instead acting as private "law merchants" whom individuals would engage to settle disputes.

It is important to note a couple of things about this definition of regulation. Observe first that the precise source of a governmental directive is not determinative of whether it is a regulation. Regulation can come from any branch of the government – executive, legislative, or judicial (or, of course, from an independent administrative agency, such as the SEC, that may not fit cleanly within any of the branches).

Second, note that only those threat-backed governmental directives that are aimed *solely* at raising revenue, redistributing wealth, or some other objective besides correcting welfare-reducing defects in private ordering are excluded from the definition of regulation. Many governmental directives raise revenue, redistribute wealth, or express legislators' views *but also* seek to mitigate a wealth-reducing defect in private ordering (a "market failure"). A gasoline tax, for example, might raise revenue *and* attempt to correct for negative externalities – carbon emissions – associated with gasoline consumption. (As we'll see, such externalities may reduce overall social welfare, and are properly deemed defects in private ordering.) Similarly, a penalty for failure to carry health insurance may be aimed at raising revenue, redistributing wealth from the young and healthy to the older and sicker, *and* preventing adverse selection, a result of the market failure we'll consider in Chapter 8. Given that correction of a market failure is one – though not the only – apparent aim of both the gasoline tax and the penalty for failure to carry health insurance, laws or rules imposing such taxes or penalties would be considered regulation for purposes of this book. Most aspects of the basic federal income tax, by contrast, have only revenue-raising and redistribution aims and therefore would not be considered regulation.

One may wonder why the redistribution of wealth is not included as a "regulatory" objective. After all, an inequitable distribution of wealth might be deemed a defect in private ordering, the sort of thing regulation seeks to fix. Why limit regulation (for purposes of this book) to efforts to correct those private ordering defects that reduce overall social welfare?

There are several reasons for drawing the line like this. As an initial matter, observe that doing so in no way impugns redistributive efforts. To say that governmental directives aimed solely at redistribution are not regulatory is not to say that they are illegitimate or even ill-advised. This book takes no position on the propriety of redistributive governmental commands; it just wouldn't label them "regulation."

Limiting regulation to threat-backed governmental directives aimed at correcting private ordering defects *that reduce overall welfare* offers several practical benefits. For one thing, it helps maximize this book's appeal by focusing on the policy objective that commands the greatest overall support. Most people agree that private ordering defects that make society poorer are generally bad and should be remedied if the cost of correction is less than the wealth saved. There is much less consensus on governmental efforts to pursue equality of end-states among citizens. Allowing creative and productive individuals to accumulate wealth creates a socially desirable incentive to be productive and creative, and, for that reason, many people think government should limit its redistributive efforts. Defining regulation as this book does allows us to focus on how the government should pursue a goal that nearly all people believe it should seek. Doing so also makes our inquiry – how to regulate? – much more manageable. If we deem equality of end-states a regulatory objective, then we must answer a nearly intractable question: How should policymakers trade-off an increase in equality against a decrease in overall social welfare? Limiting our inquiry to how to regulate *so as to maximize social welfare* saves us from having to compare incommensurable values (efficiency and equity). Finally, there is great benefit in knowing how to regulate to maximize welfare *even if* one chooses to pursue another objective. Policymakers who decide to implement a policy that furthers end-state equality at the expense of social welfare should at least have a sense of what they are sacrificing. They must decide whether it is better to command specific behaviors aimed at equalizing end-states or to regulate to maximize social welfare and then just engage in direct redistribution. This book could assist them with that inquiry.[4]

Once we define regulation as threat-backed governmental directives aimed at correcting private ordering defects that diminish total social welfare, four questions naturally arise. Three are obvious: (1) What are the well-recognized defects in private ordering?; (2) How do they diminish social welfare?; and (3) What tools are available for correcting them? The fourth arises as soon as one realizes that corrective efforts, like medical treatments, often have "side effects" that may overwhelm their benefits. Given that fact, we should ask (4) How might our corrective tools themselves decrease social welfare?

The bulk of this book focuses on these four questions. We will consider six conditions that may cause problems for private ordering, and we will examine how each may generate welfare-reducing outcomes. We will also catalogue the major tools available for addressing the various conditions and the potential maladies those tools may occasion.

Before we get to all that, though, we will set up an overarching model through which we may process our learning about private ordering defects, the social harms they cause, the available corrective tools, and their possible side effects.

---

[4] The book's conclusion revisits the trade-off between maximizing social welfare and achieving a more equal distribution of wealth. Readers who are put off by the efficiency focus announced here might wish to give the book's last few pages a quick read.

2

The Overarching Model

Virtually every harm-causing human action creates some benefit for someone – usually the actor, at least. Some types of conduct, though, always or
nearly always create more harm than benefit. Take, for example, battery – the
intentional, offensive touching of another's body. Even if the batterer derives
some perverse pleasure from punching his victim, we can confidently assume
that his action causes a net harm because any fleeting pleasure the batterer
experiences is likely to be outweighed by the physical and emotional pain
experienced by the victim, her loved ones, and other potential victims whose
anxiety increases with the prevalence of battery. This is not to say that the net
harm occasioned by an instance of battery is what makes battery wrong; ethical
theorists have long disputed whether and to what degree the morality of an
action turns on its consequences, and we need not address that matter here.
We need only recognize that some actions always or almost always occasion
net reductions in human welfare. Within that group are intentional torts such
as battery, assault, and false imprisonment, as well as most of the traditional
crimes (murder, rape, larceny, etc.).

Other types of harm-causing human behavior, by contrast, may sometimes
reduce but sometimes enhance net social welfare. Suppose a rancher delays
mending a broken fence in order to upgrade his barn. If there is no rush on
the barn improvements, they are of relatively low value, and the likelihood
that escaped cattle will cause extensive damage to a neighbor is great, then
the rancher's delay is probably a net "bad." By contrast, if an immediate barn
improvement is necessary for the rancher to secure an otherwise unobtain-
able benefit, and if the likely harm to the neighbor from delayed fence-
mending is minor because a cattle escape is improbable or the neighbor's
property is of low value, then the rancher's conduct likely results in a net
"good." Similarly, a singer who disappoints you by breaking her promise to
sing at your wedding seems to have acted badly, but if the singer reneged

because she recently became a YouTube sensation and has been asked to perform at the Super Bowl halftime show, her promise-breaking likely enhances net social welfare.

The common law – the body of precedent that has emerged as judges over time have decided discrete cases – has long afforded different treatment to "always-bad" conduct such as battery and "mixed-bag" conduct such as negligence and promise-breaking. Because we need not worry about overdeterring always-bad conduct, the punishments for crimes are often, though certainly not always, more severe than the harms suffered by the victims. Similarly, courts frequently award punitive damages – money damages in excess of the monetary value of the victim's loss – for intentional torts such as battery. By contrast, if one causes harm by acting in a manner that is merely negligent (e.g., failure to repair a fence restraining cattle), he will be required to compensate any injured persons for their loss, but he won't have to pay punitive damages. And if a person breaches a contract, she will have to pay the breach victim only an amount that will leave him as well off as he would have been had the broken promise been kept. These rules prevent overdeterrence by preserving a person's incentive to act in a risky manner or to break a contractual promise if the likely benefit of doing so exceeds the cost the mixed-bag action is likely to create.

It is useful to consider the common law's disparate treatment of always-bad versus mixed-bag behavior for two reasons. First, doing so helps us see that most regulation, at least as defined in this book, addresses mixed-bag conduct. At the outset, we defined regulation to include directives aimed at correcting welfare-reducing defects in private ordering, and we stipulated that common law rules protecting persons and property are part of the scheme of private ordering. Since the common law of crimes and torts has long forbidden and imposed punishment for most forms of always-bad behavior, prohibitions on such behavior (including subsequent legislative codifications of common law rules, such as the larceny and rape provisions of state criminal codes) are beyond the ambit of this book. That implies that our focus will be on statutes, rules, and judicial decisions, adopted primarily in the twentieth century and beyond, that govern *mixed-bag* behavior.

A second reason for beginning with the common law's disparate treatment of always-bad versus mixed-bag conduct is that it highlights the central problem this book seeks to address: How should policymakers craft legal directives so as to prevent the bad aspects of mixed-bag behavior without simultaneously forbidding or discouraging the good aspects? Common law courts grappled with that issue in fashioning remedies for wrongs. Always-bad conduct could be punished beyond making the victim whole (because there's little reason to worry about overdeterring such conduct), but for mixed-bag conduct, the defendant was typically required merely to compensate his victim for her loss (so future actors wouldn't be dissuaded from engaging in similar conduct when the harm from doing so, borne by the victim, was less than the benefit received by the actor). Because regulation tends to be explicitly forward-looking and often involves some detailed, prescriptive order rather than just a general obligation to pay if you cause harm, the need to avoid overdeterrence of mixed-bag conduct is particularly great in the regulatory context.

Consider a few examples of conduct subject to regulation:

- Hoping to raise money for her next project, a producer of documentary films sets up a website and sells interests in her next film's proceeds. Investors may read about the proposed project, view some of the documentarian's prior work, and make modest payments for small shares of the film's profits.

- A petroleum exploration company develops a new, seemingly cheap extraction technique. The technique involves shooting high-pressure vapor deep into the earth to dislodge trapped deposits of oil and natural gas. The spent vapor, accompanied by a good bit of subterranean material, is then exhausted from the ground.

- A dominant producer of computer microchips offers a 20 percent discount on all the chips a computer manufacturer buys from it as long as the manufacturer purchases at least 70 percent of its microchip requirements from the producer. The discounted price is above the producer's cost, so it could be matched by an equally efficient microchip producer. But if the "loyalty discount" succeeds in winning too many sales from the discounter's rivals, it might cause their scale of production to fall so much that their average cost per unit rises and they become less formidable competitors.

These examples have several things in common. In each, an adverse outcome is possible: investors could be duped into funneling money into an unsound project; air and groundwater contamination could occur; the market for microchips could become less competitive so that prices rise. Each example also involves (as we will discuss) a classic market failure – information asymmetry, an externality, market power. Given the potential adverse outcomes stemming from market failures (i.e., welfare-reducing defects in private ordering), each example is a prime target for regulation.

More pertinent to the discussion at hand, the three examples also involve the sort of mixed-bag behaviors that present a challenge to policymakers. In each case, failure to restrict the behavior at issue could allow a bad outcome, but imposing restrictions that are too strict could thwart arrangements that are, on net, socially beneficial. If anyone claiming to be a filmmaker (or other creator/entrepreneur) can set up a website and sell shares of future proceeds, all sorts of charlatans are likely to appear. And if that happens, legitimate creators and entrepreneurs may have a harder time raising money for their endeavors. At the same time, if the government were to impose an all-out ban on soliciting investors for projects-in-progress, many worthy projects might not be funded. The key is to select a policy that prevents the bad without thwarting the good.

The same goes for the second and third examples. With respect to the second, if the government were to allow use of the new extractive technology with no restrictions, environmental contamination would surely result. But if the government banned all underground injections aimed at extracting petroleum, the current North American energy boom, largely the result of hydraulic fracturing, would come to a quick end. With respect to the third example, if the microchip producer were given free rein to offer any discounts it wanted, it might squelch existing competition and prevent new competitors from getting established, thereby precluding consumer-friendly competition. But if the government restricts discounting too much, it may deprive consumers of the immediate "bird in the hand" of lower prices, even when the discount at issue doesn't really threaten the "bird in the bush" of market competition.

The point here is a simple but important one: Because regulation restricts mixed-bag behavior, it will always involve trade-offs. The $64,000 question is how policymakers should proceed to ensure that they strike those trade-offs in a manner that creates as much social welfare as possible.

THE ULTIMATE GOAL

The previous discussion showed that regulations may err in two directions. They may prohibit or dissuade conduct that should be allowed or encouraged, or they may fail to condemn activities that should be precluded. Economists refer to the former sort of error – inappropriate condemnation, a false positive – as a "Type I" error. The latter sort of error – inappropriate failure to condemn, a false negative – is a "Type II" error. The social losses from Type I and Type II errors, taken together, are "error costs." (To keep things simple, we'll refer to inappropriate condemnation of good behavior as a "false conviction" and inappropriate failure to condemn bad behavior as a "false acquittal.")

If regulators could anticipate every permutation of behavior, assess in advance its social desirability, and express with precision which instances should be allowed and which forbidden, both false convictions and false acquittals, and thus all error costs, could be avoided. Unfortunately, policy-makers are not omniscient, and language has its limits. It is impossible, as a practical matter, to set forth prospective rules that will proscribe all, but only, "bad" instances of mixed-bag conduct. Errors (and error costs) are inevitable.

The incidence of errors may be reduced, however, by making rules more nuanced. Consider a law school classic: the park sign reading "No vehicles in the park." If interpreted literally, that directive is over-inclusive. It would ban bicycles, fire trucks, and ambulances. An astute regulator might therefore include "(except bicycles and emergency vehicles)." But what about garbage trucks and cement trucks brought in to repair sidewalks? The parenthetical exclusion might be expanded to read "(except bicycles and emergency *or maintenance* vehicles)." But what if the local VFW wants to display a World War II-era tank on Memorial Day? Should the parenthetical read "(except bicycles, emergency or maintenance vehicles, *and tanks*)?"

Nuance isn't free. It's costly for regulators to anticipate and properly express exceptions, and the more complicated they make the rule in an effort to reduce errors, the harder it is for those being regulated – "regulatees," we'll call them – to learn what's allowed and to plan their conduct accordingly. It's also harder for adjudicators to assess whether a violation has occurred. The costs associated with making rules more complex – regulators' costs of drafting the rules, regulatees' costs of interpreting them and making compliant plans, and adjudicators' costs of assessing compliance – are incurred in decid ing whether a particular action will be taken and, if so, condemned. Accordingly, we may refer to them as "decision costs."

False conviction error costs, false acquittal error costs, and decision costs are in inexorable tension. Shrinking the scope of a rule's prohibition to avoid false convictions enhances the risk of false acquittals. Conversely, expanding the prohibition to avoid false acquittals threatens an increase in false convictions. Attempting to minimize both false convictions and false acquittals simulta-neously by adding in exceptions and other nuances raises decision costs.

For a contemporary example of these inevitable trade-offs, consider the so-called Volcker Rule, authorized by Section 619 of the 2010 Dodd–Frank financial reform law.[1] That rule, named for former Federal Reserve Chairman Paul Volcker, who first proposed it, prohibits federally insured

---

[1] Dodd-Frank Wall Street Reform and Consumer Protection Act of 2010, Pub. L. 111–203, 124 Stat. 1376, § 619 (codified at 12 U.S.C. § 851).

banks from making "proprietary trades" – trades in securities or derivatives where the purpose is to enhance the trading bank's profits by benefiting from short-term price changes. The idea is that a stable commercial banking sector is essential to the health of the entire financial system, and banks that have federal backing should not be allowed to engage in risky, speculative trading for no reason other than enhancement of their own profits. Chairman Volcker himself anticipated a short-and-sweet rule. Upon seeing the first draft of the rule, he remarked, "I'd write a much simpler bill. I'd love to see a four-page bill that bans proprietary trading and makes the board and chief executive responsible for compliance. And I'd have strong regulators. If the banks didn't comply with the spirit of the bill, they'd go after them."[2]

Unfortunately, Chairman Volcker's laudable objective proved difficult to translate into an administrable rule that would ban bad instances of proprietary trading without also discouraging good instances. For one thing, the rule needed to provide leeway for banks to engage in legitimate "hedging" transactions – proprietary trades made in order to reduce a specific risk associated with another of the trading bank's financial positions. Too broad a prohibition would make it difficult for banks to manage investment risk, injuring their depositors. Too narrow a prohibition would permit shrewd bankers to engage in the very sort of risky proprietary trading Chairman Volcker sought to prohibit. To avoid over- and under-inclusivity, the drafters of the Volcker Rule opted for nuance. Lots of it. The end result was a 1,077-*page* rule that may minimize error costs but only by raising decision costs substantially.

The point here is not to disparage the Volcker Rule. It is simply to highlight the inexorability of the tension among false conviction error costs, false acquittal error costs, and decision costs. As in a game of whack-a-mole, pushing down costs in one spot causes them to rise somewhere else.

But sometimes costs don't rise *as high* in their new spot as in their old spot. For example, shrinking the scope of a prohibition may increase false acquittal error costs, but by less than it reduces false conviction error costs. Or creating a highly tailored loophole to prevent some inappropriate condemnation without eliminating liability for truly bad acts may enhance a regulation's decision cost, but by less than it reduces the rule's overall error cost. Sometimes, reducing a rule's complexity (loopholes, etc.) will lower decision costs by more than it raises error costs. So while there are always *trade-offs* between false conviction error costs, false acquittal error costs, and decision costs, some rules result in lower total costs than others. That observation suggests a goal to which policymakers should aspire: Craft directives to minimize the sum of

---

[2] See James B. Stewart, Volcker Rule, Once Simple, Now Boggles, N.Y. *Times* (Oct. 21, 2011).

error and decision costs. Doing so will ensure that society gets the most bang for its regulatory buck.

This ultimate goal – minimize the sum of error and decision costs – is really just a form of cost–benefit analysis. It's more sophisticated, though, than the simplistic cost–benefit analysis with which many people are familiar. Under that version, policymakers ask simply whether the benefits of a proposed policy exceed its costs, where those costs are taken to include the out-of-pocket costs of implementation and the losses from thwarting certain beneficial behavior. Suppose, for example, that Policy A, a requirement that widget factories install a new pollution control technology, would cost the factories $50 million out-of-pocket, would eliminate operations that create value of $10 million, and would create benefits (reduction in illness, etc.) worth $70 million. Policy A would seem to create value of $10 million and would be appropriate under a simplistic cost–benefit analysis.

That form of cost–benefit balancing, though, fails to account for a key cost of adopting the policy under consideration. Costs are simply foregone opportunities. If a widget "costs" $10, for example, then one must forego $10 worth of other consumption in order to obtain that widget. A cost of adopting Policy A, then, is the value that could have been obtained from implementing an alternative policy instead.

Suppose Policy B, which would require widget factories to adopt some other pollution control technology, would create benefits of $50 million but impose out-of-pocket compliance costs of only $20 million and losses from thwarted operations of only $5 million. Because it would create $25 million in net benefits as opposed to Policy A's $10 million, Policy B would be the superior policy. And having Policy B as an option would cause Policy A to fail cost–benefit analysis *if* the analysis accounted for the opportunity cost of alternative policies. (In that case, Policy A would occasion a net loss of $15 million. While it would create benefit of $70 million, it would impose costs of $50 million out-of-pocket, $10 million in foregone benefits from thwarted operations, *and* $25 million in benefits that could have been achieved had Policy B been implemented instead.)

The ultimate goal set forth above thus improves upon the simplistic cost–benefit analysis often invoked in debates over proposed regulations. If we prescribe an approach that doesn't just ask "Do the benefits of a policy exceed its costs?" but instead directs "Pick the approach that minimizes the sum of error and decision costs," we will ensure that we are taking account of the opportunity costs of selecting one regulatory approach over its alternatives. At the end of the day, we're still doing cost–benefit analysis; we're just doing it better.

GETTING THERE

It's all well and good to state that regulators should endeavor to minimize the sum of error and decision costs, but how, as a practical matter, should policy-makers proceed in pursuing that goal? Most obviously, they would need to bring "on screen" the key costs and benefits that will determine the magnitude of a proposed policy's error and decision costs. Moreover, it would not be enough to consider regulatory proposals in isolation. To assess the opportunity cost of selecting one regulatory option over another, policymakers would need to have some sense of how net welfare would differ under all regulatory alternatives. Of course, the cost of performing all this analysis must be kept in check; at some point, the incremental cost of further investigation by regulators exceeds the incremental benefit the additional study provides, so additional investigation just isn't worth it. The key, then, is to gather as much welfare-related information as can be cost-effectively gathered on all potential regulatory options, and then select the option that minimizes the sum of error and decision costs.

That sounds like a daunting task, but decisionmakers routinely perform similar analyses in other contexts. Take physicians. A doctor seeing a patient with a new ailment should aim to select not just a remedy that will leave the patient better off (i.e., will create more benefit than cost) but *the* remedy that creates the greatest expected net benefit for the patient. And the doctor needs to act quickly and efficiently; she can't dither incessantly over potential remedies, suffering "paralysis by analysis."

To perform the task before her, the physician marches methodically through a number of steps. First, she identifies the patient's *symptom*, the adverse effects experienced by the patient but not by healthy people. Next, she seeks to *diagnose the cause* of the symptom: What is it about this patient that leads him to suffer those adverse effects? After that, she *catalogues the available remedies* for correcting the cause of, or perhaps just alleviating, the symptom. She then *assesses the net benefits* of each remedy, taking into account expected benefit to the patient, the difficulty (and perhaps monetary cost) of imple-menting the therapy, and potential side effects. She ultimately selects the remedy that will provide the greatest net benefit to the patient.

The central claim of this book is that policymakers, when crafting regula-tions, should follow the lead of physicians. When confronted with a call to regulate, they should first identify the symptom – the adverse effect citizens confront within the scheme of private ordering. They then should seek to determine the cause of that symptom: Why has private ordering failed in this case to maximize social welfare? The regulator should then catalogue available remedies. Some may be "palliative" only, alleviating the symptom but failing to address the underlying disease. Others will seek to address not just the symptom but also the reason for it. Having catalogued the remedies, the regulator should investigate and make an informed judgment as to the net benefits of each. This process will bring on screen the information needed to minimize the sum of decision and error costs.

Most of the rest of this book aims to assist policymakers as they proceed through the steps described above. We will examine five sets of circumstances – "diseases" – that often lead to adverse effects and have traditionally been invoked to justify regulation. Those are the classic market failures of externalities, public goods, market power, and information asymmetry, as well as a long-recognized defect (agency costs) resulting from two of those market failures. We will then consider a novel, but increasingly prominent, non-market failure-based justification for regulatory intervention: people's apparent cognitive and volitional limitations. For each of these defects, we will consider the "symptoms" they present, why those symptoms appear, what remedies are available for addressing each, and the remedies' implementation costs and potential "side effects."

First, though, we turn to consider the state of "health" against which all these symptoms and diseases stand in contrast.

3

The Private Ordering Ideal

We defined regulation as governmental directives aimed at correcting private ordering defects that diminish total social welfare. We therefore need some sense at the outset of the way things work under *non-defective* private ordering.

Because we defined private ordering to include the judge-made common law rules of torts, property, contracts, and criminality – rules aimed at protecting people's bodies and property and allowing them to enforce agreements – we know that the private ordering infrastructure provides general protection for people's "stuff." Ideally, private ordering also leads to the optimal production of the things people desire. That is because when property rights are well defined and transferable, and individuals are able to strike trustworthy exchange agreements, markets will emerge and channel productive resources to their highest and best ends – production of the goods and services individuals value the most.

So why does this happen? Most of us learned the basics in Economics 101: Demand curves slope downward and to the right; supply curves, upward and to the right; and production levels and prices settle at the optimal level, the point at which supply and demand intersect. But what does all that really *mean*? To understand market failures – the diseases that cause the symptoms that often justify regulation – one must comprehend what's behind all these curves and graphs.

The first thing to see is that people differ in the degree to which they value different things. Take plastic. Suppose that roughly a pound of plastic is used in an artificial hip implant, a laptop computer, a pair of hiking boots, and fifty disposable drinking cups. Most likely, the hip implant manufacturer would ascribe greater value to a pound of plastic than would the producers of laptops, hiking boots, and cups. That's because the implant producer could use the plastic to make a product for which consumers would pay a huge amount – many thousands of dollars. Even if the price of a pound of plastic were to skyrocket one hundred fold from $0.50 to $50.00, the implant maker would still buy plastic. After all, adding $49.50 to the price of an artificial hip is unlikely to drive away any implant buyers.

At the other end of the spectrum, the cup maker values plastic the least because the amount he could earn from transforming the plastic into his product is pretty low. If the price of plastic were to rise just twenty fold, from $0.50 to $10.00 per pound, the cup manufacturer, knowing he would make very few sales if he raised by $9.50 the price of a fifty-pack of cups, would probably stop buying plastic.

Producers of laptops and hiking boots are somewhere in the middle. Depending on the price-sensitivity of the buyers of their products, they would probably continue buying plastic in response to a twenty fold increase in prices (from $0.50/lb to $10/lb). But if the price of plastic were to rise one hundred fold (to $50/lb), most makers of hiking books would likely drop out of the market, and producers of some low-end laptops might do so too, depending on the volume of sales they'd lose by raising their prices to account for the $49.50 increase in their costs.

The most obvious thing to see here is the so-called law of demand – that there is an inverse relationship between the price of a product and the quantity demanded. When some set amount of a product is produced, the individuals who value that product the most will compete for the available supply by offering higher prices to the seller. When the amount produced is low, prices get bid up to high levels as buyers who value the product the most (e.g., hip implant makers) vie against each other for the limited offerings. When there are lots of units on hand, buyers don't have to compete as vigorously, prices fall, and those valuing the product less (e.g., plastic cup makers) enter the competition. Thus, we derive the familiar downward-sloping demand curve in Figure 3.1. That curve reflects that, as price falls, the quantity demanded grows.

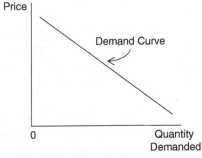

FIGURE 3.1 Demand Curve

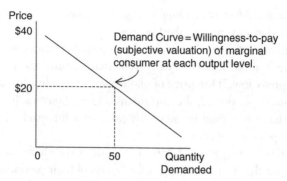

FIGURE 3.2 What the Demand Curve Represents

More important for our purposes, though, is *what this curve represents*. Every point on the curve denotes the amount that the last person to buy a unit – the "marginal consumer" – would have to pay if that particular quantity of units were auctioned off one-by-one. (For example, in Figure 3.2, the person buying the fiftieth unit would have to pay $20 to acquire the unit for himself. If this were a real auction, units 1–49 would have sold for more than $20; consumers valuing the product at less than $20 would have already dropped out of the bidding.)

If there were lots of buyers at the auction, one would expect the marginal consumer's actual willingness-to-pay to come very close to the "market-clearing price" – i.e., the price the marginal consumer had to pay for the last unit sold. That is because if his willingness-to-pay were higher than that amount, he probably would have purchased one of the earlier auctioned units; if it were less, he would not have made the bid he won. Thus, the demand curve represents, for each unit produced, the amount the marginal consumer – the person to buy that unit if the units were auctioned off one-by-one – would be willing to pay for the unit. And, of course, one's willingness-to-pay (or "reservation price," to use economic jargon) represents the amount of subjective value he attaches to the thing. (If you derive $5 of value from owning a widget, you would be willing to pay up to $5 for that widget.) The upshot of all this is that the demand curve for a product represents the actual value that product would create if it were produced.

While production creates value, it is not an unmitigated good. Using resources to make one thing means those resources cannot be employed for other purposes. Production therefore always involves foregone opportunities, which, as we've said, are costs.

The incremental cost to make one more unit of a product or service – i.e., that unit's "marginal cost" – will vary as additional units are produced. If production requires one-time fixed costs, such as building a factory, then the marginal cost of the first unit produced may be quite high. Subsequent units will have much lower marginal costs, since the producer won't have to incur again the fixed costs expended in producing the first unit. But as more and more units are produced, the marginal cost of an additional unit of output will start to rise. That is because the producer will first utilize the easiest-to-obtain inputs and will resort to less readily available, and thus costlier, inputs only when those that are easily obtained have been exhausted.

Suppose, for example, that a corn farmer owns 900 acres of land. Of those acres, 400 are flat and arable, 300 are slightly hilly and rocky, and 200 are wetlands. The farmer will first cultivate the arable land. If he exhausts that property but still wants to expand output, he will turn to the next-most readily available land, the hilly/rocky acreage. He will have to expend greater effort cultivating that land. If he wants to expand even further after planting all his hilly/rocky land, he will turn to the wetlands, which must be drained at great expense before they can be planted. The farmer's marginal cost of producing corn will thus rise as he is forced to use land that is costlier to develop. Similarly, if a factory owner wants to expand output by increasing the hours his factory operates, his incremental costs are likely to rise. To run the factory at night, the owner will likely have to pay his workers an increased over time salary to compensate them for foregoing valuable family time. (Such a foregone opportunity is a cost for which factory workers will demand reimbursement.)

We see, then, that the marginal cost of producing one more unit of a product or service eventually tends to rise as additional units are produced. Figure 3.3 illustrates this point graphically.

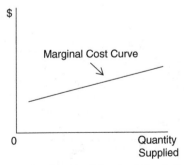

FIGURE 3.3 Supply (Marginal Cost) Curve

Astute readers may observe that the marginal cost curve in Figure 3.3 resembles the old supply curve from Econ 101. As well it should! They're really the same thing. The supply curve, you may recall, represents how much of a thing producers would be willing to supply at different price levels. Most of us learned, correctly, that the curve illustrates that as prices go up, producers are willing to supply more. But if we drill down a bit, we see that the supply curve reflects much more. A producer should be willing to supply an additional unit of whatever she makes *if* the price for which she could sell that unit is at least as great as the incremental cost of producing the unit. In other words, the price at which a producer would supply an additional unit – the information graphically represented in a supply curve – *equals* the marginal cost of the unit. The supply curve for a product is its marginal cost curve.

Now that we have explored what's really represented by both a demand curve (i.e., the amount by which the marginal consumer values each unit produced) and a supply curve (i.e., the marginal cost of producing each unit), we can see how private ordering usually results in the optimal production of goods and services. As most of us learned in Econ 101, in a competitive market with fully informed buyers and sellers, market output and price will tend to settle at the point at which the demand and supply curves intersect (points Q_C and P_C in Figure 3.4). Producers would not cease production short of that point (say, just before point Q_1) because any producer that made an additional unit could sell it for a price (P_1) exceeding his marginal cost (MC_1). But producers would not produce beyond point Q_C (say, to point Q_2), because the incremental cost of producing an additional unit would exceed the price that unit would command (e.g., $MC_2 > P_2$). Q_C and P_C are the equilibrium

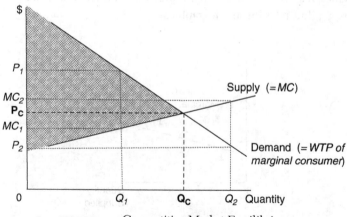

FIGURE 3.4 Competitive Market Equilibrium

output and price levels – the levels that will naturally attain if producers and consumers pursue their own interests and there are no market failures.

Production to, but not beyond Q_C, also happens to make the best possible use of society's resources. Every unit produced prior to the Q_C unit creates more value (represented by the demand curve) than would the next-best use of the resources required to produce that unit, a use that constitutes a "foregone opportunity" and is thus reflected in the marginal cost/supply curve. Producing units beyond Q_C, by contrast, squanders opportunities to use the required resources in ways that would create greater value than would the production of additional units of the product at issue. We see this in the fact that, to the right of Q_C, the supply curve, representing the value of opportunities foregone because of production of each additional unit, exceeds the demand curve, representing the value each additional unit creates. The shaded area, showing the difference between the cost of deploying resources to produce these units and the value the units create, represents wealth that is created from allocating resources in this fashion. Allocating the resources in a different manner would result in less total wealth.

In sum, the private ordering ideal, through the common law, protects people's stuff and allows them to enter into enforceable exchange agreements. The ability to trade property then facilitates the emergence of markets, which, when working well, channel society's resources to their highest and best ends, maximizing the wealth those resources will produce.

Unfortunately, markets sometimes fail to work well. We turn now to consider the various sets of circumstances in which systematic market failure may occur and, for each, the potential fixes available to policymakers.

4

Externalities

Suppose you own a small wine and cheese shop in a charming Midwestern college town called Columbia. It's a beautiful Saturday morning in late April, and you rise early to open the shop. When you arrive at the store, you see that the business next door, an upscale café, has installed large planters around its patio, which happens to abut your own outdoor seating area. Even as tender shoots, your neighbor's plantings are lovely. You know the planters will be gorgeous once the plants mature. This will be great for your own patio business, you think.

Around noon, you receive a call from your landlord. Your lease on the shop space is up for renewal soon, and the landlord informs you that, in light of increased demand for downtown retail space, she is going to raise your rent by 20 percent. You're upset, but not surprised. Over the last eighteen months, several condominium complexes have gone up in the area, and young professionals have been pouring into downtown. Most of the new downtown residents are new to Columbia, having moved to take jobs at a new Google affiliate that recently opened in town.

Mid-afternoon, the newly constructed Brookside development, a high-end student apartment complex located across the street from your shop, hosts a bash to celebrate the seasonal opening of its rooftop swimming pool. Hoping to drum up interest among students looking for housing for the fall, Brookside has hired a DJ to blast music from the pool deck. Within minutes, the patrons who have flocked to your patio to enjoy some wine and cheese (and newly planted spring flowers) vacate the premises. You don't make another patio sale for the rest of the day.

You, my friend, have been the victim and the beneficiary of "externalities." An externality occurs when some of the cost or benefit of an activity is experienced by someone "external" to the activity. The annoyance and business losses you suffered because of Brookside's raucous pool party were negative

Costs or benefits spill over from some external thing

externalities – cost spillovers. So was your rent increase occasioned by the opening of the Google facility (though, as we'll see, that was a special type of negative externality that is less troubling). The extra business you enjoyed because of your neighbor's new planters constituted a positive externality, a benefit spillover. Your neighbor bore the full cost of providing those planters, but could not capture all the benefit – some trickled your way.

SYMPTOMS/DISEASE

With most of the market failures we will consider, the adverse effects (the symptoms) and the cause of those effects (the disease) are distinct concepts. For example, with information asymmetry, the subject of Chapter 8, the primary symptom – an absence of high-quality products or services of a certain sort – is quite different than the disease – the fact that the sellers of those products and services have far more information about quality than do potential buyers. We usually have to connect a few dots to see exactly how a market failure occasions the adverse effects that result.

With an externality, though, one symptom is closely related to the disease. When the externality is negative, there is an apparent injustice to the party bearing the spilled-over cost. It simply wasn't fair, for example, for Brookside to disrupt your business with its loud pool party. When the externality is positive, the injustice is suffered by the party that created the benefit but couldn't fully capture it. It wasn't fair to your café neighbor, for instance, that you should benefit from its planters even though you didn't contribute to their creation. So one symptom of externalities – the unfairness to the bearer of the externalized cost or creator of the externalized benefit – is immediately obvious from and nearly synonymous with the disease – spilled over costs or benefits.

Another symptom of externalities, though, is less apparent. Recall from the previous chapter that in the private ordering ideal, markets channel productive resources to their highest and best uses, resulting in the optimal production of goods and services. An assumption of the private ordering ideal is that decisionmakers bear the full costs and benefits of their choices. When they are able to offload some of the costs of their decisions or are incapable of capturing all the benefits, optimal market output will not occur. That means society as a whole will be poorer than it otherwise would be.

To see why this is so, let's make some adjustments to the models we considered in the previous chapter. If a producer of some activity is able to foist some of the cost of her conduct onto others, then there will be a divergence between her *individual* marginal cost curve (reflecting the costs she faces) and the curve representing the *total* marginal cost of her production. The producer's

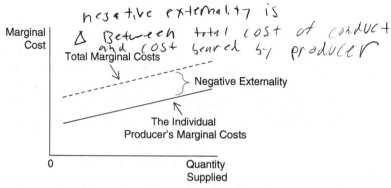

[handwritten annotation:] nesative externality is Δ Between total cost of conduct and cost beared by producer ✓

FIGURE 4.1 A Negative Externality

individual costs will be systematically lower than the total cost she produces. As illustrated in Figure 4.1, the negative externality is the difference between the total cost of her conduct and the amount of cost she actually bears.

This divergence between total and individual marginal costs affects overall output. In general, a person will continue to engage in an activity as long as the added benefit she derives from doing the action one more time (or to one greater degree) exceeds the added cost she incurs in repeating (or increasing the intensity of) the action. That is why the marginal cost curve, which represents the incremental cost of making an additional unit, is normally equivalent to the supply curve, which represents a producer's willingness-to-supply at different price levels: If an additional unit of production will command a price (or confer a benefit on the producer) that is at least equal to the additional cost of making that unit, the producer will make the unit. Willingness-to-supply equals marginal cost.

But a producer's willingness-to-supply a unit turns on whether the price (or other benefit) she would receive for that unit is sufficient to cover *her* costs. That means the supply curve will equal the producer's individual marginal cost curve, not the total marginal cost curve. If a producer is able to foist some of the cost of production onto others, so that her marginal costs are systematically lower than the total marginal costs, she will produce *beyond* the point at which the incremental cost of a unit of production equals the benefit that unit creates. All units of production beyond that point create greater total cost than total benefit. They squander wealth.

[handwritten left margin:] Squanders wealth

Figure 4.2 illustrates these points. If the producer bore all the cost of her production, she would produce to Q_C, the point at which the benefit she would receive for the last unit of production (the price that would prevail given the demand curve, which represents buyers' willingness-to-pay) equals her cost of producing that unit. Production past that point would cost the producer more than she would receive in additional benefits; stopping short of that point

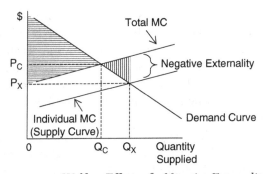

FIGURE 4.2 Welfare Effects of a Negative Externality

would forego profits she might otherwise earn. With a negative externality, though, the producer is able to offload some of her costs, so her individual marginal cost curve is lower than the total marginal cost curve. When deciding how much to produce, she compares her costs to the benefits she expects to receive, and she thus produces to point Q_X. Stopping short of that point foregoes profits on units that cost the producer less than the benefits they would provide for her. From a *societal* standpoint, however, production of all units between Q_C and Q_X involves waste: The total incremental cost of each unit, as reflected in the total marginal cost curve, exceeds the value that unit ultimately produces, as reflected in the demand curve. While the horizontally shaded area of the graph represents the wealth created from producing units up to Q_C (i.e., value to consumers as represented by the demand curve, less the cost of achieving that value as represented by the total marginal cost curve), the vertically shaded area represents social waste resulting from the production of units Q_C to Q_X (i.e., the difference between the higher cost of producing those units and the lower value they create).

We've described the dynamic here in terms of the production of goods or services, but a negative externality may lead to wealth losses even when the actor isn't making something to sell. In blaring music, for example, the owner of Brookside wasn't constructing new apartments to lease. He did, however, have to make a decision about how much volume to "produce," and that decision required consideration of incremental costs and benefits. If he played the music at the level appropriate for an elevator or department store, he would fail to attract passing students to the promotional party. Turning the music up a bit would win him a significant benefit (more potential tenants at the promotional event) and probably wouldn't impose significant costs (e.g., driving away students who are sensitive to loud music). At some point, though, a unit of additional volume could repel more students than it would attract.

The Brookside developer thus had to select an optimal volume level. Since some of the costs of additional volume were borne by his neighbors, the Brookside developer did not account for those costs in deciding how loud to play the music. As a result, he set the volume too high from a societal standpoint: The last few units of volume increase – say, from seven to ten – likely annoyed the neighbors by more than it enhanced Brookside's promotional efforts. Welfare was destroyed.

What about the other negative externality you experienced that day in April? You had to pay higher rent as a result of Google's decision to open a facility in Columbia. Technically, Google externalized onto you some of the costs of opening its Columbia facility. It's doubtful, though, that this sort of externality should be deemed a market failure.

As an initial matter, the injustice we often associate with externalities seems absent here. Was Google's creation of all sorts of new jobs "unjust" because its job creation would require you to pay higher rent or move your shop elsewhere? If you somehow constrained local business expansion so that Columbia's downtown population, and thus your rent, remained stable, wouldn't *you* be imposing costs on Google and the young professionals that would otherwise move to Columbia to take Google jobs? Your insistence on a low rent would victimize Google and its potential employees.

As explained in greater detail later, negative externalities typically involve *reciprocal* potential harms: The actor imposing a cost on another may harm that other, but if the other could ban the actor's conduct, she would "harm" the actor. In light of the inevitability of harm to one party or the other, policymakers would generally do well to focus not on the apparent injustice of an externality, but on whether it leads to a decrease in social welfare.

When Google opened a new facility and lots of young professionals sought housing in downtown Columbia, landlords raised rents, causing a loss for current downtown residents. That loss, though, was precisely offset by a gain to the landlords. Moreover, the higher rent levels downtown signaled to real estate developers that more resources should be devoted to developing downtown living spaces. Rather than *mis*allocating resources – diverting them from their highest and best uses – the externality here channeled resources *toward* their highest value ends. Economists refer to this sort of externality, one where the adverse effects on "victims" consists of a change in prices, as a "pecuniary" externality.[1] Because they typically do not reduce overall social welfare – and,

---

[1] Non-pecuniary externalities are sometimes referred to as "technological" externalities. Unless otherwise specified, when we speak of externalities here, we refer to technological externalities only.

in fact, enhance it by encouraging productive resources to be reallocated to more valuable uses – such externalities normally do not warrant regulation.

Now, one of the externalities on that April day inured to your benefit: Your wine and cheese shop saw an increase in business because of the neighboring café's plantings. Does such a positive externality raise concerns (besides the apparent unfairness of your being enriched at the expense of another)? Indeed, even positive externalities may result in a decrease in social welfare.

As we've now said several times, people regularly have to decide "how much" of an activity to engage in. When your neighbor decided to spiff up her patio, she could have just cleaned things well, or perhaps also planted a pot, or maybe some long planters (either cheap plastic, moderately priced clay, or expensive stone). She might have bought cheap, easy-to-maintain plants from Wal-Mart, or she could have upgraded to exotic, high-maintenance plants from an upscale nursery. She could have chosen to add some potted trees or to install speakers to play background music, in which case she would have faced choices about tree and speaker quality.

When your neighbor made all these decisions, she compared incremental costs and benefits. She reasoned that going from a dirty to a clean patio would cost her very little and would substantially enhance her café's appeal. Adding low-end plants in cheap containers would cost a bit more than basic cleaning but would bring in a number of additional customers – perhaps not as many as basic cleaning, but enough to generate additional revenue that would more than cover the cost of the plantings. Upgrading further to long clay planters with more exotic plantings would probably generate just enough additional revenue to cover the added cost of the upgrade. Further upgrading to stone planters or adding potted trees and speakers, your neighbor concluded, would not generate enough additional revenue to cover the additional cost. Your neighbor therefore gave her patio a thorough cleaning and added mid-grade clay planters with exotic plants, but she didn't install trees or speakers.

The benefits your neighbor enjoyed because of her efforts, though, were not the only value those efforts produced. You (and probably her other neighbors) also profited from her efforts. Had she taken into account the benefit you and the other neighbors experienced, she might well have planted those trees and installed speakers. Indeed, it could be that the total marginal benefit resulting from tree planting and speaker installation would exceed the marginal cost of those activities. If so, then the neighbor's failure to plant trees and install speakers reduced overall welfare from what it might otherwise have been.

Figure 4.3 below illustrates how positive externalities make society poorer. The top line represents the total marginal benefit of an activity. Most of the

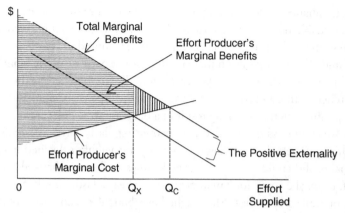

FIGURE 4.3 Welfare Effects of a Positive Externality

time, early increments of an activity create more benefit than later units – think of eating a pie (where the first few bites are delightful but continued consumption eventually becomes sickening) or cleaning your house (where you first take care of really obvious problems, like dirty clothes on the floor, before moving to tasks with a less dramatic impact). Reflecting people's tendency to take high-value steps first, the total marginal benefit curve slopes downward to indicate that additional units of an activity generate less additional benefit. The bottom curve, the individual producer's marginal cost, slopes upward, because most actors do the cheap and easy things first (e.g., they pick up their clothes), and then turn to the sort-of-hard tasks (e.g., vacuuming), and perhaps eventually turn to difficult, tedious tasks (e.g., cleaning the baseboards or dusting between the window blinds). The key to the graph is the divergence between the *total* marginal benefit curve, which reflects all the marginal benefits of the actor's conduct, and the individual marginal benefit curve, which represents the lower level of benefit the actor himself receives. That divergence is the positive externality.

Because the actor captures only the benefits reflected in the individual marginal benefit curve, he will intensify his efforts at an activity only until the point at which his marginal cost of a unit of effort equals his own marginal benefit. That is point Q_X on the graph. From the individual actor's standpoint, continued units of effort cost more than they provide in benefits. If *all* benefits were accounted for, however, the actor would intensify his efforts to point Q_C, for all the units of effort between Q_X and Q_C actually create greater benefit than they cost to provide. By not providing that effort, the actor fails to create the social wealth represented by the vertically shaded area. (He does, though, create the value represented by the horizontally shaded area.)

To summarize, externalities may cause society to be poorer than it otherwise would be. They may also create injustices, though assessing the unfairness of an externality is difficult given the reciprocity of potential harms. Externalities that are only pecuniary – that impose costs on others by changing relative prices – should generally be of little concern to regulators.

We turn now to consider the remedies available for addressing externalities and the implementation difficulties and side effects those potential remedies entail.

AVAILABLE REMEDIES AND THEIR IMPLEMENTATION DIFFICULTIES AND SIDE EFFECTS

The textbook example of an externality is environmental pollution. The factory that belches smoke and odors and spews contaminants onto its neighbors quite obviously does not bear all the costs of its operations. We might therefore look at actual and proposed means of addressing environmental pollution to get a sense of the range of potential remedies for externalities.[2] Versions of those remedies could also be employed to address externalities outside the environmental context.

Before turning to potential regulatory corrections, though, we should first recognize that the common law, which we have classified as an aspect of private ordering and thus beyond the scope of regulation as we have defined it, has long provided significant protection against negative externalities. The ancient common law principle *sic utere tuo ut alienum non laedas* ("so use your own so as not to injure another's property") underlies several tort doctrines that police negative externalities. The law of nuisance, for example, prohibits unreasonably using one's property in a manner that substantially interferes with another's use or enjoyment of her own. Rules on trespass forbid intentional, unjustified invasions of others' property. The doctrine of strict liability for abnormally dangerous activities requires a person who has engaged in conduct that can't be made safe (e.g., dynamite blasting) to compensate those he harmed, even if he used reasonable care to prevent any harm. Taken

---

[2] Because pollution involves cost spillovers, the discussion here will focus primarily (though not exclusively) on potential remedies for negative externalities. Positive externalities are usually addressed either by subsidization, which is discussed below, or by having the government perform the externality-causing activity. When the government uses tax revenue to engage in an activity subject to positive externalities, it is not engaging in "regulation" as we have defined the term for purposes of this book. We will therefore spend little time here on positive externalities.

together, these flexible, judge-made doctrines go a long way toward preventing negative externalities and the social losses they create.

Practical enforcement and bargaining difficulties, though, may prevent the common law from achieving optimal deterrence of negative externalities. If a polluting factory imposes a small but significant amount of harm on each of a thousand neighbors, for example, no single neighbor may incur the expense of a lawsuit to stop the conduct at issue, even though the total amount of uncompensated damage (and the inefficiency resulting from the externality) is substantial. Even if that difficulty could be overcome through the class action mechanism, a pure common law approach may not be optimal. Because the outcomes of class action lawsuits are unpredictable and potentially catastrophic, the factory owner would likely prefer to compensate his injured neighbors up front in exchange for a release from liability. Negotiating with hundreds of neighbors, though, would be extremely costly, particularly since each neighbor would have an incentive to be the last holdout so as to extract the greatest possible compensation. As a practical matter, up-front liability protection might be impossible to procure, and the risk resulting from its absence could cause the factory owner either to abandon construction altogether or to build a smaller factory than he might otherwise develop. Regulation might generate a better outcome. So what are the regulatory options?

Command and Control

The traditional means of regulating negative externalities, at least in the environmental context, has been for the government simply to impose limits on each producer's spillovers and punish those who exceed their limit. Nixonera environmental statutes such as the Clean Water Act and Clean Air Act largely take this tack. Each producer is subject to emission limitations, generally expressed in a permit and based on the emission reductions attainable using the "best available" pollution control technology. An expert governmental agency (usually the EPA or its state counterpart) commands a maximum activity level from each regulatee and controls its operations to ensure attainment of the goal. The approach is thus often referred to as "command-and-control." The standards employed are called "technology-based" standards because they are based on, and frequently require adoption of, particular control technologies.

Command-and-control has two salutary effects. First, it reduces the magnitude of the externality – the difference between individual and total marginal costs. It does this by inducing the producer to adopt some control technology,

two effects

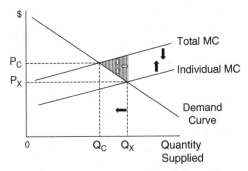

FIGURE 4.4 Command and Control

which simultaneously raises the producer's marginal cost while reducing the total marginal cost imposed. Second, it often induces the regulatee to reduce the level of its spillover-causing activity so as to comply with its permit. Figure 4.4 illustrates the effect of this one–two punch. As the producer's own marginal costs rise and the total costs fall, and as the producer's overall output level constricts, the vertically shaded triangle representing externality-induced wealth loss shrinks.

Despite its prominence in American law, command-and-control involves some significant drawbacks. For one thing, it unrealistically assumes that regulators can know and effectively process a tremendous amount of information. Command-and-control requires some governmental entity to decide by how much each regulatee must reduce its spillovers. Because those making efforts to cut back on spillovers typically take the available low-cost, high-impact actions before turning to higher-cost, lower-impact measures, externality reduction exhibits the familiar pattern of increasing marginal costs and decreasing marginal benefits. Accordingly, regulators ought to require externality reduction to the level at which the marginal cost of the last unit of reduction just equals the marginal benefit achieved; any other level would be wasteful. But that means regulators must know both the marginal costs and the marginal benefits of achieving different levels of externality-reduction. That's a tall order, especially since the marginal costs and benefits of different levels of externality-reduction are likely to differ among regulatees. Imposing a single standard for all entities of the same type, as often occurs, squanders resources if some could cheaply reduce further while others must incur great costs – costs exceeding the benefits created – to achieve just the prescribed level of spillover reduction.

The difficulty here is an instance of a problem that afflicts regulation generally. At the end of the day, regulation involves centralized economic planning: A regulating "planner" mandates that productive resources be allocated away from some uses and toward others. That requires the planner to know the relative value of different resource uses. But such information, in the words of Nobel laureate F.A. Hayek, "is not given to anyone in its totality."[3] The personal preferences of thousands or millions of individuals – preferences only they know – determine whether there should be more widgets and fewer gidgets, or vice-versa. As Hayek observed, voluntary trading among resource owners in a free market generates prices that signal how resources should be allocated (i.e., toward the uses for which resource owners may command the highest prices). But centralized economic planners – including regulators – don't allocate resources on the basis of relative prices. Regulators, in fact, generally assume that prices are *wrong* due to the market failure the regulators are seeking to address. Thus, the so-called knowledge problem that afflicts regulation generally is particularly acute for command-and-control approaches that require regulators to make refined judgments on the basis of information about relative costs and benefits.

In addition to this implementation difficulty, command-and-control approaches may give rise to a number of unintended consequences or "side effects." If the regulatory approach is technology-based, as many command-and-control rules are, it may retard innovation by locking in existing technologies. A command-and-control directive that actually prescribes a particular technology – e.g., the use of certain scrubbers by coal-fired power plants – reduces the incentive to discover cheaper, more effective means of reducing spillovers. Why develop the technology if you can't use it? If the command-and-control directive does not mandate use of a particular technology but instead prescribes a level of performance that is achievable using that technology, then regulatees may have an incentive to develop technologies that are less expensive – i.e., that achieve the prescribed level of spillover more cheaply than the technology on which the performance standard is based. But regulatees still have little incentive to develop technologies that cost more but achieve a much greater reduction in spillovers. Even if those more expensive technologies involve lower costs per unit of reduction, they will provide little benefit to regulatees if they cost more to implement than does the inferior technology on which the prescribed performance standard is based. Why develop such technologies?

A second side effect of command-and-control is, like the knowledge problem, applicable to a great many regulatory interventions. Command-and-control

[3]   F.A. Hayek, The Use of Knowledge in Society, 35 *Am. Econ. Rev.* 519, 520 (1945).

typically involves detailed orders directing regulatees to do particular things a certain way. The approach can thus be useful to businesses seeking to gain advantages over their rivals. A firm might, for example, lobby the government to require all competitors within the sector to adopt some technology that the firm already utilizes, or it could seek a ban or limitation on some conduct that is of particular advantage to its rivals. It might pursue rules hobbling producers of substitutes for its product, as when alcoholic beverage producers lobby against marijuana liberalization or hotel groups try to ban Internet room rentals on websites such as Airbnb.

While one might initially expect regulators pursuing the public interest to resist efforts to manipulate regulation for private gain, that assumes that government officials are not themselves rational, self-interest maximizers. As scholars associated with the "public choice" economic tradition have demonstrated, government officials do not shed their self-interested nature when they step into the public square.[4] They are often receptive to lobbying in favor of questionable rules, especially since they benefit from regulatory expansions, which tend to enhance their job status and often their incomes. They also tend to become "captured" by powerful regulatees who may shower them with personal benefits and potentially employ them after their stints in government have ended.[5]

Moreover, there is often little counter-lobbying against protectionist regulations. When a regulation disadvantages not established rivals but only fledgling competitors or potential entrants into the market, there may be no one to lobby against the regulation. Even if the regulation would ultimately injure consumers by squelching nascent competition, they would be unlikely to invest resources in defeating the regulation. Consumer harm is widely dispersed, and individual consumers have little incentive to make lobbying efforts that will largely inure to the benefit of others. The discrete and insular

---

4   The public choice approach to analyzing political decision-making simply transfers the rational actor model of economic theory (i.e., individuals act as rational self-interest maximizers) to the realm of politics. It assumes that the motivations of actors in the political process – from voters to lobbyists to bureaucrats to politicians – are no different from those of people participating in grocery, housing, or car markets. Voters "vote their pocketbooks"; lobbyists seek the money and prestige that comes from securing competitive advantages for their clients; bureaucrats strive for job advancement, with its enhanced power and income; and politicians seek election and re-election. As explained below, all these parties may seek to mask this "crass" self-interest by paying lip-service to altruistic considerations. But make no mistake: Self-interest lurks beneath the surface. In the memorable words of Nobel laureate James Buchanan, public choice is simply "politics without romance."

5   For a particularly vivid recent account of regulatory capture, see Nolan McCarty, *Five Things the Goldman Tapes Teach Us About Financial Regulation*, *Wash. Post* (Sept. 30, 2014).

beneficiaries of protectionist regulation, by contrast, stand to reap substantial per capita benefits from lobbying efforts and are therefore likely to make them. Experience has shown that regulations involving the sort of "concentrated benefits and diffuse costs" described here are particularly likely to be enacted. Protectionist rules that impede nascent competition are thus common under command-and-control regimes.

Two types of losses result from the sort of interest-group manipulation public choice predicts. First, when command-and-control does squelch competition, firms obtaining a regulatory advantage may gain market power that deprives consumers of benefits and reduces overall social welfare. (We will consider in Chapter 7 exactly what market power is and how it creates "deadweight loss," a pure sacrifice of wealth.) Second, when firms spend money lobbying for protectionist rules, rather than invest in product development or simply lower their prices, wealth that otherwise could have been created is squandered. Thus, to the extent that command-and-control encourages interest group wrangling, it generates waste.

A classic tale of command-and-control's manipulation by interest groups is recounted in the wonderfully titled book, *Clean Coal, Dirty Air: Or How the Clean Air Act Became a Multibillion Dollar Bail-out for High-Sulfur Fuel Producers.*[6] The 1970 Clean Air Act imposed certain effluent limitations based on the level of cleanliness attainable using the best available pollution control technology. EPA's air-quality standard for coal-fired power plants based the attainable level of cleanliness on the assumption that a plant would burn, and thus control sulfur emissions from, coal produced in the East (West Virginia, Kentucky, etc.). Many coal-fired plants found that they could achieve the required level of cleanliness relatively cheaply simply by switching to low-sulfur coal mined in the West (Wyoming, Montana, etc.). Eastern power plants incurred higher shipping costs from using western coal, but those costs were much lower than the cost of installing the scrubbers necessary to reduce emissions from eastern coal.

Not surprisingly, eastern coal producers were unhappy with widespread switching to western coal. They therefore lobbied Congress for new rules requiring all coal-fired plants to install scrubbers. If all plants had such scrubbers, then western coal would lose its advantage over eastern coal, eastern power plants wouldn't incur the higher cost of transporting coal from the West, and eastern coal producers could maintain their market position.

---

[6] Bruce Ackerman and William T. Hassler, *Clean Coal, Dirty Air: Or How the Clean Air Act Became a Multibillion Dollar Bail-out for High-Sulfur Fuel Producers* (New Haven, Connecticut: Yale University Press, 1981).

It can be difficult to persuade Congress (or any other democratically accountable authority) to mandate higher-cost operations for nakedly protectionist reasons, so the eastern coal interests needed political cover. They got it from western environmentalists, who wanted to see the relatively clean coal-fired plants in the West reduce their emissions further by scrubbing even their lower sulfur emissions. A rule requiring all plants to install scrubbing technology regardless of the type of coal used would achieve that goal. Of course, it would substantially raise costs – and for little additional benefit, at least in the East. It would also protect the production of dirty, eastern coal.

In the end, the eastern coal/western environmentalist coalition achieved its goal: Congress amended the Clean Air Act to require not attainment of some level of cleanliness (e.g., 10 parts per million of x), but instead some level of emission reduction (e.g., a 40 percent reduction in your emissions of x). Members of Congress also concocted a legislative history (House committee reports, etc.) implying that the new goal could not be met by just switching fuel sources. Thus, implementation of scrubbing technology was effectively required for all power plants, even though the same level of environmental benefit could have been achieved much less expensively had eastern plants been allowed to meet air quality goals by switching their fuel sources.

The sort of "strange bedfellow" cooperation that precipitated the scrubber rule is not at all uncommon. Wealthy business interests often desire the imposition of a command-and-control directive that can give them an advantage over their rivals or otherwise insulate them from competition. Raw protectionism, though, is unseemly. Politically accountable legislators and regulators do not want to be seen nakedly favoring one group over another. Business interests that would benefit from the rule therefore often seek out some politically attractive (or at least palatable) "face" to make an altruistic case for the rule at issue. Economist Bruce Yandle has dubbed this dynamic the "Bootleggers and Baptists" effect, in honor of the two groups that in the early twentieth century pushed hardest for liquor prohibition: the Baptists, who emphasized the evils of alcohol and made a passionate and public "pro-social" case for prohibition, and the Bootleggers, who privately pushed prohibition in the hopes of squelching competition and gaining the ability to earn monopoly profits on their illegal booze. Whenever bootleggers and Baptists find themselves aligned, watch out!

Taxes/Subsidies

Several of command-and-control's drawbacks result from, or are exacerbated by, the fact that the approach involves highly detailed directives. Because command-and-control requires the regulator to make precise decisions about each regulatee's activity level – judgments that require comparing the marginal costs and benefits of reducing spillovers by one amount versus another – the knowledge problem is particularly acute for command-and-control. Technology lock-in is especially likely when a regulatory approach mandates particular equipment or bases the level of permitted spillovers on what is achievable using it. And the more a regulatory approach limits regulatees' freedom to operate as they choose, the more useful the approach is as a protectionist device and thus the more susceptible it is to interest group manipulation and other public choice concerns. For command-and-control, the devil really is in the details.

Recognizing as much, economists have often suggested that regulation be less detailed and prescriptive. When it comes to negative externalities, regulators could refrain from ordering regulatees to take or avoid precise actions and instead require them simply to pay an amount equal to the cost their activity imposes on others. In the case of positive externalities, the government might use the public purse to pay the benefit-creator an amount reflecting the value of benefits conferred on the general public.

Economist Arthur Cecil Pigou most famously advocated for this approach. In his 1920 book, *The Economics of Welfare*, Pigou described how "divergences between social and private net product," what we now call externalities, tend to make society poorer. When externalities exist, he reasoned, "[n]o 'invisible hand' can be relied on to produce a good arrangement of the whole from a combination of separate treatments of the parts. It is therefore necessary that an authority of wider reach should intervene."[7] Specifically, Pigou concluded, "[i]t is ... possible for the State, if it so chooses, to remove the divergence in any field by 'extraordinary encouragements' or 'extraordinary restraints' upon investments in that field. The most obvious forms which these encouragements and restraints may assume are, of course, those of bounties and taxes."[8] In other words, the government should tax activities that create negative externalities and subsidize those that create positive externalities, thereby ensuring that the actors at issue bear the full cost and receive all the benefit of their conduct. If they do, they'll act optimally, taking all actions that generate benefits in excess of cost and none that don't. Thus was born the idea of "Pigouvian" (or sometimes "Pigovian" or "Pigonvian") taxes and subsidies, the effects of which are illustrated in Figures 4.5 and 4.6.

---

[7] A.C. Pigou, *The Economics of Welfare* (London: Macmillan and Co., 1920), 195.
[8] Ibid. at 192.

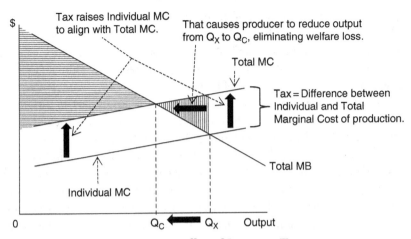

FIGURE 4.5 Effect of Pigouvian Tax

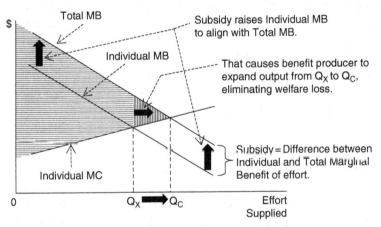

FIGURE 4.6 Effect of Pigouvian Subsidy

Many governments, especially those in Europe, have utilized Pigouvian taxes to address a number of environmental concerns. Norway, for example, imposed a tax on sulfur in mineral oil as far back as 1971, about the time the major command-and-control environmental statutes were enacted in the United States. Norway has since imposed taxes on non-refillable beverage containers, pesticides, lubricating oil, lead in petroleum, nitrogen and phosphorous in fertilizers, and carbon dioxide from numerous sources. Germany has similarly imposed a number of so-called green taxes. Austria, Portugal, and the Netherlands charge progressive automobile registration fees that exact greater amounts from owners of inefficient cars. And even the United States, which has not widely embraced Pigouvian taxes as a means of environmental protection, levies a "gas guzzler" tax on automobiles that emit a high volume of pollutants per mile. While the carmakers pay the tax, they ultimately pass it along to consumers in the form of higher prices.

Outside the environmental context, Americans are subject to a number of Pigouvian "sin taxes" on unhealthful products and services such as cigarettes, alcohol, and indoor sun-tanning. Paternalistic impulses – a desire to encourage people to make choices that are "good for them" – undoubtedly inspire some policymakers to support these taxes. But supporters also seek to justify the taxes on the ground that they internalize externalities resulting from the fact that people who engage in the vices being taxed account for a higher proportion of public health care (and perhaps public safety) expenditures.

Pigouvian taxes have even been considered in the financial sector. For example, in proposing a bank tax following the 2008 financial crisis and subsequent bailouts of financial institutions, President Obama emphasized that the tax would force "too big to fail" banks to take account of, and limit, some of the costs their risk-taking imposes on the public. He explained: "[T]he bigger the firm – and the more debt it holds – the larger the fee. Because we are not only going to recover our money and help close our deficits; we are going to attack some of the banking practices that led to the crisis."[9]

The Economist stated the Pigouvian rationale for the proposed bank tax more clearly:

> [A] tax on size would seek to correct for the large negative externality associated with the systemic risk presented by too-big-to-fail banks. The larger a bank gets, the less likely the government is to allow it to fail, and the more shielded it is from potential losses. Size therefore generates some significant social costs, particularly since the negative externality encourages firms to take on too much risk. A tax on bank size would get firms to internalise the social cost.[10]

For an example of Pigouvian subsidies, consider efforts to encourage the development of electric vehicles. Federal and state policymakers reasoned that early purchasers of expensive electric vehicles would create public benefits –

---

[9] Weekly Radio Address of President Barack Obama (Jan. 16, 2010).
[10] The Risk Externality, *The Economist* (The Free exchange), (Jan. 12, 2010). It is worth noting, of course, that government policy of deeming some firms too big to fail – a policy that was arguably strengthened by the 2010 Dodd-Frank Financial Reform Act – tends to encourage the sort of risk-taking the proposed bank tax aimed to reduce. (More about this in Chapter 8.)

chiefly, a market for zero- and low-emission vehicles – that buyers could not appropriate for themselves. In recognition of that positive externality, the federal government provided a $7,500 tax credit for the purchase of an electric auto-mobile. Numerous states have offered similar subsidies. California, for exam-ple, paid its citizens up to $5,000 for buying a standard battery electric car. Illinois residents could earn a tax credit of $4,000; Coloradans, up to $6,000. And these sorts of incentives weren't limited to "blue" and "crunchy" states. States as geographically and politically diverse as Georgia (up to $5,000), Louisiana (up to $3,000), Maryland (up to $1,000), Oklahoma (up to $1,500), Pennsylvania (up to $3,000), South Carolina (up to $2,000), and deep red Texas (up to $3,500) lined up to offer subsidies for purchasing electric vehicles.

Pigouvian taxes and subsidies may offer a number of advantages over a command-and-control approach to reducing externalities. Most obviously, a Pigouvian strategy doesn't threaten to lock in particular technologies. Because a Pigouvian strategy, unlike command-and-control, mandates neither specific controls nor technology-based performance standards, there is no reason to worry that it will discourage the development of cheaper or more effective spillover-reducing technologies.

The knowledge problem also appears to be less severe for a Pigouvian strategy than for command-and-control. When a command-and-control regime involves performance standards (e.g., emit no more than 0.5 parts per million), regula-tors must know the marginal costs and benefits of different levels of spillover-reduction. If regulators instead mandate particular technologies (e.g., install a #3 XYZ filter on each exhaust), then they must know the marginal costs and benefits of utilizing each technology versus its closest substitutes. A Pigouvian approach requires less information. For negative externalities, regulators need to know only the difference between individual and total marginal costs, and for positive externalities, only the difference between individual and total marginal benefits. The regulator then sets the tax or subsidy to equal that difference and allows regulatees themselves – using their personal, "man on the spot" knowl-edge of benefits and costs – to decide how much spillover-causing activity to engage in and how, if at all, to reduce any spillovers.

A Pigouvian approach is also likely to cause less welfare loss from manip-ulation by special interests. The more a regulatory approach directly controls the activities of those who are regulated, the more it can be hijacked to provide private benefits to some regulatees over others. For example, if a firm that has developed some spillover-reducing technology successfully lobbies for a rule requiring all its rivals to utilize the same technology (or to attain an emissions level currently achievable only using that technology), it can put those rivals out of business until they come up with all the money for the new technology and actually implement it. Since a Pigouvian approach gives regulatees a choice – eliminate spillovers *or* pay a per-unit penalty – it is less likely to cause firms to suspend or abandon their operations. It should therefore generate less deadweight loss from competition reduction and inspire a lower level of wasteful lobbying activity, lessening the twin harms from interest group manipulation of the regulatory system.

In addition to mitigating command-and-control's primary downsides, a Pigouvian strategy may offer affirmative benefits. Because Pigouvian taxes raise revenue for the government, they may permit the reduction of more distortive taxes. High marginal tax rates on earned income, for example, tend to discourage additional work. High capital gains rates decrease investment. By allowing for lower marginal tax rates on ordinary income and capital gains, Pigouvian taxes may permit the government to raise the revenue it needs with less adverse impact on economic growth. (Of course, as Pigouvian taxes achieve their goal of inducing people to shift away from the externality-causing behavior, the amount of revenue they generate falls and may need to be replaced by a more distortive tax. Unless its rate rises continuously, a Pigouvian tax cannot simultaneously maintain revenue and reduce the externality it targets.)

A Pigouvian strategy may also enable cheaper and quicker externality reduction. Command-and-control generally utilizes a single type of mechanism for reducing spillovers: a technological fix that achieves some degree of spillover reduction per unit of activity. Moreover, newly implemented command-and-control rules often "grandfather" old sources of spillovers so that the rules apply only (or more strictly) to new sources.[11] Pigouvian taxes, by contrast, reduce spillovers two ways: They encourage the development and adoption of spillover-reducing technologies, *and* they encourage an overall reduction in spillover-causing activity. They also apply equally to new and old sources of spillovers, so significant replacement of old sources with new sources is not required to achieve a substantial reduction in spillovers.

To get a sense of the potential magnitude of these benefits of Pigouvian taxes, consider a recent study comparing the federal Corporate Average Fuel Economy (CAFE) standards, a command-and-control approach to regulating automobile emissions, to a Pigouvian gasoline tax. CAFE standards require automobile manufacturers to design and sell fleets of vehicles that achieve a certain average fuel efficiency (e.g., 39 miles per gallon for certain model groupings). In existence since 1978, CAFE standards are the primary approach used in the United States to reduce the externalities associated with

---

[11] The Clean Air Act, for example, requires new sources of air pollution to limit emissions far more than is required of old sources.

automobile fuel consumption. Gasoline taxes are relatively low in the United States and have generally not been justified on Pigouvian grounds but as means of raising revenue for road construction. Many European nations, by contrast, impose much higher gasoline taxes and justify them as a way to reduce the externalities associated with automobile fuel consumption.

According to a recent study by researchers from the Massachusetts Institute of Technology (MIT), Americans could reduce automobile emissions more cheaply and quickly by moving in the European direction. The MIT researchers compared different means of achieving a 20 percent reduction in gasoline consumption (and thus greenhouse gas emissions) between 2010 and 2050. One means, a "fuel economy standard" (FES), would mimic the current CAFE standards. Another option would be a gasoline tax set at the level needed to reduce consumption by the requisite amount. The researchers concluded that the gasoline tax could achieve the target level of fuel consumption at as little as *one-fourteenth* the cost of the CAFE standards approach.

As explained in *Energy Futures*, the magazine of the MIT Energy Initiative:

> The FES [i.e., CAFE standards] regulation affects only new vehicles, so its beneficial effect requires that those vehicles be bought and driven in significant number. The FES regulation is the most costly when fuel economy increases are phased in gradually. The timing of the required standards is critical. If the fuel economy standards ramp down gradually in the early years, achieving the cumulative 20% reduction requires introducing high levels of vehicle efficiency in the final compliance years – an increasingly expensive proposition. . . .
>
> [T]he gasoline tax incurs the least cost because it elicits responses on several fronts. It provides a strong incentive for consumers to buy fuel efficient vehicles, adopt biofuels if they are cost-effective, and sharply curtail travel in both new and used vehicles.[12]

While Pigouvian strategies offer a number of advantages over command-and-control, they pose some difficulties. As an initial matter, Pigouvian taxes can be harder to implement politically. For example, despite widespread agreement among economists that a gasoline tax would be preferable to CAFE standards as a means of reducing the externalities associated with automobile fuel consumption, imposition of a Pigouvian gasoline tax has proven politically infeasible in the United States. Perhaps voters don't trust politicians to offset higher gasoline taxes with tax reductions elsewhere

[12]   Nancy W. Stauffer, US passenger cars, *Energy Futures* (Autumn 2011), at 11, 13–14 (available at www.energy.mit.edu/wp-content/uploads/2016/06/MITEI-Energy-Futures-Autumn-2011.pdf).

(especially since, as noted, revenues from Pigouvian taxes tend to fall and have to be replaced). Or perhaps gasoline taxes, which voters experience every time they visit the pump, are more politically salient than income and capital gains taxes, which voters generally confront only once a year. Whatever their reasons, Americans have traditionally been less inclined than Europeans to embrace Pigouvian taxes.

A Pigouvian strategy may also generate adverse distributional effects. Items typically subject to Pigouvian taxes – unhealthful foods, fuel, excessive product packaging, etc. – are usually either consumable goods or inputs, such as gasoline, that are heavily used in the production and distribution of such goods. Because poorer citizens tend to spend greater proportions of their incomes on consumption, a scheme that substitutes Pigouvian taxes for more distortive taxes on income and capital gains may raise the relative tax burden borne by individuals with lower incomes.

[margin note: regressive tax]

In addition, Pigouvian approaches sometimes entail higher administrative costs than command-and-control. It may be easier, for example, to set and monitor compliance with performance standards or technology requirements than to calculate and collect taxes on spillover-causing activity. If the tax is collected at the consumer level (e.g., $0.25 per can of sugared soda or $1.00 per gallon of gasoline), administrative costs should be minor. But where the tax is collected from upstream producers (e.g., $1 per kilogram of carbon emitted from your smokestacks), attaining compliance could be rather costly, perhaps costlier than just assuring that technological controls are in place.

Other drawbacks for a Pigouvian approach are the two difficulties that afflict most government interventions into private ordering: the knowledge problem and public choice concerns. Although those difficulties are usually less severe for Pigouvian strategies than for command-and-control, they still exist. Indeed, Pigou himself recognized as much.

Issuing a warning to those who would ignore government's own limitations and compare actual unregulated states of affairs to an unrealistic and idealized regulatory alternative (an approach economist Harold Demsetz would later term the "Nirvana Fallacy"[13]), Pigou wrote:

> In any industry, where there is reason to believe that the free play of self-interest will cause an amount of resources to be invested different from the amount that is required in the best interest of the national dividend, there is a *prima facie* case for public intervention. The case, however, cannot become more than a *prima facie* one, until we have considered the qualifications, which governmental agencies may be expected to possess for intervening

[13] Harold Demsetz, Information and Efficiency: Another Viewpoint, 12 *J. L. & Econ.* 1 (1969).

advantageously. It is not sufficient to contrast the imperfect adjustments of unfettered private enterprise with the best adjustment that economists in their studies can imagine.[14]

Pigou then proceeded to identify institutional constraints that could prevent regulators from achieving the ideal outcome imagined by economists:

> [W]e cannot expect that any public authority will attain, or will even whole-heartedly seek, that ideal. Such authorities are liable alike to ignorance, to sectional pressure and to personal corruption by private interest. A loud-voiced part of their constituents, if organised for votes, may easily outweigh the whole.[15]

Pigou thus recognized that the two drawbacks that plague most regulatory interventions – the knowledge problem ("ignorance") and public choice concerns ("sectional pressure and ... personal corruption by private interest") – may indeed afflict his own preferred type of intervention.

With respect to the knowledge problem, regulators employing a Pigouvian scheme may not need to identify the optimal technology or level of spillover-reduction – matters that would require a great deal of widely dispersed information about the marginal costs and benefits of different outcomes – but they still need to answer a difficult question: By how much do the total and individual marginal costs or benefits of an actor's behavior differ? That question would be vexing enough if the difference were constant at different output levels, but that is likely not the case. Guesswork is inevitable, and a mistake in setting the appropriate size of the Pigouvian tax or subsidy will lead to a less than ideal outcome.

Pigouvian strategies may also generate the sort of special interest manipulation public choice predicts. One way for firms to gain a competitive advantage over their rivals is to saddle those rivals, or the rivals' customers, with a special tax. If a firm can concoct an account of how such a tax would internalize an externality, it can usually find some public interest-minded "Baptists" to help distract attention from the private benefit the tax will confer on its bootlegging proponent. So, for example, producers of bottled waters, juices, or teas might fund a lobbying campaign for taxes on sugary sodas. They could justify the taxes as a means of reducing the externality that results when people consume too much sugar and then look to the public to subsidize the expenses stemming from their diabetes or obesity. They might enlist both health advocates and fiscal hawks to make the public case for the tax, and they could of course offer donations to the campaigns of supportive politicians.

[14] Pigou, *The Economics of Welfare*, supra note 7, at 331–32.   [15] Ibid. at 332.

Special interest manipulation of Pigouvian subsidies is even easier. Given that it's less unseemly to pursue government support for one's own socially beneficial offering than to seek to hobble one's rival with a tax, there is less need to find an attractive front person to make the public case for subsidies that confer competitive advantages. Moreover, counter-lobbying is less likely for subsidies than for taxes. Subsidy schemes do not directly target competitors for harm, so rivals are less likely to invest resources in opposition. Nor is significant taxpayer opposition likely, given the "concentrated benefits, dispersed costs" dynamic described above. Firms pushing for Pigouvian subsidies may therefore enjoy a relatively easy road to success.

Not surprisingly, then, one needn't search far to find examples of Pigouvian subsidies whose existence or magnitude seem more the result of effective lobbying than of a genuine effort to enhance social welfare. It's hard to believe, for example, that paying a whopping $12,500 ($7,500 from the federal government plus $5,000 or so from some states) to the wealthy buyer of a $90,000 Tesla electric automobile can be justified on externality grounds. It's even harder to believe that social welfare is enhanced when the federal government covers *the entire cost* of an electric golf cart the manufacturer has tweaked to be street-legal. That, however, is exactly what resulted when the Pigouvian subsidy for electric cars was extended to "neighborhood electric vehicles."[16] The benefit spillovers that result from purchasing a Tesla or a tricked-out golf cart are surely less than the lavish rewards the government confers on those who make such purchases. But Tesla and the neighborhood electric vehicle manufacturers – not to mention the gated community residents who tend to buy their products – are a politically powerful bunch.

Define Property Rights and Facilitate Markets

Three premises underlie command-and-control and Pigouvian approaches to ameliorating the harm from negative externalities. First, both assume that such externalities involve a clear victimizer (e.g., the owner of a polluting factory) who imposes costs on an innocent victim (e.g., the factory's downwind neighbor). They then reason that forcing that victimizer to do something – either limit her spillovers or pay some sort of spillover tax that encourages her to alter her behavior – will lead to the right, or at least a closer-to-right, outcome. Finally, they assume that the government must do the forcing.

[16] See Kathy Kristof, Free Golf Cart – But Call It a "Low-Speed Neighborhood Vehicle," *CBS Moneywatch* (Dec. 21, 2009).

Nobel Prize-winning economist Ronald Coase called into question each of these assumptions.[17] Coase first observed that external costs are not produced solely by one of the parties and borne solely by the other. Instead, externalities generally result from decisions by both parties. To be sure, downwind neighbors wouldn't wheeze and experience noxious odors if the factory didn't operate. Yet, the factory's operation would pose no problem if the neighbors didn't reside downwind from it. The factory's insistence on operating may harm the neighbors, but the neighbors' insistence on living where they do and enjoying pristine air harms the factory. The harms are reciprocal: Each party is both victim and victimizer.[18] It's therefore inappropriate to reflexively label one party the victimizer and then command it to change its behavior or burden it with a tax.

Indeed, as Coase showed, doing so may lead *away* from the optimal outcome, contrary to the second assumption of command-and-control and Pigouvian approaches. Suppose, for example, that a music producer purchases property next to an automobile repair garage. The producer plans to build a recording studio at the end of the lot closest to the garage but finds that the garage, while not especially loud, produces noises that will show up on sound recordings. The producer therefore successfully lobbies the city council to impose a noise ordinance banning sounds over a certain decibel level or perhaps imposing a hefty tax on such noises. The result is that the garage owner has to either shut down or install sound insulation that, while expensive, would be cheaper than any taxes or fines for noncompliance. If, as is likely, the music producer could avoid the problem more cheaply by building its recording studio at the other end of the lot or installing its own sound insulation at a lower cost, then the city's command-and-control or Pigouvian strategy will have squandered wealth. The better outcome would be to have the cheaper cost-avoider – in this case, the music producer – take whatever steps are necessary to minimize the external cost.

When property rights are clearly defined and enforceable, the parties are free to exchange them, and transaction costs are sufficiently low, this is the result that will obtain even without government intervention. That statement

---

[17] See R. H. Coase, The Problem of Social Cost, 3 *J. L. & Econ.* 1 (1960).

[18] If the notion that a downwind neighbor shares responsibility for the harm sounds strange, imagine that the factory has been in operation for decades and employs a majority of the residents of the impoverished island where it is located. The neighbor recently bought property next to the factory, plans to open a luxury resort catering to ultra-wealthy Americans and Europeans, and demands that the factory shut down. While the reciprocal harm is particularly clear in this example, it really exists in any instance of external cost, where each of the parties could avoid the conflict by altering its behavior.

is, in a nutshell, the so-called Coase Theorem. It undermines the third premise underlying command-and-control and Pigouvian approaches: the assumption that *the government* must force cost internalization by either commanding spillover reduction or taxing spillovers.

Coase's point here may be best explained with an illustration. Suppose that any invasion of sound into our hypothetical recording studio will corrupt recordings and that both the garage owner and the music producer could take steps to prevent such invasion from occurring. Relocation of the studio is impracticable, but the producer could install some soundproofing insulation, as could the garage owner. If neither party were to take any measures to mitigate the spillover (i.e., the garage made as much noise as it wanted, and the producer did nothing to protect itself), 100 decibels of sound would invade the studio. Each party, though, could equip its facility's walls with up to five levels of soundproofing insulation, each of which would reduce the spillover by 20 percent (from 100 to 80 decibels, from 80 to 60 decibels, etc.). The costs of implementing such soundproofing technology would differ between the two parties. The garage could reduce its sound spillover to zero at a cost of $25,000. The producer could fully insulate so as to block out any and all noise from the garage for $20,000. Obviously, the more one party insulated, the less the other party would need to do so. Table 4.1 sets forth the costs each party would face with different amounts of sound emanating from the garage.

The optimal outcome, given each party's costs of reducing the externality here, would be for the garage owner to insulate to the point at which the garage's sound spillover was reduced to 60 decibels, with the music producer then soundproofing the studio to protect against sound invasions of up to that level. The total cost of achieving that outcome would be $16,000 ($4,000 for the garage owner, $12,000 for the music producer). Summing the parties' costs

TABLE 4.1. *Costs of Soundproofing and Noise Abatement by Emission Level*

Amount of Sound Spilling Over from the Garage	Garage's Abatement Cost	Music Producer's Soundproofing Cost
100 dB	$0	$20,000
80 dB	$1,000	$16,000
60 dB	$4,000	$12,000
40 dB	$9,000	$8,000
20 dB	$16,000	$4,000
0 dB	$25,000	$0

at each of the possible levels of sound spillover reveals that every other outcome would involve greater total costs.

An assumption of command-and-control and Pigouvian approaches is that regulation – some sort of prescriptive mandate or a tax – is required to achieve the optimal outcome. But suppose that no such regulation exists and that the only rules governing the parties' behavior are the common law and any contracts the parties may have entered. Suppose further that the common law of the parties' jurisdiction adheres strongly to the *sic utere* maxim and would give the music producer the right to force the garage to reduce sound spillovers to zero.[19] Would the garage owner shut down or incur abatement costs of $25,000?

Probably not. The right to emit just 20 decibels of noise is worth $9,000 to the garage (the difference between abatement costs of $25,000 and $16,000), and such a level of sound spillover would cost the music producer only $4,000. The garage owner and music producer could thus strike a mutually beneficial bargain in which the garage owner paid more than $4,000 but less than $9,000 for the right to emit 20 decibels of noise. The right to go from 20 to 40 decibels, then, would be worth up to $7,000 to the garage owner, while imposing only $4,000 in additional costs on the music producer. Again, we would expect the parties to cut a deal allowing the garage to emit the additional decibels in exchange for at least $4,000. Raising the limit from 40 to 60 decibels would save the garage owner $5,000 and impose only $4,000 in cost on the music producer, so the parties could work out yet another mutually beneficial deal. They would not, however, agree that the garage owner's sound spillovers could rise from 60 to 80 decibels. The right to emit that extra noise would save the garage owner only $3,000 but would saddle the music producer with an additional $4,000 in soundproofing costs. It seems, then, that a simple common law rule granting the music producer the right to complete quiet would likely result in the optimal outcome: 60 decibels of spillover sound.

Suppose, though, that the common law of the relevant jurisdiction recognizes a "coming to the nuisance" defense that denies legal relief to people who move next to noisy operations (and probably pay discounted prices for their properties). In effect, such a rule would grant the garage the right to emit the full 100 decibels.

As strange as it seems, the final outcome should be the same as if the right were allocated in the opposite direction. Reducing the spillover from 100 to 80

---

[19]   Recall that the ancient common law principle *sic utere tuo ut alienum non laedas* ("so use your own so as not to injure another's property") underlies many tort doctrines involving real property. Jurisdictions vary in the extent to which they embrace the principle.

decibels would benefit the music producer by $4,000 while costing the garage only $1,000. The parties should thus strike a deal in which the producer pays the garage between $1,000 and $4,000 for that level of reduction. Going from 80 to 60 decibels of spillover, then, would cost the garage $3,000 and would benefit the music producer by $4,000. Again, a mutually beneficial bargain should emerge. Reducing spillovers from 60 to 40 decibels, however, would create greater cost to the garage ($5,000) than benefit to the music producer ($4,000). The parties would not bargain for that level of reduction. In the end, then, they should strike a deal achieving the optimal outcome – 60 decibels of reduction by the garage, with the studio soundproofing against that level of noise – without regulation and regardless of how the law allocates the property right between the parties.

Now, this assumes that property rights are clearly defined and transferable and, crucially, that the cost of striking these bargains is zero. If bargaining instead involves significant transaction costs, Coase observed, the optimal outcome may not result. Assume, for example, that it costs each party $5,000 to negotiate, execute, and enforce an agreement altering the common law's initial allocation of entitlements. Suppose further that the prevailing rule recognizes the coming to the nuisance defense and therefore allows the garage to emit the full 100 decibels. To secure an agreement by the garage owner to reduce its sound spillovers to the optimal level of 60 decibels, the music producer would have to pay the garage owner at least $9,000 ($4,000 to cover the cost of insulating the garage, plus $5,000 to cover the garage owner's transaction costs). The benefit to the music producer, however, would be only $3,000 ($8,000 in soundproofing savings, minus $5,000 of transaction costs for the producer). The producer therefore wouldn't pursue this agreement.

Nor would the optimal outcome be achieved if the law fully embraced extreme *sic utere* and gave the music producer the right to ban all sound spillovers. Procuring the right to emit 60 decibels of sound would cost the garage owner $17,000 ($12,000 to cover the music producer's soundproofing costs, plus $5,000 to cover the producer's transaction costs), while benefiting him by only $16,000 ($21,000 in reduced abatement costs, minus $5,000 of transaction costs for the garage owner). The garage owner wouldn't enter such a foolish bargain. Indeed, for every possible level of sound spillover – 20, 40, 60, 80, or 100 decibels – the net benefit to the party seeking alteration of the common law rule (i.e., insulation costs avoided minus that party's transaction costs) would be less than the cost the alteration would impose on the other party (i.e., the sum of that party's enhanced insulation costs and transaction costs). Under these circumstances, no "Coasean bargain" would occur.

It is, of course, the magnitude of transaction costs that determines whether parties are likely to strike Coasean bargains. If such costs are low – say, $1,000 per party in our example – an optimal bargain could still result regardless of the initial allocation of the entitlement.[20] When transaction costs are higher, but not so high as to preclude all Coasean bargaining, an agreement to achieve the optimal outcome may occur only if the right is initially allocated to one party but not the other. Suppose, for example, that each party faces transaction costs of $3,000. If the law gives the garage the right to emit the full 100 decibels, no bargain is likely. Achieving the optimal result would require the music producer to pay a minimum of $7,000 (the sum of the garage's abatement and transaction costs) to secure a benefit of only $5,000 (the producer's cost savings less his transaction costs). Every other bargain would be even less attractive to the music producer, so the common law allocation would endure. If, however, the law gave the right to the music producer, the parties would likely bargain for the optimal outcome. The music producer would benefit from allowing 60 decibels of spillover if he was paid at least $15,000 (his soundproofing plus transaction costs), and an agreement allowing that level of spillover would benefit the garage owner by $18,000 (his reduction in soundproofing expenses less his transaction costs). We would expect such a bargain to occur.

Coase's fundamental insight is that when there is a conflict over a legal right, the cost to the party who is denied that right isn't really "external" to the party to whom the right is allocated. Because costs are ultimately foregone opportunities, an entitled party that fails to transfer all or a portion of its right to the denied party in exchange for compensation incurs a real cost – the amount the denied party would have been willing to pay for the right at issue. If that amount, which reflects the value the denied party ascribes to the right at issue, would exceed the loss the entitled party would incur in transferring its right (or a portion thereof), then the entitled party will agree to the transfer, and the social cost of the inevitable conflict between the parties will be minimized. Such a transfer will not likely occur, however, if the parties' combined

---

[20]　In such circumstances, if the common law gave the right to the garage, achieving the optimal level of sound spillover (60 decibels) would require the music producer to pay the garage owner $5,000 ($4,000 to cover the garage's insulation costs, plus $1,000 to cover the garage owner's transaction costs) to secure a benefit of $7,000 ($8,000 in soundproofing cost reduction, minus $1,000 of transaction costs for the producer). Such a bargain would likely occur. If the law instead gave the right to the music producer, achieving the optimal outcome would require the garage owner to pay the music producer $13,000 ($12,000 to cover the producer's soundproofing costs, plus $1,000 to cover his transaction costs) to secure a benefit of $20,000 ($21,000 in soundproofing cost reduction, less the garage owner's transaction costs). Again, we would expect the deal to occur.

transaction costs would outweigh the surplus created by the trade. The real problem, then, isn't externalities. It's transaction costs! Reducing those, not externalities themselves, may be the optimal regulatory solution.

Many legal scholars have regarded the Coase Theorem as a theoretical curiosity with little relevance for regulation as we have defined it.[21] They concede that Coase's insights may offer guidance to courts tasked with defining property rights and resolving discrete disputes over entitlements. (One such guideline is that an adjudicator should allocate a disputed right to the party most likely to bargain for it, thereby minimizing transaction costs.) But regulation, most scholars have assumed, generally comes into play in contexts in which transaction costs are so high that Coasean bargains are unlikely.

Take air pollution, for example. Suppose a newly developed community of 1,000 homes is located downwind from a smoke-spewing factory and that the law of the jurisdiction includes a coming to the nuisance defense that effectively gives the factory the right to continue its traditional operations. Even if the most efficient outcome were for the factory to install pollution-eliminating technology, the homeowners and factory would not likely strike that bargain. In addition to facing the expense of investigating options and negotiating an agreement with the factory, the homeowners would confront a vexing coordination problem. While the homeowners would need to contribute to cover the factory's expenses, each individual homeowner would have an incentive not to pony up, hoping that others would make up for her deficiency. If the fundraising campaign succeeded without her contribution, she would benefit from declining to contribute. If it would fail even with her contribution, her failure to contribute would be inconsequential. Only in the unlikely event that her contribution would determine the success of the fundraising campaign would it be in her individual interest to contribute. She would therefore be unlikely to pay anything, hoping instead to free-ride on her neighbors' efforts. Substantial free-riding of this sort, though, would prevent the deal from being consummated. Moreover, the mere expectation of such free-riding might prevent homeowners from even attempting to pay off the factory.

A similar problem would exist if we reversed the assumptions, making pollution the efficient outcome but giving the homeowners a right to pristine air. To secure the right to pollute, the factory would have to pay each homeowner an amount exceeding the cost the pollution would impose on her. The most the factory owner would be willing to pay the homeowners as a group would be the amount it would cost him to eliminate the pollution altogether, minus his transaction costs. The last homeowner to agree to allow the pollution would probably be paid the most; she could hold out for an amount just shy of the difference between what the factory owner had already paid to other homeowners and the maximum amount he would be willing to pay. Each individual homeowner would therefore have an incentive to delay striking a deal in order to be the last hold-out. But if many homeowners adopted that strategy, the factory owner would likely fail in his quest to buy the right to pollute. It seems, then, that strategic behavior – a transaction cost – will tend to thwart Coasean bargains in situations involving conflicts among large numbers of individuals. And since regulation typically occurs in such situations, many scholars reason, the Coase Theorem is of little relevance to regulation.

There are at least three responses to such thinking. The first is to point out that bargains requiring significant coordination among multiple parties do occur with some regularity. A classic example involves bees. In a famous article, Nobel Prize-winning economist James Meade asserted that there are positive externalities associated with honeybee pollination of apple orchards so that, absent government intervention, there will be suboptimal amounts of both beekeeping and apple production.[22] Landowners hosting beehives, Meade observed, can't capture the benefit of the pollination their bees provide neighboring orchardists. At the same time, landowners who plant apple trees can't capture the benefits their nectar production confers on beekeepers. Meade argued that a Pigouvian taxation and subsidy scheme was necessary to correct for these externalities and thereby promote optimal levels of apple cultivation and beekeeping. He assumed that privately ordered arrangements among beekeepers and orchardists would prove too difficult to negotiate and enforce.

It seems Meade was wrong. As economist Steven Cheung demonstrated, apple farmers in Washington, a leading apple producing state, regularly pay beekeepers to maintain hives on the farmers' property for pollination purposes.[23] Moreover, social norms have emerged to combat free-riding wherein orchardists rely on their neighbors' hives for pollination. Cheung explained:

> [I]f a number of similar orchards are located close to one another, one who hires bees to pollinate his own orchard will in some degree benefit his

[22] J. E. Meade, External Economies and Diseconomies in a Competitive Situation, 52 *Econ. J.* 54 (1952).

[23] Steven N. S. Cheung, The Fable of the Bees: An Economic Investigation, 16 *J. L. & Econ.* 11 (1973).

neighbors. .... [I]n the absence of any social constraint on behavior, each farmer will tend to take advantage of what spillover does occur and to employ fewer hives himself. Of course, contractual arrangements could be made among all farmers in an area to determine collectively the number of hives to be employed by each, but no such effort is observed.

Acknowledging the complication, beekeepers and farmers are quick to point out that a social rule, or custom of the orchards, takes the place of explicit contracting: during the pollination period the owner of an orchard either keeps bees himself or hires as many hives per area as are employed in neighboring orchards of the same type. One failing to comply would be rated as a "bad neighbor," it is said, and could expect a number of inconveniences imposed on him by other orchard owners. This customary matching of hive densities involves the exchange of gifts of the same kind, which apparently entails lower transaction costs than would be incurred under explicit contracting, where farmers would have to negotiate and make money payments to one another for the bee spillover.[24]

Further research has revealed that when the external benefits conferred on beekeepers by orchardists (nectar) exceed those the beekeepers confer on the orchardists (pollination), it is the beekeepers who do the paying.[25] Apple blossoms produce little nectar, so in Washington more benefit flows to the orchardists than to the beekeepers, and the orchardists pay the beekeepers for housing their hives on the orchardists' land. Orange blossoms, by contrast, produce gobs of valuable nectar, so beekeepers in Florida have traditionally paid the owners of orange groves for the right to keep hives on their property.[26] It seems, then, that pollination and nectar production don't produce the intractable externality problems Meade assumed.

So-called neighborhood assemblages provide another example of coordinated transactions that seem implausible in the economics classroom but, in the real world, happen all the time. In an assemblage, a real estate developer buys up all the parcels of land in an area – e.g., an entire subdivision – to build a larger structure like a shopping center. The developer faces a hold-out problem similar to that confronting a factory owner who wishes to buy the right to pollute from numerous downwind neighbors: Each homeowner has an incentive to be the last to sell, so she can extract the highest possible price from the buyer. Despite this difficulty, many neighborhood assemblages, each

[24] Ibid. at 30.
[25] See Michael Munger, Orange Blossom Special: Externalities and the Coase Theorem, Econlib.org (May 5, 2008) (available at www.econlib.org/library/Columns/y2008/Mungerbees .html).
[26] Apparently, this practice has recently changed as the total honeybee population has declined and beekeepers' services have thus become more valuable.

involving dozens of landowners, have succeeded in densely populated areas such as the Chicago suburbs. Given the potential value at stake, assemblers and their lawyers have been quite motivated to develop means of overcoming the hold-out problem. Perhaps they've used "most favored nations" clauses that give each seller the right to any higher per-acre price paid to another seller, thereby enabling the developer to credibly threaten to reject a hold-out's demand for a premium price. Or maybe they've employed contingent contracts in which none of the land is purchased unless all owners agree to sell. Experimental evidence has shown that the use of such contracts can virtually eliminate the hold-out problem by increasing the social pressures on potential hold-outs.[27] Regardless of how neighborhood assemblers have managed to succeed, the important point for present purposes is that they have done so.

Examples like these do not suggest that free-riding, hold-out problems, and other transaction costs aren't serious hurdles to privately ordered solutions to externalities. We still shouldn't expect that Coasean bargains between polluters and millions of Los Angeles homeowners will generate the optimal level of air quality in Southern California. The examples do remind us, though, that evidence trumps theory and that policymakers shouldn't be too quick to dismiss the possibility of efficient private ordering simply because of theoretical hold-out and free-rider problems.

A second response to scholars who would confine Coase's insights to the adjudicatory, non-regulatory context is to observe that regulation is not limited to situations in which transaction costs would be so high as to preclude Coasean bargains. Indeed, regulatory measures are often imposed to address purported externalities in contexts in which such bargains are likely to occur, and often have occurred.

Consider smoking bans. In recent years, hundreds of local and state governments have enacted regulations banning cigarette smoking in "public" places, which are defined to include not only publicly owned facilities but also privately owned properties to which members of the public are invited (restaurants, bars, hotel lobbies, etc.). A chief justification for these regulations has been that smoking by patrons imposes a negative externality on non-smokers. But Coasean bargaining, perhaps implicit, tends to eliminate any such externalities.

On the issue of smoking in privately owned places to which the public is invited, there is an inevitable conflict between the proprietor and some group

[27] Sean M. Collins and R. Mark Isaac, Methods to Overcome the Hold-Out Problem in Land Acquisition: An Experimental Economics Study, Florida State University Institute for Energy Systems, Economics, and Sustainability (Jan. 2011 Working Paper).

of potential patrons. If the proprietor insists on a no smoking policy, she will conflict with smokers; if she instead permits smoking, she will clash with non-smokers. Her demands harm the disfavored group, but if that group's demands were satisfied, she (and members of the favored group) would suffer harm. We have, then, the sort of reciprocal harm that exists whenever there are complaints of negative externalities.

Conditions are also right for Coasean bargaining. The right to determine indoor smoking policy is well defined in the common law (it belongs to the establishment owner). It is transferable (the owner can change the smoking policy at will). Transaction costs are low (whatever customers the proprietor favors "pay" her by patronizing the establishment and buying her wares; no explicit negotiation is required; patrons simply "vote with their feet"). If the initially disfavored group is willing to pay more than the initially favored group – i.e., if altering the smoking policy from the owner's preferred position would increase her profits – the owner transfers the right. Sometimes the outcome that is most efficient (and thus profit-maximizing, and thus selected) involves a compromise in which both sides bear some cost, as when a restaurant offers smoking and non-smoking sections. The important point is that the owner is motivated and, under the common law, equipped to strike the optimal outcome. There is simply no need for regulation to correct an externality here.

Or take workplace safety regulation. That, too, is often justified as a means of correcting an externality. For example, in an article entitled *The Necessity of OSHA*, Professor Sidney Shapiro argued that without workplace safety regulation "[a] portion of the cost of production – the workers' illnesses – . . . 'spills over' to the employees in the sense that they, not the factory, will pay for the consequences of becoming ill." This, he continued, causes an inefficiency:

> There is a market failure because the price of the product made by the factory does not reflect the costs paid by the workers concerning their illnesses. The underpricing of the product leads to overproduction. Because the price is lower than it would be if the factory paid for the spillover cost, consumers will purchase more of it than otherwise. The market is not efficient because more of the product is sold than if it were properly priced.[28]

Again, though, there are good reasons to believe that bargaining among the parties will minimize external costs in this context. Under the common law, the right to set risk levels was well defined (allocated to the employer) and transferable (she could accede to worker demands for more protections).

---

[28]   Sidney A. Shapiro, The Necessity of OSHA, 8-SPG *Kan. J. L. & Pub. Pol'y* 22, 22–23 (1999).

Because employers regularly hire workers and adjust salaries, they can easily negotiate the level of avoidable risk as part of compensation discussions, which means transaction costs are low. Not surprisingly, then, economists have long asserted that employers bargain over – and pay for – risk.[29] Indeed, one of the most robust empirical findings in all of labor economics is that employers must pay "compensating differentials" for exposing their workers to risk.[30] Even when workers' compensation laws require employers to pay for on-the-job injuries, employers typically pay risk premiums to account for injury costs not covered by the workers' compensation system (pain and suffering, etc.), and those premiums tend to rise as workers' compensation becomes stingier and fall as it becomes more generous.[31] In effect, then, employers and workers engage in Coasean bargains over risk. Though the common law traditionally gave risk-determination rights to employers, employees "buy" those rights, or a portion thereof, by reducing their compensation demands. Both employers and their workers have an incentive to bargain for the optimal outcome – that in which the employer takes all, but only, cost-effective safety precautions.

[29] Adam Smith, for example, explained as far back as 1776 that "[t]he whole of the advantages and disadvantages of the different employments of labor and stock must, in the same neighborhood, be either perfectly equal or tending toward equality. ... The wages of labor vary with the ease or hardship, the honorableness or dishonorableness of employment." Adam Smith, *An Inquiry into the Nature and Causes of the Wealth of Nations* 99–100 (1776, London: Thomas Nelson; reprinted 1937, New York: The Modern Library).

[30] See, e.g., Richard Thaler and Sherwin Rosen, The Value of Saving a Life: Evidence from the Labor Market, in *Household Production and Consumption* 265–98, (Nestor Terleckyj ed.) (Cambridge, MA: National Bureau of Economic Research, 1976); W. Kip Viscusi, *Employment Hazards: An Investigation of Market Performance* (Cambridge, MA: Harvard University Press, 1979); Charles Brown, Equalizing Differences in the Labor Market, 94 *Quarterly J. Econ.* 113 (1980); W. Kip Viscusi, Occupational Safety and Health Regulation: Its Impact and Policy Alternatives, in *Research in Public Policy Analysis and Management* 281, 281–89 (John P. Crecine ed.) (Greenwich, Connecticut: JAI Press, 1981); Richard J. Arnould and Len M. Nichols, Wage Risk Premiums and Workers' Compensation: A Refinement of Estimates of Compensating Wage Differentials, 91 *J. Pol. Econ.* 332 (1983); Stuart Dorsey and Norman Walzer, Workers' Compensation, Job Hazards, and Wages, 36 *Indus. & Lab. Rel. Rev.* 642 (1983); Greg J. Duncan and Bertil Holmlund, Was Adam Smith Right After All? Another Test of the Theory of Compensating Wage Differentials, 1 *J. Lab. Econ.* 366, 374 (1983); Henry W. Herzog, Jr. and Alan M. Schlottmann, Valuing Risk in the Workplace: Market Price, Willingness to Pay, and the Optimal Provision of Safety, 72 *Rev. of Econ. & Statistics* 463 (1990); Felice Martinello and Ronald Meng, Workplace Risks and the Value of Hazard Avoidance, 25 *Canadian J. Econ.* 333, 343 (1992); Michael Moore & W. Kip Viscusi, Doubling the Estimated Value of Life: Results Using New Occupational Fatality Data, 7 *J. Pol'y Analysis & Mgt.* 476 (1988).

[31] See Michael Moore and W. Kip Viscusi, *Compensation Mechanisms for Job Risks: Wages, Workers' Compensation, and Product Liability* (Princeton: Princeton University Press, 1990), 23, 46–54.

As with indoor smoking, there is no externality here that is unlikely to be alleviated through bargaining.

None of this is to say that smoking bans and workplace safety regulations are never justified. Other defects in private ordering – say, information asymmetries (discussed in Chapter 8) or endogenous preferences (discussed in Chapter 9) – may be significant enough in these contexts to warrant a regulatory fix. But if that is the case, then the fix should be aimed at those maladies, not at externalities. Given the low transaction costs in these contexts, Coasean bargains should address any externality concerns.

A third response to those who dismiss the Coase Theorem's relevance to regulation is to observe that even in contexts in which transaction costs are so significant that pure Coasean bargains are unlikely, policymakers may harness Coasean insights to achieve efficiencies. Consider, for example, emission permit trading, known colloquially as "cap and trade." Under a permit trading scheme, the government does not command individual regulatees to utilize particular technologies or meet individual performance standards. Nor does the government impose a tax equal to the difference between the total and individual marginal costs of an activity, as in a Pigouvian scheme. Instead, the government sets a total limit on the aggregate emissions of all regulatees, distributes emission permits that, taken together, allow emissions up to the total limit, and permits regulatees (and others, including environmentalists seeking to reduce overall emissions) to trade those permits. Emitters for whom reduction is particularly costly will be willing to pay the most for permits; those for whom emission reduction is cheaper can benefit by selling their permits and reducing their emissions accordingly. The result is that we achieve the target level of aggregate emissions at the lowest possible cost.

Permit trading exhibits aspects of all three regulatory approaches considered in this chapter. As with command-and-control, regulators determine the aggregate amount of pollution allowed, not just the fee per unit emitted. As with Pigouvian taxes, polluters may choose either to cut their emissions or pay. The essence of emissions trading, though, is distinctly Coasean: The government defines property rights and facilitates exchanges that result in the "cheapest cost-avoider" taking the lead in minimizing social cost.

Of course, there are potential downsides to a permit trading scheme. Because regulators determine the maximum aggregate amount of the activity at issue, cap-and-trade regimes confront the difficult knowledge problem facing command-and-control. Regulators do not need to determine just the difference between the individual and total marginal cost of an activity; instead, they must estimate the marginal costs *and benefits* of the activity at issue so that they can determine what quantity maximizes social welfare.

Moreover, if the activity at issue is one that causes greater harm if concentrated in one area, trading schemes may increase the social loss resulting from a set amount of the activity. For example, aggregate emissions of five tons of some toxin may cause no health problems if the emissions are widely distributed throughout the country but could cause grave harms if permit trading resulted in their being released in one small area. When such "hot spots" are a concern, permit trading may prove problematic.

Despite these concerns, permit trading appears to offer significant benefits over the dominant American approach to mitigating externalities, command-and-control. Consider, for example, the acid rain provisions of the Clean Air Act's 1990 amendments. Those provisions eschewed additional individual lim-itations on sulfur dioxide emissions in favor of a scheme that would cap total emissions and distribute tradeable pollution permits among the nation's 3,200 coal-fired power plants. When the amendments were adopted, the estimated cost of achieving the mandated reduction (one-half the level of 1980 emissions) was $6.1 billion per year. The actual annual cost of achieving that goal appears to have been around one-quarter of that amount. Moreover, coal-fired plants achieved their mandated reduction by 2007, three years before the target date.

Despite such successes, efforts to impose a cap-and-trade scheme for reg-ulating greenhouse gases have so far failed. That failure, however, seems more the result of skepticism concerning the *objective* of greenhouse gas reduction (e.g., does it make sense to spend vast sums of money to reduce greenhouse gases when climate science is uncertain, other major emitters aren't abating, and future innovation may well moot the problem?) than about the means of achieving it. If regulating greenhouse gases is indeed cost-justified, cap-and-trade is likely the way to go.

LESSONS FOR POLICYMAKERS

The analysis in this chapter suggests that policymakers, in deciding whether and how to exercise governmental power to address an externality, should ask the following series of questions, in roughly the order presented:

- Does the activity at issue involve a significant net spillover in costs or benefits? Many times, an activity will create some costs not borne by the actor *but also* some benefits that the actor cannot capture. If the spilled-over costs and benefits are of roughly equal magnitude, then there may be no need to address the spillovers at all; they'll self-correct.[32]

- Is the externality the result of an increase or decrease in prices? If it's a pecuniary externality only, then it doesn't actually lead to a misallocation of productive resources and generally should be ignored (though the government might offer some form of safety net for individuals disadvantaged by the price effect).

- To what extent are Coasean bargains occurring? If property rights are well defined, enforceable, and transferable, and if transaction costs are relatively low, one would expect parties to bargain in a way that minimizes external costs. We saw this in restaurants and hotels prior to the advent of smoking bans, when different proprietors were opting for different smoking policies in response to varied consumer preferences. Evidence similarly suggests a significant amount of bargaining over workplace safety levels. Where we see this sort of bargaining, regulation aimed at alleviating externalities may be unnecessary and, if it thwarts Coasean bargains, even destructive of wealth. (Again, there may be *other* reasons to regulate even where Coasean bargains are occurring, but those reasons involve different market failures that typically call for different regulatory solutions.)

- Is it possible to encourage Coasean bargains? Governments can often facilitate private ordering by better defining property rights or taking steps to reduce transaction costs. Given that any regulation aimed directly at reducing externalities will involve some downsides (e.g., the knowledge problem, public choice concerns), the optimal solution may be not to address the externality head-on but instead to remove barriers that prevent parties from bargaining for whatever outcome minimizes external costs.

- Would a command-and-control, Pigouvian, or hybrid (e.g., cap and trade) scheme create a net social benefit? If so, which approach would create *the greatest* net benefit? To answer these questions, policymakers

---

[32] For this reason, Nobel Prize-winning economist and *New York Times* columnist Paul Krugman may have erred in calling for "progressive taxation that goes beyond the maximization of revenue" to combat the negative externalities rich people impose on the rest of the population when they engage in conspicuous, resentment-inducing consumption. See Paul Krugman, Having It and Flaunting It, N.Y. *Times* (Sept. 24, 2014). A consistent theme of Krugman's writing has been that the nation's macroeconomic woes result from inadequate consumption (insufficient aggregate demand). See, e.g., Paul Krugman, The War on Demand, N.Y. *Times* (Jan. 24, 2011). If he's right on the latter point, then what he deems excessive consumption by the rich actually creates positive externalities that may well offset any resentment-based negative externalities he observes.

should assess the degree to which the implementation difficulties and side effects discussed above will afflict each potential regulatory solution. In particular, they should ask:

- To what degree is technological lock-in a concern? If an innovative technology might reduce the externality in the future, then there may be a significant downside to adopting a technology-based command-and-control regime that discourages technological experimentation.

- How much information is required to implement the policy? Do regulators have, or can they cost-effectively obtain, that information? And what will be the downsides if they're mistaken? In general, the more prescriptive the approach, the more information regulators need to implement it appropriately.

- What is the potential for the regulatory approach under consideration to be used to create entry barriers or other competitive disadvantages? Again, this concern generally increases with the prescriptiveness of the regulatory approach under consideration.

By methodically answering these questions when presented with a demand to regulate instances of purported spillover costs or benefits, policymakers can ensure that they have appropriately diagnosed the disease, examined the range of potential remedies (including doing nothing), and selected the policy most likely to minimize adverse outcomes. They can thereby minimize the sum of decision and error costs from externality regulation.

We turn now to the traditional market failure most closely related to externalities: public goods.

5

Public (and Quasi-Public) Goods

It's a sunny Fourth of July in your delightful Midwestern hometown. You're off work for Independence Day, and the weather couldn't be better. You know summer's dog days are fast approaching, so you resolve to savor as much outdoor time as you can.

Fondly recalling the many hours you spent fishing with your grandfather, you decide to honor his memory with an afternoon at your old fishing spot, a lake created by a dam on the river that runs through your town. *That lake was just swarming with bass*, you recall. You plan to fish until late afternoon and then head to a friend's house to eat hot dogs, watch fireworks, and revel in being an American.

Fishing gear packed, you hop in your car and turn on the radio. The dial is set to your local public radio station, which you used to enjoy but increasingly find irritating. *Every show on that station is so biased*, you think. You turn the dial to another talk radio station, one that claims to be fairer and more balanced. The problem with that station is the commercials – there are way too many of them. You decide to switch over to satellite radio, to which you've recently subscribed. *How have I lived without this?*, you ponder. There are just so many options: 80s music, dance hits, various flavors of country (new, old, "alt"), political talk (left-leaning, right-leaning, down the middle), clean comedy, not-so-clean comedy . . . where to begin?

Reggae tunes, beamed from space, blare from your radio as you drive along the banks of the river through town. *Visitors passing through might not even know there's a river here*, you think. Decades ago, the town built an elaborate system of levees to prevent flooding. The levees are so tall that they block views of the water from Old River Road. *I suppose the road's name would tip them off*, you conclude.

A little past downtown, the levees end and you can finally see the river. New subdivisions full of cookie-cutter houses now straddle it. *I'd be scared to buy a place down here*, you think. A small flood wouldn't reach the houses, but every couple of decades a big one comes along. *Hope they have flood insurance!*

A few miles out of town, the lake comes into view. Marveling again at the beauty of the place, you're disappointed to see lines of cars along the shore. *Oh well*, you think. *I should have expected as much on a gorgeous Independence Day.* You park, unload your gear, and hike around the lake until you find an unoccupied spot on the shore. You quickly tie on your best lure and cast out a line. Then another. And another.

After several hours without so much as a bite, you decide to call it quits. You pack up your gear, hike back to your car, and tune to a satellite radio station playing British alternative rock music produced from 1982 to 1988. Singing along to your favorite Morrissey tune, you head to a local supermarket to pick up some food and drink for the barbeque. You're amazed at the store's selection of hot dogs and bratwursts. Passing over wieners of various substances (pork, turkey, beef, soy), you settle on traditional pork beer brats. *What brew would go well with these?*, you think. Back behind some creamy British ales, a bunch of micro-brewed wheat beers, and a collection of various stouts (oatmeal, coffee?, chocolate?!), you spot a section of green-bottled Czech pilsners. *Perfect.*

The cookout ends up being far more enjoyable than the fishing. *(There used to be so many fish in that lake!)* After sampling a smorgasbord of cylindrical meat products and beers from all over the world, you and the other cookout guests turn your lawn chairs toward downtown and take in the local fireworks show, which is choreographed to music broadcast on that annoying public radio station. *A near perfect Fourth of July*, you think.

Perhaps unbeknownst to you, you spent your Independence Day enjoying some "public" – as well as a few "quasi-public" – goods.

WHAT ARE PUBLIC AND QUASI-PUBLIC GOODS?

A public good is a good or service that is "non-excludable" and "non-rivalrous." Non-excludable means that it is impossible, or at least impracticable, for the producer of the amenity to prevent non-payers from enjoying it. Production of a public good therefore entails positive externalities – spillovers of benefits that cannot be captured by their creator. Non-rivalrous means that one person's consumption of the amenity does not diminish the consumption opportunities of others. There's no need for consumers to fight over who gets to enjoy something if one person's enjoyment doesn't diminish another's ability to enjoy the same thing. *entails positive externalities*

Two things should be apparent about these two features of public goods. First, they are independent of each other. Because excludability and rivalrousness are distinct concepts, it's possible to exhibit one characteristic but not the other. Second, the two features are matters of degree. A good or service may be *partially* excludable or rivalrous, so it makes sense to think about the degree or "strength" of a good's excludability or rivalrousness. In light of these considerations, it is useful to divide goods and services into four quadrants depending on whether they exhibit (1) weak excludability and weak rivalrousness, (2) strong excludability but weak rivalrousness, (3) weak excludability but strong rivalrousness, or (4) strong excludability and strong rivalrousness. *See graph*

"Pure" public goods comprise the first category, exhibiting both weak excludability and weak rivalrousness. The fireworks display that closed out your Fourth of July was such a good: the producer couldn't prevent people in the surrounding area from watching the show (weak excludability), and one viewer's watching of the show didn't diminish anyone else's opportunity to enjoy it (weak rivalrousness). The levees along the river, as well as the public radio programming you used to enjoy but now find irritating, were also pure public goods. Again, even non-contributors could enjoy both amenities, and one person's enjoyment wouldn't cause another to be excluded.

The second category – strong excludability but weak rivalrousness – would include the satellite radio programming you listened to on your drive. By scrambling its signal for all but its subscribers, the satellite radio provider is able to exclude non-payers from enjoying what it has produced. But its product is still non-rivalrous; your enjoyment of Morrisey and The Cure created no impediment to any other subscriber's enjoyment of the same tunes. Goods and services exhibiting strong excludability but weak rivalrousness are sometimes dubbed "club goods," reflecting the fact that the producer uses its power to exclude to create a "club" of authorized (i.e., paying) consumers.

The lake you visited falls into the third category, exhibiting weak excludability but strong rivalrousness. Lying on public property and reachable from numerous points, the lake and the fish it contained were broadly accessible by members of the general public. Each visitor's consumption of the lake amenity, however, reduced consumption opportunities for other visitors. Each additional power boat, for example, reduced the open area in which other boats could pull water-skiers or enjoy wake-free solitude. And each time one visitor reeled in a bass, the potential for another visitor to do so was reduced. Goods and services exhibiting weak excludability but strong rivalrousness are generally called "commons goods," because they often involve commonly

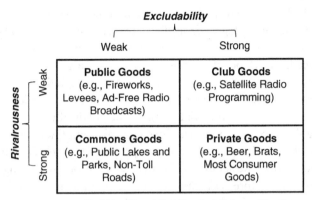

FIGURE 5.1 Public, Quasi-Public, and Private Goods

owned property, such as public parkland. (Indeed, public greenspaces are sometimes referred to as "commons" – e.g., the Boston Common.)

Goods and services that exhibit neither of the hallmarks of public goods – those that are both strongly excludable and strongly rivalrous – are called, not surprisingly, "private goods." Most consumer products and services, including the beer and brats you purchased for your July 4th barbeque, fall into this category.

Figure 5.1 illustrates the categories of public and quasi-public goods, and provides examples of goods and services falling within each.

SYMPTOMS/DISEASE

Think back over your Independence Day. Some of the amenities you enjoyed – brats, beer, satellite radio programming – were available in great abundance. Some others – levee protection, fish down at the lake – weren't. This is, in general, the adverse symptom that results from public (and some quasi-public) goods: There isn't enough of the amenity available relative to consumer demand.

But let's be more precise. How much of a good or service is "enough"? If we're aiming to maximize the value achievable from productive resources, we'll want for a good or service to be produced if, but only if, the subjective value it brings to those who consume it (which determines their reservation price, the amount they would be willing to pay for the thing) exceeds the cost of producing the thing (including the value of things that could have been produced had the required resources been put to other ends).[1] We'll also want people to consume something only if the value they derive from doing so

---

[1] Because costs are foregone opportunities, a cost of producing X is the inability to produce Y, which requires the same resources as X.

exceeds the loss suffered by others who then cannot consume the same thing. Welfare-reducing shortages occur when either (1) consumers would be willing to pay more for a good than its cost of production, yet the good remains unproduced; or (2) people consume goods, making them unavailable to others, despite the fact that the value the consumers derive is less than the value that would have been created if the goods had been left for others.

When it comes to public and quasi-public goods, these sorts of welfare-reducing shortages are common. Flood control exemplifies the first variety – underproduction. Recall that once you got out of town on Old River Road, the levees ended. Residents of the new subdivisions straddling the river could cut their future costs and reduce their immediate flood insurance expenditures by having levees constructed along their section of the river. If we added up the benefit each unprotected homeowner would get from levee protection, thereby deriving the homeowners' aggregate willingness-to-pay (reservation price) for levees, it's likely that the sum would exceed the cost of building levees. Yet, no levees were built. Potential value was squandered.

Your old fishing spot illustrates the second sort of shortage problem – over-consumption. Back when the area was less populated, that lake was chock full of bass. It has now been so overfished that throwing out a line is hardly worth the effort. Yet people continue to flock to the lake, as you saw on July 4th.

Welfare-reducing shortages are just a symptom that tends to accompany public and some quasi-public goods. To address the problem effectively, we need to identify the disease that regularly causes such goods and services to be in short supply. A moment's reflection suggests that the real culprit is the fact that producers and consumers don't experience all the benefits and costs of their production and consumption – i.e., that there are externalities involved in producing and consuming public and some quasi-public goods. Those externalities exist when the amenities at issue are non-excludable.

Consider again underproduction shortages, exemplified by the absence of downriver levees. The value a levee would produce for each unprotected homeowner would exceed that homeowner's pro rata share of the total cost of levee construction. But since a homeowner will be protected even if he or she doesn't contribute to the construction, each has an incentive not to contribute and to let the neighbors shoulder the burden. With too many free-riders, contributing homeowners may be unable or unwilling to pay enough to finance the levee. If contributors could exclude non-payers from protection, each homeowner would pay up to his or her reservation price, and there would be enough money for the levee. It is thus a non-excludability-induced positive externality – the inability of the homeowners producing the levee to exclude

free-rider problem is an externality

overconsumption is a negative
externality from lack of excludability (handwritten annotation)

non-contributors and thereby capture all the benefits of their efforts – that creates the welfare-reducing levee shortage.

Overconsumption shortages, exemplified by the overfished lake, similarly result from externalities. Suppose that the fish in the lake reproduce at a rate where the fish stock will remain relatively constant with ten or fewer fishermen per day. (More than ten depletes the fish faster than they can reproduce, but with fewer than ten, the fish multiply so much that they face food constraints and begin to die off.) Under these conditions, adding an eleventh fisherman will reduce total welfare if the benefit that fisherman enjoys is less than the cost he imposes by reducing the fishing stock below replacement levels. Of course, each fisherman beyond number ten imposes some cost on himself when he chooses to head to the lake; each, after all, has an interest in maintaining a healthy fish stock. Despite that self-inflicted harm, though, fishermen are likely to crowd the lake – well beyond ten per day – because each captures *all* the benefit of his conduct (the enjoyment of fishing plus the fish he catches) while sharing the cost of his activity (the reduction in future fish stocks) with everyone who fishes at the lake. The cause of your July 4th fishing troubles, then, was a negative externality resulting from the fact that fishermen cannot easily be excluded from the lake.[2]

Comparing our categories of goods confirms that externalities resulting from an inability to exclude are to blame for the welfare-reducing shortages that accompany public, and some quasi-public, goods. Private goods, such as brats and beer, are both rivalrous and excludable and are available in abundance. Quasi-public club goods like cable television shows and subscription satellite radio programming are non-rivalrous but excludable, and they, too, seem to be optimally available. By contrast, non-rivalrous and non-excludable public goods (such as flood protection) and rivalrous but non-excludable commons goods (such as fish in publicly owned water bodies) are regularly subject to shortages from underproduction and/or overconsumption. This suggests that the real culprit – the common thread running through shortage-prone, but missing from abundantly produced, goods – is non-excludability, which leads to externalities. (As we'll soon see, non-rivalrousness is relevant in

---

[2] We might alternatively view this situation as one involving *positive* externalities. Consider things from the perspective of a fisherman who is contemplating whether to limit his fishing in order to help preserve or replenish the fish stock. Each fisherman who does so bears all the cost of his decision (the immediate fish foregone) but captures only a small portion of the benefit he creates (a more stable fish population that will enable better fishing in the future). As we saw in Chapter 4, when an activity inures largely to the benefit of people besides the actor, individuals tend to do "too little" of it. Because conservation of non-excludable goods is such an activity, such goods tend to be underconserved (i.e., overconsumed), leading to welfare-reducing shortages for potential future consumers.

determining the appropriate policy response to non-excludable goods, but it's not the cause of the adverse symptom that tends to accompany such goods.)

non-rivalrousness is key

AVAILABLE REMEDIES AND THEIR IMPLEMENTATION DIFFICULTIES AND SIDE EFFECTS

Given that externalities resulting from non-excludability are the disease giving rise to the adverse symptom associated with public and quasi-public goods, our consideration of available remedies will focus primarily on the two categories of non-excludable goods: pure public goods and quasi-public commons goods. We'll see that while some form of government intervention may (but won't necessarily) be the optimal response for both types of goods, the interventions most appropriate for pure public goods are not typically *regulatory* interventions. Commons goods, on the other hand, may warrant the same sort of regulatory responses as negative externalities generally. First, though, a brief word on the category of quasi-public goods for which no departure from private ordering is needed.

Club Goods

Because a club good is non-rivalrous, it by definition cannot be overconsumed, so its consumption alone entails no negative externalities.[3] Because it is excludable, its producer can prevent free-riders from enjoying its benefits, so its production doesn't involve a debilitating level of positive externalities. Lacking significant externalities in their consumption and production, club goods typically exist in abundance, and there is generally no need for an affirmative government response to prevent welfare-reducing shortages. It is important to note, though, that certain *institutions* need to be in place in order to preserve the excludability that facilitates optimal production of club goods.

I am speaking primarily of property rights.[4] Consider a large movie theater. Most nights, there are more than enough seats available for viewers, so the amenity at issue – a place to watch an exhibited film – is a non-rivalrous but excludable club good.[5] Despite the non-rivalrousness of the amenity they are

---

[3] A club good's consumption may, of course, lead to negative externalities if the consumption generates some adverse by-product (e.g., noise pollution from playing a non-rivalrous musical composition too loudly). The externality, though, results not from the mere consumption of the good but from the by-product produced.

[4] Contract rights – e.g., the right to enter into an enforceable agreement to allow access to a club good in exchange for payment – are also essential to the optimal production of club goods.

[5] When there's a blockbuster that attracts more potential viewers than available seats, the amenity may become rivalrous. Most evenings, though, it is not.

supplying, people regularly build and operate large movie theaters because they know they can collect money from anyone who consumes the amenity they are providing. They can do that only because their property interest in the theater includes the right to exclude non-payers. It is thus property rights – and specifically the right to exclude – that ensures the optimal production of large movie-watching venues.

That's easy to see when we're talking about a tangible amenity such as theater seating, but the same principle also applies to non-rivalrous intangible goods such as song compositions and recordings, television programming, literary works, and plans for building new inventions. The creation of such "information goods" – valuable amenities capable of being digitized and thereby widely shared – will entail significant positive externalities (and will thus occur at suboptimal levels) unless there is some way for the creator to charge users for their consumption. That, in turn, requires that the creator have the right to exclude non-payers from enjoyment of the amenity. The creator must, in other words, have a property right in her creation.

This is, of course, the policy rationale for the intellectual property laws (copyright, patent, etc.). By enabling the creators of information goods to exclude non-payers, the intellectual property laws transform such goods from pure public goods, which tend to be underproduced absent government intervention (e.g., flood control levees), into quasi-public club goods, which are typically available in abundance (e.g., satellite radio programming).

Because secure property rights in tangible and intangible assets are essential to the production of club goods, there may be a significant downside to legal changes that reduce property protections, particularly broad rights to exclude. When it comes to tangible property (real and personal), there is currently little enthusiasm for reducing property protections or curtailing property owners' rights to exclude. Intellectual property, though, is another story. Reformers regularly call for new laws reducing the scope or duration of intellectual property protections. Such reformers typically emphasize that broad rights to exclude non-payers from accessing information goods – particularly patents – may entail an immediate efficiency loss, since the marginal cost of providing the goods to additional users is zero or negligible, while the benefit those users attain is significant. We will consider this concern about "deadweight loss" in more detail in Chapter 7 (discussing market power). For present purposes, though, it is important to observe that cutting back on intellectual property rights to avoid one welfare loss may create another, larger one, given that intellectual property rights are necessary to transform information goods from routinely underproduced public goods into abundantly available club goods.

If property rights – real, personal, and intellectual – are needed to assure optimal production of goods that would otherwise be public goods, should we deem such rights to be "regulation"? They are, after all, institutions calculated to alleviate a wealth-reducing defect. They are not, though, institutions aimed at correcting wealth-reducing defects *in private ordering*. Property rights in tangible property are an ancient feature of the common law and are thus, in the scheme this book employs, *an aspect* of private ordering. We wouldn't say, for example, that the basic property doctrines allowing a theater owner to prevent non-payers from entering her space are "regulations." By the same token, the intellectual property rights that enable a songwriter to exclude non-paying consumers from the amenity she has created should probably not be deemed regulatory. Such rights are provided for in the US Constitution and have been part of the legal landscape for centuries.[6] While they may facilitate a regulatory objective, they would not constitute regulation as we have described it.

In any event, the important thing to see here is that secure property rights – whether or not they amount to "regulation" – are key to ensuring the production of club goods, which would otherwise be underproduced public goods. Regulators tempted to curtail such rights to achieve other objectives, such as the elimination of licensing requirements that make it hard to develop and market new consumer products utilizing lots of patented technologies, should keep in mind the classic physicians' mantra: "First, do no harm."

Pure Public Goods

The inability to exclude non-contributors is the feature that distinguishes often underproduced public goods from generally abundant club goods. Before using government power to secure public good production, then, policymakers should ensure that the amenity at issue really is non-excludable. In particular, they should keep two points in mind.

The first is that a non-rivalrous amenity is not a public good simply because the producer cannot exclude *some* consumers – even a great many – from its enjoyment. Take broadcast radio programming. On first glance, it might appear that a producer of that non-rivalrous amenity would have no way to exclude

---

[6] See U.S. Const. Art. I, Sec. 8, cl. 8 ("The Congress shall have Power ... To promote the Progress of Science and the useful Arts, by securing for limited Times to Authors and Inventors the exclusive Right to their respective Writings and Discoveries").

non-payers; after all, anybody with an antenna can receive a radio signal and enjoy the associated programming. There is one group of consumers, though, that can easily be excluded by the radio broadcaster: advertisers. Producers, who have the right to control programming content, can exclude all advertisers except those willing to pay for brief units of air time. Advertisers' payments, then, finance creation of the programming at issue, with radio listeners effectively "reimbursing" advertisers by listening to their pitches. The lesson here is that as long as there are *some* consumers who (1) can be excluded from an amenity and (2) collectively value that amenity enough to finance its creation, the amenity is not a public good and should not be treated as such.

A second point policymakers should remember is that technological change may transform amenities from one type of good into another. Again, radio programming provides an example. Until recently, *advertising-free* radio was a public good because it was non-rivalrous and non-excludable for all classes of consumers.[7] But technological developments allowing radio signals to be encrypted, beamed from space, and then decrypted using relatively inexpensive receivers opened up new possibilities. The US FCC responded to these developments by allocating a portion of radio spectrum in the S band (2.3 GHz) to "digital audio radio broadcasts." When CD Radio, Inc. (later Sirius) and American Mobile Radio Corp. (later XM) acquired licenses to broadcast over that band, satellite radio was born. Advertising-free radio was transformed from a non-rivalrous, non-excludable public good to a non-rivalrous but excludable club good. Programming proliferated, and consumers can now listen to virtually any genre of music or talk radio – advertising free – by paying a small monthly fee.

This observation about technological change highlights two lessons. The first is that policymakers should regularly revisit policies aimed at addressing non-excludable goods to ensure that they remain warranted in light of technological developments rendering the amenities excludable. Public goods may have become club goods (as in the case of advertising-free radio), and non-excludable commons goods may have become excludable private goods (as when the invention of barbed wire enabled western landowners to exclude roaming cattle from their property).[8] Policies adopted at one time,

---

[7] By definition, advertising-free radio cannot be consumed by advertisers – at least not in their capacity as advertisers – so the only consumers were listeners, who could not be practicably excluded.

[8] For a fascinating account of how the invention of barbed wire, and the consequent enhancement of the ability to exclude, altered appropriate public policy in the American West, see Terry L. Anderson and P. J. Hill, The Evolution of Property Rights: A Study of the American West, 18 *J. L. & Econ.* 163 (1975).

such as government funding for advertising-free television and radio, may no longer be justified – at least, not on the ground that they are necessary to secure a public good – when technological developments lower producers' costs of excluding non-payers.

A second lesson is that technological developments enabling excludability may not be *sufficient* to transform public and commons goods into club and private goods; regulatory adjustment may be needed as well. With advertising-free radio, for example, the development of technologies permitting excludability did not enable satellite radio until the FCC allowed potential satellite radio providers to license portions of the radio spectrum. Policymakers should always remain attuned to regulatory barriers that prevent non-excludable amenities from being transformed into excludable goods. Remember, non-excludability is the enemy.

Once policymakers have determined both that there are no excludable consumers (such as advertisers) likely to finance some non-rivalrous amenity and that technological developments are unlikely to render the amenity excludable, what should they do? Economists have often jumped to the conclusion that the government should produce (or at least finance the production of) the amenity at issue. Consider, for example, this passage from a law school text authored by five acclaimed economists:

> It is apparent that public goods will not be adequately supplied by the private sector. The reason is plain: because people can't be excluded from using public goods, they can't be charged money for using them, so a private supplier can't make money from providing them. ... Because public goods are generally not adequately supplied by the private sector, *they have to be supplied by the public sector.*[9]

That last claim seems demonstrably false. A moment's reflection calls to mind all sorts of public goods that are supplied by private actors without government coercion. For example:

a)   Having one's downtown be free of orphans and impoverished beggars is a benefit that is both non-rivalrous and non-excludable, yet privately funded orphanages, homeless shelters, and soup kitchens are common.

b)   A beautiful, well-kept garden provides a vista that multiple users can enjoy without depletion (non-rivalrous) and from which passersby cannot easily be barred (non-excludable), yet many homeowners in populated areas

9   Howell E. Jackson, Louis Kaplow, Steven Shavell, W. Kip Viscusi, and David Cope, *Analytical Methods for Lawyers* (La Habra, California: Foundation Press, 2003) 362–63 (emphasis added).

expend significant sums, not to mention hours of hard labor, tending their yards.

c) A highly educated citizenry tends to make better political decisions and to generate a richer cultural environment – both benefits that are non-rivalrous and largely non-excludable – yet people routinely spend great sums educating their children.

d) Private groups regularly clean up roadsides, even though the benefit they are creating is not depleted as more drivers use the road (non-rivalrous) and cannot be limited to people who contribute to the clean-up (non-excludable).

e) Millions of people make donations on so-called "crowd-funding" websites to fund projects such as community theater spaces, thereby creating the non-excludable, non-rivalrous benefit of more cultured communities.

These five examples highlight several common situations in which private actors, lacking access to (or refraining from using) state power, create public goods. Homeless shelters, soup kitchens, and orphanages (example (a)) are often established and operated privately by groups of individuals whose moral or religious convictions lead them to make charitable contributions. Private provision of garden vistas and youth education (examples (b) and (c)) occur because the *personal* benefit the provider receives from creating the amenity at issue is greater than her cost of doing so; if, for example, you receive tremendous personal happiness from having a beautiful yard or a well-educated child, you will spend a great deal on yardwork or tuition – even though much of the benefit of your expenditure inures to others. Private groups sometimes clean up roadsides (example (d)) not only as acts of charity but also because doing so entitles them to public recognition on "adopt a spot" road signs.

We can see from examples (a) through (d), then, at least three situations in which private provision of public goods regularly occurs: (1) when the amenity at issue so appeals to conscience that individuals with moral or religious convictions are likely to pony up funding; (2) when some individuals have personal preferences (i.e., high enough reservation prices for the amenity at issue) that justify their bearing all the cost of the amenity, despite the spillover of benefits onto others; and (3) when some organization has successfully tied participation in the provision of a public good to some sort of excludable benefit (e.g., favorable publicity, etc.). Example (e) demonstrates how the forces that often lead to private provision of public goods – charitable inclinations, idiosyncratically strong preferences for an amenity, the tying of excludable benefits to public good provision – can be combined *and then amplified* through the use of creative contracting.

Consider a typical project observed on a recent visit to the Kickstarter website (www.kickstarter.com). Brooklyn-based Heritage Radio Network provides a non-excludable, non-rivalrous amenity: Internet-based radio programming focused on food ("the world's only food radio station broadcasting 39+ weekly shows"). The Network recently employed Kickstarter to solicit funds to redesign and rebuild its website, which used a soon-to-expire computer code. In its pitch for donations, the Network exploited potential donors' charitable inclinations by emphasizing the benefits conferred on society as a whole: "Your support will not just help move forward conversations that make real change in the food world; it will bring that dialogue into the 21st century." The Network further highlighted how individuals with strong preferences for the amenity being funded would personally benefit from its creation: "[T]hrough the power of technology, you can listen to any of our episodes as podcasts on demand – wherever you are, whenever you want, always for free." Solicitors also tied excludable benefits to provision of the public good: Small contributors would "[b]e immortalized in Heritage Radio Network's backer hall of fame on the new site," medium contributors would achieve such immortality *and* receive an invitation to a party at the network's headquarters, and larger contributors would attain even greater private benefits.[10]

The Kickstarter platform then enabled Heritage Radio Network to address a problem that often thwarts private efforts to provide public goods. People who might otherwise be willing to contribute to such goods, either for charitable reasons or because of idiosyncratically strong preferences for the amenities at issue, may not give if they are concerned that the contemplated projects will fail and their contributions will be squandered. A homeowner living near an unprotected portion of a river, for example, will worry that the organizers of a private levee project may ultimately end up with insufficient funding, resulting in either no levee or one that is too short to provide adequate flood protection. Despite the substantial private benefit she would attain from levee construction, a homeowner may choose not to contribute to the effort because she's worried that her donation will be effectively squandered. If other homeowners reason similarly, the voluntary levee project is destined to fail. Private providers of public goods thus need some way to assure potential donors that their contributions will not go to waste.

A mechanism often used by such providers – and a key to Kickstarter's business model – is the "assurance contract." In an assurance contract, project

---

[10] See Heritage Radio Network: Website Rebuild Project, www.kickstarter.com/projects/heritager adionetwork/heritage-radio-network-website-rebuild-project/description (visited May 14, 2015).

organizers promise potential donors that if sufficient funds are not raised (or committed), the organizers will return (or refrain from collecting) the donors' contributions. In Heritage Radio Network's solicitation, for example, potential donors were assured that their credit cards would not be charged the amount they pledged unless donors collectively pledged $35,000 – enough money to complete the project – by a certain date. That assurance protected donors from having their contributions squandered if the Network failed to raise enough money to complete its website redesign.[11]

A variation on the assurance contract may be even more helpful in facilitating the private production of public goods. Even when a solicitor of funds has assured donors that their contributions will be returned if the financing effort doesn't succeed, individuals with charitable inclinations or idiosyncratically strong preferences for the amenity at issue will still be reluctant to commit funds if they believe the fundraising effort will ultimately fail. Why go through the rigmarole of making a donation and tie up the committed funds for some period of time if the project at issue is unlikely to make it? Of course, if too many potential donors think this way, failure of the fundraising effort becomes a self-fulfilling prophecy. Accordingly, organizers of efforts to finance public goods need some way to get enough initial funds committed that the project appears likely to succeed and will appeal to less enthusiastic donors.

A "dominant" assurance contract can assist project organizers with this first-mover problem. Under such a contract, an entrepreneur seeking to provide a public good promises potential donors that if the project fails for lack of sufficient funding, their funds will be returned *and* they will be paid some amount (or given some other tangible benefit). The latter promise induces initial donors to pony up and get the ball rolling. As economist Alex Tabarrok has explained, "Pledging is now a no-lose proposition – if enough people pledge you get the public good and if not enough pledge you get the prize. A contract like this makes it a dominant strategy to pledge and so the public good is funded."[12]

It seems, then, that the aforementioned claim that public goods "have to be supplied by the public sector" is just wrong. But perhaps we're being unfair to the quoted economists. After all, they didn't say the public sector must provide public goods *if they are to be provided at all*; rather, they asserted that such

---

[11]   Allow me to end the suspense: Heritage Radio Network's Kickstarter campaign was a success. The Network raised $40,388 – more than enough to finance its website redesign.

[12]   Alex Tabarrok, A Test of Dominant Assurance Contracts, *Marginal Revolution* (Aug. 29, 2013) (available at http://marginalrevolution.com/marginalrevolution/2013/08/a-test-of-dominant-assurance-contracts.html#sthash.ifnhYgJl.dpuf). For more on dominant assurance contracts, see Alexander Tabarrok, The Private Provision of Public Goods Via Dominant Assurance Contracts, 96 *Pub. Choice* 345 (1998).

goods "are generally not adequately supplied" by private actors and therefore "have to be supplied by the public sector." The implication is that because private provision of public goods tends to be inadequate, public provision of such goods must be the optimal approach.[13]

Assessing that claim requires some thought about how to identify the optimal approach to securing public goods. One might think that the optimal approach would be the one under which every unit whose marginal benefit exceeds its marginal cost, but no unit beyond that point, is produced – in other words, the approach that generates the ideal, or theoretically welfare-maximizing, level of production. But that is the old Nirvana Fallacy we discussed in Chapter 4. Theoretical perfection is impossible in our fallen world, so policymakers should strive not for ideal production (no approach can attain that) but for the best *achievable* outcome. They should catalogue available policies (when it comes to public goods, they are chiefly government provision of the amenity at issue or reliance on private sector provision), assess outcomes under each, and select the approach that generates the highest level of welfare. That is the optimal approach. And there are certainly reasons to doubt that government provision of non-rivalrous, non-excludable amenities is always optimal. In particular, both the knowledge problem and public choice concerns once again rear their ugly heads.

When the government provides a public good, officials must decide, among other things, *how much* to produce. With some public goods – say, a lighthouse – there may not be many choices: one or zero. But most public goods – national defense, fire protection, flood control systems, public art – can be produced in different amounts (and even a lighthouse can be built to different heights and with lights that reach different ranges). Should our town have three fire trucks or ten? Should we install two giant sculptures downtown or six? Should the levee protect against only fifty-year floods, or should we build it high enough to protect us from the hundred-year deluge? Private providers of public goods confront similar questions, of course, but because they rely on voluntary participation by contributors, they face a constraint that will prevent overprovision: contributors' willingness to support the project at issue.[14]

---

[13] Even economists who are unwilling to say that public goods "have to be supplied" by the government generally maintain that government provision is the optimal solution – i.e., the one that will generate the highest net benefits for members of society. The leading law and economics text, for example, maintains that *"efficiency requires* that ... nonrivalrous and nonexcludable goods should be controlled by a large group of people such as the state." Robert Cooter and Thomas Ulen, *Law and Economics* (New York: Pearson Addison Wesley, 4th edn., 2003) 108 (emphasis added).

[14] If the plans get too elaborate, contributors motivated by charitable impulses will stop giving. Those who are contributing because of idiosyncratically strong preferences or in order to attain

Government planners with access to the public fisc lack a similar mechanism to tell them enough is enough.

That is particularly problematic given that the funds the planners are spending are coerced from individuals who may not support the particular public good at all or, at a minimum, may want less of it. Pacifists, for example, are appalled at current levels of military spending; conservative Christians, at public funding of art projects such as the 1987 photograph "Piss Christ" (for which the artist received $15,000 from the National Endowment for the Arts); many secularists, at abstinence-only sex education (for which federal funding is available). In light of inevitably divergent preferences among taxpayers and the absence of any feedback mechanism other than the ballot box, government planners are likely to make significant mistakes in deciding how much of a public good to produce.

But what about that ballot box? Won't it punish (and ultimately prevent) mistakes about how much of a public good should be provided? Not very well. For one thing, an election assesses *everything* the candidates have done and promised, and therefore sends only a muted signal about any particular expenditure of public funds. What's more, government officials' decisions to spend tax revenues on public goods exhibit a feature that makes them particularly impervious to political correction. While many or most members of society receive some benefit from government provision of public goods (e.g., protection from fire or flooding, a more aesthetically pleasing downtown), some individuals and groups enjoy *special* benefits that are not generally available. Firemen and levee builders receive business opportunities from government provision of fire and flood protection, artists, from enhanced expenditures on public art projects. While these special benefits are concentrated on small and discrete groups, their costs are borne by taxpayers as a whole. As you will recall from Chapter 4, government programs involving concentrated benefits and diffuse costs tend to persist even when they reduce total welfare by imposing marginal costs in excess of marginal benefits. Such programs are resilient because small, easily organized interest groups have much to lose if the program is curtailed and will fight curtailment accordingly, whereas each individual beneficiary of curtailment – each taxpayer whose money is being wasted – receives only a tiny personal benefit from cutting back on the program and is thus unlikely to expend resources to secure that end.

In light of the knowledge problem and the potential for manipulation by special interests, government provision of public goods creates a need for

some excludable tied benefit will limit their contributions to the amount of subjective value they expect to attain from the project.

careful monitoring. And therein lies the irony: The monitoring of government provision of public goods *is itself a public good*. It is non-rivalrous, for when you enjoy my monitoring of public officials, your neighbor's ability to do so remains undiminished. It is non-excludable, for if I monitor officials to protect my own interest, I can't prevent you from benefiting from my efforts. This suggests that monitoring of government efforts to provide public goods – an activity that is essential to ensuring that government production approaches ideal production – will be systematically underproduced. Government provision of public goods, then, is no silver bullet.

Of course, none of this implies that government provision is never the optimal policy response to a particular public good. The point is simply that both government and private provision of public goods are likely to diverge from the ideal production level. The optimal approach is the one that is likely to diverge *less*. With respect to national defense, government provision is almost certainly optimal. Free-rider problems would likely hold private provision of national defense well below the ideal level, and while the knowledge problem and public choice concerns could generate some overproduction of government-provided defense services, any inefficiencies there would be dwarfed by those resulting from reliance on the private sector. Most publicly viewable art projects, by contrast, are probably best provided by the private sector. Although such art projects are susceptible to free-riding, people's charitable inclinations, idiosyncratically strong preferences, and desire for excludable benefits that are frequently tied to the project at issue (e.g., a plaque listing donors) often lead to significant sums for publicly viewable art. Moreover, conflicting preferences among taxpayers are likely to lead to an intractable knowledge problem (How many art projects should be funded? Which ones?), and the concentrated benefits/diffuse costs problem will make it difficult, as a political matter, to cut back on public art programs. Flood protection may be somewhat in the middle. Free-rider problems exist, but many communities – especially smaller ones with more communitarian social norms – have witnessed private levee projects. A good starting point for policymakers confronted with a non-excludable, non-rivalrous good is to ask whether *this type of public good* is regularly provided by the private sector in *this type of community*. Policymakers should always remember, though, that there are pros and cons to both private and government provision of public goods, and they should opt for the latter only when they have sound reasons to believe that it promises greater net welfare.

Commons Goods

The chief policy response to pure public goods – government provision using general tax revenues – is an interventionist, but not "regulatory," approach, at least as we use the term. At the outset, we defined regulation as a threat-backed governmental command that seeks to correct a welfare-reducing defect in private ordering by requiring the subject of the command to do something other than pay taxes for the sole purpose of raising revenue.[15] Government provision of a public good involves no threat-backed order besides "pay your taxes." It is thus not regulation under our terminology. Rivalrous but non-excludable commons goods, by contrast, may call for genuinely regulatory interventions.

We needn't linger too long over the range of regulatory options here, though. We have already examined it. Recall that commons goods like ocean fisheries and public freeways are subject to shortages – not enough fish to sustain populations, insufficient road space to drive at a reasonable rate of speed – because they are overconsumed. That is because consumers, who cannot be easily excluded from the amenities, continue to consume even after the cost of their last unit of consumption begins to exceed the benefit such consumption confers. (For example, a fisherman might catch another fish that provides him with $10 in benefit, even though removal of the fish devalues the fishery by $12 by driving the population below replacement levels.) Consumers overdo it like this because they get all the benefit of continued consumption while bearing only a portion of the cost, which is externalized – shared among all consumers of the amenity. It should come as no surprise, then, that the menu of policy options for regulating commons goods mirrors that for negative externalities generally: command-and-control, Pigouvian taxes, and defining and enforcing property rights.

Under a command-and-control regime, government officials first decide what level of aggregate consumption maximizes welfare, and then restrict each individual's consumption to ensure that such an aggregate level is achieved. With an ocean fishery, for example, the government might grant each fisherman the right to catch only a set quantity of some fish species within a certain period of time, or it might impose other behavioral constraints designed to prevent overfishing – e.g., limits on fishing seasons, boat size, fishing areas, permitted equipment. With congested roadways, a command-and-control approach might involve dictating who may drive when. Chinese officials employed such an approach during the 2008 Olympic Games, when

---

[15] A Pigouvian tax amounts to regulation because its point is not simply to raise revenue. The basic federal income tax, by contrast, is not regulation as this book defines it.

drivers were allowed on Beijing's roads only every other day, depending on whether their license plates ended in even or odd numbers.[16]

A Pigouvian approach to commons goods attempts to secure the welfare-maximizing level of consumption using taxes rather than strict consumption limitations. In theory, the tax should reflect the amount of cost spillover from a unit of consumption – i.e., the difference between the consumer's marginal cost and the total marginal cost of consumption. (Recall Figure 4.5.) In practice, however, it is quite difficult to implement such a tax schedule. The divergence between individual and total marginal cost tends to grow as consumption increases; with a fishery, for example, driving the population a fish or two below replacement levels may not be that harmful, but as the population dwindles removing an additional fish may significantly damage the stock as a whole. A perfect Pigouvian system would require officials both to estimate how the divergence between individual and total marginal cost changes with increased consumption *and* to collect different (higher) per-unit amounts as consumption increases. In light of those informational requirements and administrative difficulties, most Pigouvian schemes don't even attempt perfection but instead crudely slap some blanket charge on all users of the commons. In London, for example, officials have sought to alleviate inner city traffic congestion by charging each non-exempt vehicle £11.50 (currently around $15) to drive within the city center during a weekday.

Of course, technological developments may reduce the information and administrative burdens of Pigouvian schemes, increasing their attractiveness. Consider, for example, the "congestion pricing" system recently implemented on two busy Los Angeles roadways: the I-110 Harbor Freeway and the I-10 El Monte Freeway.[17] Data collection over the years has shown that the maximum number of cars pass through congested freeways like these when the flow of traffic proceeds at about 45 miles per hour.[18] Data on driver responses to tolls, then, make it possible to estimate how many drivers will drop out of (or enter) tolled lanes as toll prices rise (or fall). Taking current congestion information derived from sensors in the freeways and plugging it into an algorithm allows

---

[16] Following the Olympics, Beijing adopted a (less restrictive) version of this approach. Under that version, cars must stay off the road one day per week, again based on the last number of their license plate.

[17] Similar tolling approaches have been implemented on other California roadways (e.g., State Route 91 in Orange County) and in congested areas of Florida, Minnesota, Texas, and Virginia.

[18] When congestion reduces traffic speeds below 45 mph, fewer cars make it through per hour. To achieve traffic flow at speeds greater than 45 mph, congestion must be reduced so much that fewer cars pass through within a given time period, even though each does so more quickly.

instantaneous calculation of the toll rate needed to keep the flow of traffic proceeding at 45 mph. That toll, recalculated every five minutes or so to reflect current congestion, is then posted on electronic signs along the freeways. When an automobile with a specially equipped transponder enters the toll lanes, the then-prevailing toll rate is "locked in." The commuter is charged the appropriate amount – the locked-in toll rate times the distance traveled – when she exits the toll lanes. This system of tolling represents quite an improvement over London's clumsy Pigouvian scheme.[19]

A property rights-based approach addresses head-on the disease causing the commons goods problem: externalities resulting from non-excludability. Commons goods are overconsumed because they have no owner that is capable of limiting consumption in a way that will wring the most value from the resource. The very same resource, if controlled by an owner with the ability to exclude consumers, may face no overconsumption problem at all. A private fishery, for example, is unlikely to be overfished. The owner has an *incentive* to limit consumption to value-maximizing levels since she may ultimately capture that value by selling fish or the right to fish. She has the *information* required to maximize value because market prices allow her to compare the value of fish caught today versus future fishing opportunities. Her property right in the fishery gives her the *ability* to maximize value by excluding anyone from fishing beyond the value-maximizing point. Creating property rights in an otherwise non-excludable but rivalrous amenity may thus be the best way to ensure efficient exploitation of the resource.

To see this point, consider the history of radio spectrum regulation. The public airwaves, at least in their unregulated state, are non-excludable (anyone with the proper equipment can broadcast over a particular frequency) but rivalrous (one person's broadcast will interfere with a nearby neighbor's broadcast over a similar frequency). In the early days of radio, interference – a result of overconsumption – was quite common. A 1910 letter from the Department of the Navy to the US Senate Committee on Commerce complained that each radio station

> considers itself independent and claims the right to send forth its electric waves through the ether at any time that it may desire, with the result that there exists in many places a state of chaos. Public business is hindered to the

---

[19] That is not to criticize London. The technology likely does not exist for implementing congestion pricing on its twisted inner-city streets. My point is simply that technological developments may increase the attractiveness of Pigouvian (or Coasean) schemes for regulating commons goods. The wise policymaker will regularly revisit existing command-and-control schemes to see if they ought to be replaced in light of new technologies.

great embarrassment of the Navy Department. Calls of distress from vessels in peril on the sea go unheeded or are drowned out in the etheric bedlam produced by numerous stations all trying to communicate at once. . . . It is not putting the case too strong to state that the situation is intolerable, and is continually growing worse.[20]

Congress responded to this problem with a command-and-control approach. It authorized the Secretary of Commerce, and eventually the FCC, to determine who can broadcast what, and at what frequencies.

This command-and-control approach has proven problematic. In addition to offending free speech values (the system results in the government's controlling who can broadcast what, depending on what government officials deem to be the "public interest, necessity or convenience"), the approach has run headlong into the knowledge problem. Absent prices created by competing users' bidding for rights to the spectrum, planners have little reliable information about which users can extract the most value from any particular radio frequency. They are relegated to relying on competitors' self-serving statements about how they will use the frequency to further the public interest. The upshot is that frequencies have often been allocated to uses other than those that would create the greatest value for consumers. Right now, for example, a huge amount of spectrum is allocated to broadcast television – and even more simply sits unused – even though few American households (about 7 percent) still get their television over the air,[21] and providers of wireless telephone and data services face continual capacity constraints.

The command-and-control approach to radio spectrum also invites wasteful (and unfair) political manipulation. The history of broadcast regulation is littered with examples of licenses – and license denials – that appear to have resulted from political influence. Consider, for example, the unlikely broadcast empire of the 36th US President. Lyndon B. Johnson came from a struggling farming family and worked as a teacher before entering politics. He ultimately ended up with a net worth (in 2010 dollars) of $98 million. How could that happen? It seems that then-Congressman Johnson's rise to riches began in 1943, when his wife Lady Bird purchased radio station KTBC in Austin, Texas. For many years, that "dusk to dawn" radio station had been mired in red tape. Things promptly resolved, though, when the then-embattled FCC – whose Commissioner Clifford Durr was a good friend of the Johnsons – granted the operating license to Lady Bird. Soon thereafter,

---

[20] S. Rep. No. 659, 61st Cong., 2d Sess. 4 (1910).
[21] See Consumer Electronics Association, *US Household Television Usage Update* (July 30, 2013).

Mrs. Johnson was permitted to convert KTBC to a 24-hour station, to move it down to the "uncluttered" end of the radio dial (AM 590), and eventually to quintuple its power. Congressman Johnson, in turn, went to bat for the FCC, whose powers were preserved. Thus began the media dynasty that transformed a schoolteacher from a modest farming family into the seventh wealthiest US President.

Things needn't have been like this. As far back as 1959, Ronald Coase predicted that what we now recognize as the knowledge problem and public choice concerns would bedevil the command-and-control approach to spectrum regulation, and he suggested an alternative. In an article titled simply *The Federal Communications Commission*,[22] Coase argued that regulators proved should auction off the right to use various frequencies and then allow the successful holders of the auctioned rights to resolve interference disputes and reallocate usage rights through negotiations of their own. He emphasized the point – usually associated with his subsequent and more famous article, *The Problem of Social Cost*[23] – that as long as property rights are well defined, enforceable, and transferable, and bargaining costs sufficiently low, private negotiations will lead to a valuable right (in this case, a broadcast right) being allocated to its highest and best end. (Remember Chapter 4's discussion of the garage owner and the music producer?)

For decades, Coase's recommendation was given short shrift. When he testified about his proposal before the FCC in 1959, Commissioner Philip Cross opened the questioning with this humdinger: "Tell us, Professor, is this all a big joke?" Three years later, when Coase and two other economists prepared a 200-page analysis of Coase's proposal for the Rand Corporation, the think tank worried that the analysis would have explosive political implications and therefore suppressed it – *for 33 years*. When Coase's proposal was finally taken up by an FCC Commissioner in the 1970s, two fellow commissioners contended that its odds of adoption were equivalent to "those on the Easter Bunny in the Preakness."[24] Regulators, it seems, have a hard time imagining a legal regime any different from the one they are rewarded for implementing.

In the end, though, Coase was vindicated. As technologies evolved and businesses innovated, spectrum became a more valuable resource, and applications for licenses proliferated. The FCC's command-and-control approach,

---

[22] R.H. Coase, The Federal Communications Commission, 2 *J. L. & Econ.* 1 (1959).
[23] R.H. Coase, The Problem of Social Cost, 3 *J. L. & Econ.* 1 (1960). This article is the most cited law journal article in history.
[24] See Thomas W. Hazlett, David Porter, and Vernon Smith, Radio Spectrum and the Disruptive Clarity of Ronald Coase, 54 *J. L. & Econ.* 125, 133–34 (2011).

which required the agency to engage in extensive fact-finding to determine precisely who should be allowed to do what with portions of the spectrum, became unwieldy. So-called comparative hearings could take years to complete. By 1982, the need to allocate licenses for cellular communications in the United States had so overwhelmed the regulatory apparatus that Congress permitted licenses to be issued among applicants via lottery. Such random allocation may have sped things up, but it undermined any claim that political allocation was needed to preserve the public interest. An auction system would at least ensure that spectrum would be allocated according to willingness-to-pay, a decent indicator of the relative social value competing applicants could generate with a license. Moreover – and undoubtedly of more concern to Congress – an auction system would bring significant revenue into government coffers. In light of these considerations, and following a successful spectrum auction in New Zealand, Congress voted in 1993 to authorize spectrum auctions in the United States. The FCC conducted the first such auction in 1994 and has since auctioned around 90 licenses, generating more than $60 billion in government revenues.

Coase's property rights-based approach to spectrum regulation, though only partially implemented, has created a tremendous amount of wealth. Most importantly, the approach has helped ensure that licenses initially go to the entities that will extract the most social value from them. In addition, license auctions have created social value by enabling the government to generate revenue in a manner that creates less economic distortion than do taxes. Economists estimate that the revenue from spectrum auctions has created $17 billion in social value simply by eliminating the distortive effect of otherwise needed taxes.[25] Rarely has a single piece of academic writing had so great an economic impact (in the positive sense, at least) as Coase's FCC article.

None of this is to say, of course, that a property rights approach is the optimal way to address all commons goods. Each of the available approaches imposes costs. The wise policymaker recognizes that fact, attempts to assess the costs of each possible approach (and of hybrids[26]), and selects the one most

---

[25] Ibid., at 156.

[26] Some approaches to regulating commons goods do not fit neatly into a single category – command-and-control, Pigouvian, property rights-based – but instead share characteristics of each. In a number of ocean fisheries, for example, authorities have sought to mitigate the harms of fishing season-inspired "derbies" (described in the text below) by instead imposing species-specific fishing limitations ("Total Allowable Catch") and then dividing those amounts into "Individual Transferable Quotas" (ITQs) that are allocated to, and may be traded among, individual fishermen. As with the sulfur dioxide trading scheme discussed in Chapter 4, the ITQ approach (1) resembles command-and-control, in that the total catch is set via regulatory fiat; (2) is Pigouvian, in that fishermen, by purchasing ITQs, pay a "tax" on their

likely to maximize social welfare by minimizing error and decision costs. This will generally require a case-by-case assessment, as well as an occasional *reassessment* as technological developments alter the relative costs of different regulatory approaches. In performing their assessments, wise policymakers will keep in mind each approach's typical pros and cons. Let's briefly consider those now.

Under command-and-control, welfare losses from both the knowledge problem and special interest manipulation of government power are likely to be significant, while administrative costs may – but will not necessarily – be relatively low. Because planners implementing a command-and-control approach dictate how much of a commons good each user may consume, they really need to know (if they are to maximize social welfare) (1) the incremental value each consumer would obtain from consuming an additional unit above the limit under consideration, and (2) the incremental cost such consumption would impose.[27] Of course, planners aren't privy to such consumer-specific information, and couldn't process it all even if it were available. Planners therefore set individual consumption limits using cruder measures, such as "total consumption consistent with long-term sustainability of the commons" divided by "total number of consumers." For some consumers (those attaching a high marginal value to consumption), command-and-control will permit too little of the regulated activity; for others, too much. Significant "allocative inefficiency" – welfare loss that occurs when resources are allocated away from their highest and best ends – is likely to result.

A different set of knowledge problem losses occurs when regulators fail to anticipate adverse unintended consequences of their mandates. Command and-control approaches are particularly vulnerable to such consequences because they involve inflexible mandates that drive regulatees, seeking to evade strict mandates, to take actions they wouldn't otherwise take.[28] Consider, for example, this description of the unforeseen inefficiencies spawned by command-and-control rules governing marine fisheries:

> License controls and other entry restrictions may limit the number of fishers, but they do not control the amount or intensity of fishing efforts. Mandates on the type of equipment that can be used, an effort to control

---

activity; and (3) is property rights-based, in that each ITQ-holder "owns" his right to catch and may do with it what he pleases – use it, sell it, or let it lie fallow.

[27] Welfare is maximized when the (decreasing) incremental value of the last unit consumed equals the (increasing) incremental cost created by consuming that unit.

[28] Because Pigouvian and property rights-based approaches afford more flexibility to regulatees (who may continue their conduct if they pay a tax or buy a right), they are less likely to occasion unexpected behavioral changes designed to evade the regulatory regime.

fishing efforts by mandating that fishers use less-efficient means of catching fish, encourage fishers to increase their investment in additional vessels or gear to compensate for the efficiency losses. Limits on the number of days fished encourage fishers to increase their effort on the days allowed. The results are rampant overcapitalization in fisheries and a destructive "derby" system in which each fisher races to catch as much as he or she can before the season closes.[29]

Command-and-control approaches to commons management ultimately consist of the government's granting permission to specific individuals or entities to do particular things on the precise terms set by the government (e.g., "you alone may utilize this frequency, but only for these purposes and using this equipment"; "you may capture this type of fish on these days only and using only these fishing technologies"). Because such prescriptive and inflexible orders can give a firm a leg up or hobble its rivals, businesses facing actual or potential competition will spend great sums to secure regulations that benefit them.

Such "rent-seeking" activity, a public choice concern, imposes a double whammy.[30] First, when government officials (predictably) grant or withhold permission to use commons goods because they have been lobbied, they tend to transfer commons resources away from their highest and best uses, generating yet another allocative inefficiency. In addition, the resources private firms spend on rent-seeking activity (lobbying, etc.) create no real value and are, from the standpoint of societal welfare, effectively squandered.

Lobbying   is inefficient use of resources

[29] Jonathan H. Adler, Legal Obstacles to Private Ordering in Marine Fisheries, 8 *Roger Wms. L. Rev.* 9, 15 (2002). The "race to catch" fueled by short fishing seasons makes for great drama – witness the Discovery Channel's *Deadliest Catch*, a reality television program chronicling the adventures of fishermen of Alaskan King Crab. Unfortunately, it also encourages dangerous and destructive practices. Following the first season of *Deadliest Catch*, officials in the Bering Sea fishery where the show is set sought to mitigate the harms cause by command-and-control fishing seasons by instead implementing the sort of hybrid Individual Transferable Quota approach described in note 26 above. With the fishing derby-inspired dangers reduced, the show's producers faced pressure to make their subject seem, well, "deadlier."

[30] "Rent-seeking" generally refers to efforts to obtain benefits for oneself through the political arena. In economics, the term "rent" refers to any payment to the owner of a fixed factor of production over and above its opportunity cost – i.e., the amount of benefit it would fetch in its next most profitable use. Much legitimate profit-seeking activity, then, would seem to qualify as "rent-seeking." Usually (and throughout this book), however, the term rent-seeking refers to using productive resources to persuade government officials to exercise their power of legitimate coercion in order to enhance the seeker's rents. We call rent-seeking a "public choice" concern because that body of economics, which studies how political players respond to incentives, has long emphasized the incidence and effects of rent-seeking behavior. Rent-seeking is not, however, *exclusively* a public choice concern. Even scholars who are skeptical of some public choice claims acknowledge the existence of, and potential problems from, rent-seeking.

When it comes to administrative costs, command-and-control approaches to preventing commons overconsumption will vary. Simply granting permission to do things usually isn't that difficult, so command-and-control schemes are often cheap to administer (as with China's rule allocating driving rights based on license plates). Often, though, the process for determining who may consume what is quite costly (as with the FCC's comparative hearings for allocating spectrum licenses).

Relative to command-and-control, Pigouvian schemes for regulating commons goods usually involve a lower (though still significant) informational requirement and less (though still some) potential for special interest manipulation; they are likely, though, to entail greater administrative costs. With command-and-control, regulators determine the optimal aggregate consumption level *and* dictate precisely who may consume what in order to achieve that outcome. With a Pigouvian approach, the regulator figures the optimal final outcome (e.g., the number of cars that will keep traffic flow at 45 mph) and designs some sort of tax schedule calculated to achieve it, but then allows consumers themselves – based on their private information – to determine when and whether to consume and pay the tax at issue.[31] Because command-and-control involves regulators making more decisions – both how much aggregate consumption there should be *and precisely who should cut back to achieve that level* – it imposes a heavier informational requirement and will tend to generate higher error costs. Pigouvian regulators determine ends, but their only means decision concerns the proper tax rate. While calculating a tax schedule to achieve a particular level of consumption is no mean feat, it is typically less error-prone than determining how much particular individuals, each with their own needs and desires, should be allowed to consume.

Pigouvian approaches also tend to fare better than command-and-control when it comes to public choice concerns. Because command-and-control schemes involve *personal* decisions – i.e., regulators say specifically who may and may not consume at particular levels – they are particularly attractive to special interests seeking a leg up on competitors. Targeted Pigouvian taxes may also disadvantage competitors, but, being less focused on particular individuals or entities, they are typically less effective as competitive ammunition and less susceptible to special interest manipulation. Of course, Pigouvian approaches do require someone to assess and collect taxes. For

[31] Under China's command-and-control approach to reducing traffic congestion, for example, a driver couldn't access the roads on his no-driving day (unless he was willing to risk punishment) *even if* he badly needed to travel on that day. Under the Pigouvian congestion pricing approach used in Los Angeles, by contrast, a person who gets great value from driving can do so as long as she pays the tax at issue.

that reason, they may involve greater administrative costs than command-and-control.

Compared to command-and-control and Pigouvian schemes, property rights-based approaches to regulating the commons typically involve less welfare loss stemming from the knowledge problem and public choice concerns. Under a property rights-based approach, regulators need not determine *either* who gets to consume what (as command-and-control requires) *or* the aggregate amount of consumption allowed (as required by both command-and-control and Pigouvian approaches). When the resource at issue is privately owned, the owner has an incentive to maximize its value and transfer it, in whole or in part, to whoever values it most. The owner's failure to do so saddles her with a cost: the surplus she could have earned by managing the resource differently. The owner also has access to information on the highest and best use of the resource; the different prices she is offered provide guidance on how best to manage the resource and to whom it should be transferred to maximize its value. Thus, absent barriers or costs preventing reallocation, regulators implementing a property rights-based approach need not know *anything* about preferences for a commons amenity in order to maximize its value. Moreover, because the only significant government action in property rights-based approaches consists of defining and initially allocating the property interests, such approaches present few public choice concerns. Granted, the initial allocation of rights may be subject to special interest manipulation, but after that point there is little to be gained from such shenanigans, and even the risk of manipulation at the initial allocation stage can be minimized by adopting an auction mechanism that removes regulator discretion and allocates property rights based on competitive bidding.

Of course, property rights-based approaches are not without their downsides. First, they require defining and allocating property rights – a task that is usually easy enough but may be complicated (and thus costly) depending on the nature of the commons good. It's simple, for example, to say that the owner of a restaurant or bar owns the air within her building and may thus manage its use as she sees fit (a Coasean approach to indoor air quality regulation); defining and allocating property rights to freeway space, by contrast, would be so costly as to be impracticable – at least with current technologies.[32] Perhaps more significantly, property rights-based approaches

---

[32]   If a freeway were privately owned, there would be no commons problem whatsoever. Most freeways, though, are owned by the government.

may lead to inefficient outcomes if transaction costs (1) are so significant that reallocation bargains are unlikely to occur and (2) cannot be reduced to a point at which such bargains are likely. Negotiating a transfer of spectrum rights is pretty easy; bargaining for space on a freeway isn't (though it's possible to conceive of a centralized electronic market for tradeable freeway access rights). The important point to see is that a property rights-based approach – like all the other approaches to managing commons goods – involves some potential downsides. The wise and benevolent regulator recognizes the downsides (costs) of each approach, including hybrids, and settles on the one likely to maximize net social welfare.

Before we conclude, one last point on regulating commons goods. Throughout human history and across the globe, groups of individuals have displayed a remarkable ability to manage commons goods effectively without either privatizing them or relying on government intervention. As Nobel laureate Elinor Ostrom showed in case study after case study – from grazing areas in Switzerland and Kenya, to irrigation systems in Spain and Nepal, to lobster fisheries in Maine – groups of individuals have employed agreements, social norms, and non-governmental sanctions to prevent overconsumption of commons goods.[33] The wise and benevolent regulator remains attuned to the possibility of privately ordered solutions to commons problems. She never invokes government power – coercion – unless doing so would *unambiguously* improve social welfare. And she always keeps an eye out for regulatory burdens that may preclude or discourage privately ordered solutions to commons problems.

Professor Jonathan Adler has shown, for example, that a number of private marine fishery organizations historically implemented their own conservation-minded catch limitations but thereby ran into trouble under the federal antitrust laws.[34] Those laws are designed to address another private ordering defect, market power, which we consider in Chapter 7. They laudably aim to protect consumers from collusive price increases. In pursuing that objective, though, they target effective means of preventing inefficient – and ultimately consumer-unfriendly – overconsumption of commons goods. Now (prior to

[33] See generally Elinor Ostrom, *Governing the Commons: The Evolution of Institutions for Collective Action* (Cambridge, UK: Cambridge University Press, 1990). In naming Professor Ostrom a co-recipient of the 2009 Nobel Prize in Economics, the Royal Swedish Academy of Sciences praised her for "showing how common resources – forests, fisheries, oil fields or grazing lands – can be managed successfully by the people who use them rather than by governments or private companies."

[34] See Jonathan H. Adler, Conservation Through Collusion: Antitrust as an Obstacle to Marine Resource Conservation, 61 *Wash. & Lee L. Rev.* 3 (2004).

our consideration of market power) is not the time to determine whether, and to what extent, antitrust's prohibitions should yield to competitors' concerted efforts to conserve commons goods.[35] But we should at this point acknowledge three points: that individuals and groups often concoct creative and successful means of managing the commons; that such means sometimes run afoul of rules designed to address other, perhaps less significant, problems; and that the wise regulator will consider relaxing regulatory barriers to cooperative private ordering if doing so will generate greater benefit than harm. As Professor Robert Ellickson observed at the close of *Order Without Law*, his famous book exploring privately ordered solutions to commons problems, "lawmakers who are unappreciative of the social conditions that foster informal cooperation are likely to create a world in which there is both more law and less order."[36]

LESSONS FOR POLICYMAKERS

The analysis in this chapter suggests that policymakers, when considering whether and how to intervene in response to amenities that are non-excludable, non-rivalrous, or both, should ask the following questions, in roughly the following order:

- Is the good or service routinely shortage-prone because of underproduction or overconsumption? Any legitimate government intervention would seem to require, at a minimum, an adverse symptom.
- If the amenity (1) is non-excludable, non-rivalrous, or both, and (2) seems regularly to be in short supply, then classify it. Is it a public good (both non-rivalrous and non-excludable), a club good (non-rivalrous but excludable), or a commons good (rivalrous but non-excludable)?

If the good is a club good and yet seems underproduced (such a non-rivalrous good could never be overconsumed), then seek to determine why private market actors aren't stepping up to produce the good and thereby earn a profit. Is some regulation or other government intervention infringing upon

---

[35] At least one former antitrust official believes antitrust should often stay its hand here. Professor Bruce Yandle, a former Federal Trade Commission economist, has observed that "[t]he threats of wasted and destroyed fisheries, extinguished species, and diminished water quality in rivers are real, but the possibilities that associated monopoly restrictions will impose significant costs on the economy are purely speculative and, if realized, are apt to be small and fleeting." Bruce Yandle, Antitrust and the Commons: Cooperation or Collusion?, 3 *The Indep. Rev.* 37, 50 (1998).

[36] Robert C. Ellickson, *Order Without Law: How Neighbors Settle Disputes* (Cambridge, MA: Harvard University Press, 1991) 286.

potential producers' right to exclude, a right essential to their production of the amenity at issue?

If the amenity at issue appears to be a public good:

- First check to see if it really, and necessarily, is such a good. Is there some group of consumers (like radio advertisers) who (1) can be excluded, and (2) would collectively pay enough for access to the amenity to finance its production? If so, it's not really a public good. Has technology developed (or is it likely to develop) in a way that permits excludability, as with satellite radio? If so, the optimal response may be a regulatory change (usually a liberalization) that facilitates the development and implementation of exclusion-enabling technologies.
- If the amenity really is a public good, consider whether it is nonetheless likely to be produced at significant levels without government intervention. (Again, since the good is non-rivalrous, overconsumption is not a concern.) Do we see private actors voluntarily producing the good because: (1) lots of people have ethical impulses or religious convictions that lead them to provide this sort of good; or (2) some people have idiosyncratically strong personal preferences for the amenity and will therefore provide it for themselves, derivatively benefitting everyone else; or (3) some individual or entity has tied an excludable private benefit to contributions toward the amenity at issue, thereby inducing private sector production; or (4) for some other reason? If substantial private provision is occurring, or is to likely occur, government intervention may not be required.
- If private provision appears insufficient to produce an ideal amount of the amenity, consider whether government provision would improve matters. Remember that government provision requires coercing funding from the general public (taxpayers), many of whom may not want the amenity or may want only a small amount of it. When officials, spending other people's involuntarily provided money, are deciding how much of the amenity to produce, they are operating with little guidance and are likely to make significant mistakes. Remember also that public funding always involves concentrated benefits and diffuse costs and can therefore be politically difficult to curtail. Be sure to weigh those downsides of government provision – potential welfare losses from the knowledge problem and public choice concerns – against the welfare loss that will result if the amenity, due to free-riding, remains underproduced. Between government provision and

reliance on the private sector to produce the amenity, select the approach likely to produce less total welfare loss.

If the amenity is a commons good:

- First determine whether any affirmative effort to regulate potential overconsumption is warranted. Have users developed private schemes (like those Ostrom observed) for avoiding overconsumption? Might they do so if some legal barrier – e.g., potential antitrust liability – were removed? The best approach may be to do nothing or, at most, to create some sort of safe harbor for cooperative efforts to prevent commons over consumption.
- If private cooperative efforts are unlikely to prevent overconsumption, then compare the relative costs of command-and-control, Pigouvian, property rights-based, and hybrid approaches to addressing the negative externalities associated with consumption of the amenity at issue. For each of the approaches, consider three matters:
  - *The knowledge problem.* What information is required to implement the approach effectively? How likely is it that officials will be able to attain that information at a reasonable cost? What losses will occur if they fail to collect and process the information required?
  - *Public choice concerns.* How likely is it that the approach under consideration may be exploited by firms to gain a competitive advantage? What harms will result if such rent-seeking occurs? How likely is it that the approach will create concentrated benefits and diffuse costs, making it politically difficult to amend?
  - *Administrative costs.* How difficult is it for policymakers to administer the approach at issue? For property rights-based approaches, would high transaction costs preclude reallocations of the rights at issue? If so, is there a way to lower those costs?

Having considered these various costs, select the approach that seems most likely to maximize net social welfare.

We turn now to yet another private ordering defect that stems from cost-spillovers. This time, though, the spillovers occur within consensual relationships. That fact makes a world of difference.

6

Agency Costs

In 2004, Conan O'Brien, then the host of NBC's 12:30 a.m. program, *Late Night with Conan O'Brien*, negotiated a contract under which he would eventually replace Jay Leno as host of NBC's venerable *Tonight Show*. Five years later, Leno left the 11:30 p.m. *Tonight Show* to host a different NBC program in an earlier time slot. O'Brien took over as *Tonight Show* host on June 1, 2009.

A mere seven months later, NBC was itching for a change. Leno's new show wasn't bringing in the primetime audiences the network had anticipated, and O'Brien's *Tonight Show* ratings were significantly lower than Leno's had been. NBC therefore proposed a plan: Leno would return to the 11:30 p.m. time slot for an abbreviated program, and O'Brien's *Tonight Show* would begin at 12:05 a.m.

O'Brien didn't much care for that idea. Soon after NBC floated its proposal, he released the following statement: "I sincerely believe that delaying *The Tonight Show* into the next day to accommodate another comedy program will seriously damage what I consider to be the greatest franchise in the history of broadcasting. *The Tonight Show* at 12:05 simply isn't *The Tonight Show*."[1]

In light of O'Brien's unwillingness to move his time slot, NBC decided to terminate him. The network and O'Brien ultimately agreed that O'Brien would give up the show and stay off television for a certain period of time in exchange for a $45 million severance payment.

Perhaps not surprisingly, the run-up to O'Brien's January 22, 2010 departure featured a number of sketches poking fun at NBC. In one, Jack McBrayer, who played NBC page Kenneth Parcell on the hit show *30 Rock*, interrupted

---

[1] Conan O'Brien: I Will Not Follow Jay at 12:05, *Huffington Post* (available at www.huffingtonpost.com/2010/01/12/conan-obrien-statement-i_n_420521.html).

O'Brien's monologue while purporting to give a tour of the studio. "NBC spent more time building this studio than using it," McBrayer (in page character) quipped. In another bit, Steve Carrell, who played the hapless boss on NBC's *The Office*, conducted an exit interview in which he asked sarcastic questions like, "Did anything trigger your decision to leave?" Carrell wrapped up his exit interview by shredding O'Brien's NBC identification card – to raucous applause.

In his third-to-last episode, O'Brien gave the following introduction to a somewhat odd series of sketches:

> It's looking like this could be our last week. The good news is that until NBC yanks us off the air, we can pretty much do whatever we want, and – this is the best part . . . – they have to pay for it. . . . So, for the rest of the week, we're going to introduce new comedy bits that aren't so much funny as they are crazy expensive.

O'Brien then unveiled a Bugatti Veyron (purportedly the world's most expensive car) dressed as a mouse. As the original master recording of the Rolling Stones hit "Satisfaction" played in the background, O'Brien remarked:

> Let me ask you a question. Is this appropriate music for a car that looks like a mouse? No. Does it add anything at all to this comedy bit? No, it doesn't. Is it crazy expensive to play on the air – not to mention the rights to re-air this clip on the Internet? Hell yes! That's right, ladies and gentlemen. Total price tag for this comedy bit: $1.5 million. Sorry, NBC!

The following evening, O'Brien welcomed to the stage the 2009 Kentucky Derby winner, Mine that Bird, wearing a mink snuggie and watching restricted (and exorbitantly expensive) Super Bowl footage. O'Brien claimed the bit cost NBC $4.8 million. For the finale, a hose attached to what was claimed to be a fossilized skeleton of a ground sloth (purchased from the Smithsonian Institution) sprayed a substance described as Beluga caviar onto a painting purported to be an original Picasso. Total alleged price tag for the sketch: $65 million.

As should be obvious – and as O'Brien ultimately acknowledged in response to some rather ridiculous Internet outrage – the sketches didn't really involve the expensive elements alleged and thus didn't generate the serious waste O'Brien claimed. But the important point to see is that, if O'Brien really had possessed the authority he said he had, such waste could have occurred.[2]

---

[2] I am indebted to my colleague, Royce Barondes, for pointing me to the O'Brien sketches as an example of agency costs.

Watching O'Brien's antics at the end of his *Tonight Show* tenure, my mind turned to the former Chief Financial Officer of Enron Corporation, Andy Fastow. You may remember Fastow. He was responsible for many of the shenanigans leading to Enron's ultimate demise.

In the late 1990s, Enron, which then appeared to be a wildly successful energy trading firm, was having trouble generating continued profits. Managers at the firm knew that the company's lofty stock price would tank if profits couldn't be generated, so they enlisted Fastow to help keep debt off Enron's books. Fastow accomplished this task by creating "special purpose entities" (SPEs) – separate business organizations that were set up to achieve specific objectives and maintained their own, separate accounting records. Fastow funneled Enron debts, but not the assets securing those debts, into the SPEs he created. This caused Enron to appear more profitable than it really was. Fastow then solicited investors for the SPEs, and he invested himself, earning a nifty $45 million in the process. Fastow also oversaw an accounting scheme under which Enron, exploiting a glitch in accounting rules, counted as revenue the full sale price (not the net sales revenue) of every energy contract it sold. It even goosed those figures by buying and selling the same assets over and over again, recording each full sale price as revenue. The apparent goal of all this manipulation was to keep Enron's real financial situation a secret until managers could come up with something – anything – that would generate profits sufficient to justify the company's high stock price.

It didn't work. Soon after *Fortune* magazine named Enron "America's most innovative company" for the sixth year in a row, a year after *Chief Executive* magazine named its board of directors one of America's five best, the company was revealed to be a house of cards. Its stock price plummeted, and it filed for bankruptcy. Thousands of Enron employees who had been encouraged by management to invest their retirement accounts in Enron stock endured a cruel one–two punch: They lost both their livelihoods and their nest eggs. Fastow was indicted on 98 counts of mail and wire fraud. He pled guilty to two and agreed to serve a ten-year sentence, to surrender $23.8 million in ill-gotten gain, and to cooperate with the government to bring down other Enron insiders. His wife Lea was charged with tax fraud and agreed in a plea agreement to a five month sentence.

On first glance, O'Brien and Fastow would seem to have little in common. As far as I know, Fastow is neither funny nor particularly tall (as O'Brien is). Yet, O'Brien's purported conduct at NBC, like Fastow's actual behavior at Enron, resulted in social waste – specifically, unwarranted agency costs.

WHAT ARE AGENCY COSTS?

Agency costs are the welfare losses that result from agency (and similar) relationships. To comprehend agency costs, then, we must understand what an agency relationship is. In our modern society, we often have other people do things for us. My barber cuts my hair. My stockbroker manages my investments. My lawyer represents me in court. Some of the people who do things for me effectively act *as* me and consent to my control of their objectives. My lawyer, for example, stands up in court and argues *as me*. He does this to achieve the objective I have set for him: Get me dismissed from this lawsuit without having to pay damages. My stockbroker uses my money to buy, as though she were me, the stock I have directed her to purchase. My barber, by contrast, performs a discrete service for me, but he doesn't purport to *be* me. As a legal matter, an agency relationship results when one person (the principal) manifests consent that another (the agent) act on his behalf and subject to his control, and that other person (the agent) consents to do so. Under this definition, my lawyer and stockbroker are my agents. My barber, who does something for me but never consents to act *as* me, is not my agent.

Agency relationships are ubiquitous in an advanced economy. Every business (other than the rare sole proprietorship with no employees) involves agency relationships. Employees, for example, act as the face of, and subject to the control of, the companies they work for and are therefore agents of those companies. Partners are agents of their partnerships. The directors and officers of a corporation are agents of the shareholders who have invested in the company on the understanding that its management will work to increase their returns.

Agents typically manage resources belonging to their principals. For example, an employee, in doing her job, uses property that belongs to her employer. Partners manage business opportunities that belong to the partnership. Corporate managers use shareholder money to create profit. Ultimate ownership of the value the agent creates using the principal's property, however, belongs to the principal (with the principal then typically distributing some of that value to the agent as compensation for her services). Agency relationships therefore involve a *separation of ownership and control*: The principal owns the productive resources and the value they generate, but the resources are controlled by the agent. Non-agency relationships like that between my barber and me may also involve some separation of ownership and control (e.g., my barber controls, but does not own, my hair). Non-agents, though, usually have less discretion over their customer's property and control it for shorter periods of time. The adverse effects of the separation of ownership and control are thus most pronounced in agency relationships, which is why we call the effects "agency costs."[3]

So what are those adverse effects? Return to Conan O'Brien and Andy Fastow. Each was an agent (of the shareholders of NBC and Enron, respectively). Each had control over his principal's resources. O'Brien, at least by his account, could force NBC to spend money as he chose; Fastow could cause Enron's SPEs to make payouts to their investors, including him. Each ended up using the resources under his control in a manner that benefited him personally (Fastow got cash; O'Brien, vengeance), but neither extracted the greatest possible value from the resources. Social welfare would have been greater had O'Brien and Fastow put the resources to their actual highest and best ends, rather than to those that best suited O'Brien and Fastow. The owners of the resources would have preferred that outcome because the more value their resources produce, the more they may capture for themselves. One source of loss from the separation of ownership and control, then, is allocative inefficiency: Productive resources are moved away from the use in which they would produce the most value and toward some use that maximizes the controlling agent's welfare.

But that's not the whole of it. Rational principals are aware that their agents have a tendency to use the principals' property in a selfish, not value-maximizing, manner. The principals will therefore expend resources to prevent their agents from acting unfaithfully. At the same time, agents seeking to secure or retain positions and enhance their compensation will expend resources trying to prove how faithful and diligent they really are. In the corporate world, for example, firms routinely install "internal controls" to ferret out and prevent fraud, and they spend vast sums on reputable accountants and attorneys who effectively vouch for management's job performance. Some managers procure costly certifications or licenses or agree to limit their future profit-making activities, thereby incurring an opportunity cost, in order to signal that they will not pilfer from the firm and then take up new employment elsewhere. Taken together, principals' monitoring costs and agents' bonding costs – costs incurred to prevent losses from resource misallocations by conflicted agents – comprise a second key component of agency costs.

We may thus define agency costs as the sum of (1) principals' expenditures to monitor their agents, (2) agents' costs of proving their faithfulness and

---

[3] As this analysis would suggest, agency costs may exist outside agency relationships. As a couple of leading agency cost theorists have observed, "agency costs arise in any situation involving cooperative effort ... by two or more people even though there is no clear-cut principal-agent relationship." Michael C. Jensen and William H. Meckling, Theory of the Firm: Managerial Behavior, Agency Costs and Ownership Structure, 3 *J. Fin. Econ.* 305, 309 (1976).

preventing themselves from misusing their principals' resources, and (3) the residual allocative inefficiency that occurs when agents still act unfaithfully.[4] As long as there are agency relationships (and there always will be, given the tremendous value such relationships create), there will be some agency costs. Our concern is with *unwarranted* agency costs – i.e., those that could be cost-effectively reduced.

SYMPTOMS/DISEASE   *expensive to prevent*

Given the definition of agency costs, it should be obvious what their adverse symptoms are. Business firms and other principals spend gobs of money on monitoring. They hire accountants and lawyers, provide costly ethics training, and set up expensive reporting systems and internal controls. Employees and other agents, seeking to establish and guarantee their faithfulness, procure expensive certifications and agree to costly restraints designed to prevent them from misappropriating their principals' property. Yet, despite all these monitoring and bonding costs, some opportunities to create value from principals' productive resources are still squandered as agents succumb to the temptation to put their own interests first. Most corporate scandals and responses thereto are tales of agency costs.

While the adverse symptoms of agency costs are easy to see, the disease that causes them is perhaps less apparent. On first glance, one might assume that the problem is just an externality. The separation of ownership and control means that the agent who controls productive resources doesn't bear the immediate costs of her decisions about how they should be used. Most of the loss from picking a less valuable resource use over the one that would maximize value is experienced by the principal, the owner of the resources. Much of the benefit of that pick, though, may inure to the agent. Suppose, for example, that the highest and best use of a sum of cash received by the principal is to increase research and development efforts. If the agent instead spends the money redecorating a suite of offices owned by the principal but used by the agent, there will be (at least initially) a cost spillover: The agent will bear little, if any, of the loss stemming from not increasing R&D funding, but she will capture a significant portion of the benefit of office renovations. This looks like a classic negative externality.

The externality analysis, though, neglects the fact that agency relationships are always consensual and usually contractual. If an agent makes decisions that reduce the value of her principal's resources, the principal is

---

4   Ibid. at 308.

likely to alter the relationship in some fashion. At a minimum, the principal would be expected to reduce the agent's pay by the amount of personal benefit the agent received from an unfaithful decision; doing so would not diminish the agent's total compensation from the agreed-upon level, so she would be unlikely to quit in response to the pay cut. The principal might also "punish" the bad behavior by terminating the agent, reducing her compensation by more than the amount of benefit she received, or bad-mouthing her to other potential employers. Principal response, then, can effectively internalize the costs created by agent decisions concerning the use of principal resources.

Such reasoning assumes, though, that the principal *knows* how and to what extent the agent has failed to maximize the value of the principal's resources. That will often not be the case. Principals engage agents precisely because they lack the time, energy, and ability to manage all their affairs with competence. They can't keep up with all the decisions that must be made and tasks that must be performed. They can't gather and process all the information needed to determine how best to deploy their productive resources. This implies that they will not know when and to what extent their agents have failed to wring the most value from their stuff. Nor can they know how much value an agent has obtained from any particular decision about how to allocate her principal's resources. The principal–agent relationship is thus subject to an "information asymmetry," with the agent, who is much closer to the action, possessing far more information than the principal about the highest and best ends of resource allocations, the value lost from misallocations, and the personal value such misallocations confer upon the agent. Beset by such an informational disadvantage, the principal is in a poor position to engage in the sort of "self-help" that could internalize the external costs resulting from the separation of ownership and control.

It seems, then, that agency costs result from two dynamics this book elsewhere examines separately and in greater detail: externalities (Chapter 4) and information asymmetry (Chapter 8). Separating ownership of productive resources from control thereof creates the potential for something like an externality. Principal response, always a possibility in an ongoing, consensual relationship like that of principal and agent, could internalize the costs resulting from agent decisions concerning resource use. But appropriate principal response is unlikely to occur if the principal has less information than the agent about how much value the agent has destroyed (and funneled to himself) by a resource misallocation. Because such an information asymmetry is quite common in agency relationships, unwarranted agency costs tend to persist.

[handwritten margin note: focusing on relationship between "all agents" shareholders]

AVAILABLE REMEDIES AND THEIR IMPLEMENTATION
DIFFICULTIES AND SIDE EFFECTS

While unwarranted agency costs arise in all manner of cooperative relationships, most efforts to regulate agency costs have involved the management of business organizations, usually corporations. We will therefore focus on that context here, considering potential interventions for reducing the agency costs that arise from relationships between corporate shareholders and the managers (e.g., directors and officers) who control the corporate enterprise. The shareholders are principals; the managers, agents.

In light of our analysis of the disease giving rise to unwarranted agency costs, we might expect two general types of remedies. First, planners might seek to reduce the degree to which ownership and control are separated; uniting ownership and control would mitigate the externality potential inherent in agency relationships. Second, planners might try to make it easier for principals to respond appropriately to agent infidelity; anticipating such a response, agents would be less likely to act disloyally in the first place. As it turns out, both privately ordered responses to agency costs and actual and proposed regulatory solutions have generally taken one of these tacks.

Pure Private Ordering

Before turning to regulatory interventions, let's briefly consider the private solutions that are sometimes implemented to reduce agency costs. The first type of remedy, reuniting ownership and control, can be accomplished either by giving controllers more ownership or by giving owners more control. *[handwritten margin note: giving skin in the game]* To give controllers of the corporate enterprise more ownership, business planners often provide that managers be compensated with stock (or options to buy stock). This is designed to give them more "skin in the game" and better align their personal interests with those of shareholders. Less commonly (at least in large corporations), planners endeavor to give owners more control by providing that shareholders shall have the right to vote on particular management decisions.

Both efforts to reunite ownership and control are subject to limitations. Compensating corporate managers with stock may increase the amount shareholders have to pay for managerial talent without significantly reducing managerial infidelity. A corporate executive who is paid in her own company's *[handwritten margin note: limitations]* stock – especially if its transfer is restricted, as is the case with most so-called equity-based compensation – suffers from a lack of diversification; she has really put all her eggs in one basket. If the corporation she works for goes bust, she loses both her income (her job) *and* her savings. Because paying her in stock forces her to bear a significant economic risk, she will demand additional compensation, raising the amount the shareholders must pay for managerial talent. It's not at all clear that those additional costs are justified on grounds that they secure a reduction in agency costs. After all, even a manager who is compensated entirely in stock of her company will be tempted to make decisions that don't maximize returns for the company but do benefit her personally. For example, such a manager may wish to spend corporate funds on office renovation rather than R&D, a more valuable objective, because she personally captures much of the benefit of the renovated offices while sharing the loss from foregone R&D with all the other shareholders.

The other means of reuniting ownership and control – giving stockholders more management control – runs into the problem of "rational ignorance." Business decisions, as it turns out, are complicated. Determining which potential allocation of resources is most likely to be value-maximizing often requires a great deal of study. In most large corporations, the vast majority of shareholders own such a small stake in the company that their vote (which is weighted according to their ownership interest) will have almost no influence over the ultimate decision. Recognizing as much, shareholders quite reason-ably decline to perform the investigation needed to make a sound decision. They *rationally* remain *ignorant*. Entrusting significant business decisions to shareholder voting is thus unlikely to yield value-maximizing decisions, at least in large corporations with widely dispersed share ownership.

In addition to reuniting ownership and control, business planners have sought to constrain agency costs by facilitating appropriate principal responses to agent infidelity. If agents anticipate such responses, they are less likely to act unfaithfully. There are, though, at least two barriers that limit principals' ability to respond appropriately when their agents are disloyal. The one we have discussed is information asymmetry: The principal is at an informational disadvantage, and the agent, aware of that fact, knows there's a good chance she won't get caught. The other barrier is that principals' self-help options for punishing disloyalty are largely limited to *prospective* sanctions – e.g., fire the agent, dock her pay, or reduce her future employment opportunities by bad-mouthing her to others. An agent who plans to leave her current employment, or wouldn't mind doing so, won't be dissuaded by the threat of termination or changes in the terms of her employment, and threats to her reputation among future employers may not be significant enough to counterbalance her desire for immediate pilfered profits. The second set of privately ordered solutions to unwarranted agency costs, then, consists of efforts to remove these two barriers to the sort of principal responses that tend to discourage agent infidelity.

*Corporate gatekeepers
and internal controls*

To alleviate the information asymmetry that often stymies principal responses, business planners have installed systems that monitor agent conduct and have relied upon various "corporate gatekeepers" to ferret out managerial misbehavior. Planners have set up mechanisms under which managers' financial reports are regularly audited by outside accountants. They have implemented information and reporting systems and other "internal controls." They have opted into a financing system that requires managers regularly to allow credit ratings agencies and securities analysts to inspect all manner of corporate affairs. All these endeavors help bring managerial misdeeds to light.

Contracts provide a means for overcoming the second barrier to appropriate principal response – the fact that principals' self-help options are limited to imposing only prospective sanctions on their unfaithful agents. An employment agreement may specify how a corporate manager is to act on behalf of shareholders. If the manager breaches the agreement, shareholders will be entitled to contract damages, meaning that the disloyal manager will have to *pay something* to the aggrieved shareholders. Contracts can thus assure both that managers remain accountable for their disloyal actions even after their employment comes to an end and that shareholders aren't limited to adjusting future employment terms in response to agent disloyalty.

There are limitations to both of these efforts to facilitate appropriate principal responses to agent infidelity. With respect to the first (monitoring), cost is the obvious limiting factor. Monitoring by principals, you will recall, is an *element* of agency costs. Every dollar spent on monitoring therefore adds to the total from at least one source. That is not to say, of course, that manager monitoring is always bad. Far from it. Every increment of monitoring that reduces the loss from agent disloyalty by more than it costs to implement that unit of monitoring – put differently, every monitoring effort whose marginal benefit exceeds its marginal cost – is good. At some point, though, additional monitoring efforts aren't worth the costs they impose.

Employment agreements have also proven limited in their ability to constrain agency costs in the corporation. Because indefinite promises can be difficult to enforce, contract language tends to be precise. It would be nearly impossible, though, to anticipate and precisely preclude all the acts of disloyalty a corporate manager might take. Imagine trying to craft an exhaustive list of "Thou Shalt Nots" for an officer or director of a large, publicly held corporation. The difficulty of doing so has prevented contract from playing a leading role in constraining agency costs in large corporations. As Professor Jonathan Macey has observed,

While there is a great deal of corporate law, both statutory and judge-made, there is precious little in the way of contract between shareholders and corporations. The judge-made law may masquerade as contract by invoking the idea of hypothetical bargaining, but that does not detract from what it is: non-contractual law. Simply put, the non-contractual law governing shareholder rights is literally voluminous, while the actual contracts that exist are skeletal, particularly in the publicly held corporation.[5]

So what is that "statutory and judge-made law" that largely substitutes for explicit contracts between shareholders and managers? We turn to that now.

Fiduciary Duties and Shareholder Suits

As observed, express contracts purporting to set forth the precise obligations corporate managers owe to shareholders are a rarity. That's largely because it's so difficult to anticipate and specify with precision all the things managers should and shouldn't do. Contracts typically set forth *rules* the parties are to follow in their dealings with each other. Rules entail an advance determination of what conduct is permissible; their mandates and prohibitions are fleshed out ex ante – i.e., before the person subject to the rule acts. A speed limit ("Thou shalt not drive in excess of 70 mph") is a rule. Because (1) contracts usually prescribe conduct rules; (2) fashioning rules to govern behavior requires knowing what decisions the governed party will confront and specifying how she should respond; and (3) planners cannot anticipate all the temptations a corporate manager will face, and, even if they could, would have a difficult time addressing them all in a single document, express contracting is usually not the best way to prevent managerial infidelity.

Setting forth ex ante rules, though, is not the only way to say how someone should behave. The law regularly holds people to *standards* of behavior. Under a standard, specification of precisely what is allowed or forbidden is determined ex post – i.e., after the person subject to the behavioral norm has acted. From 1995 to 1998, for example, the state of Montana scrapped its daytime speed limit, a rule, in favor of a directive that motorists drive in a "reasonable and prudent manner." That's a standard. So is the general tort law requirement that people not act negligently. It would be impossible to state in advance all the actions that might constitute negligence, so courts have just posited a standard of care – "Thou shalt act 'prudently,' 'with reasonable care,' etc." – and allowed the precise contours of that standard to be fleshed out

---

[5] Jonathan Macey, *Corporate Governance: Promises Kept, Promises Broken* (Princeton: Princeton University Press, 2008) 29.

on a case-by-case basis, after people have acted. The chief difference between a rule – the sort of prescriptive mandate one regularly sees in contracts[6] – and a standard is that the former's precise content is determined ex ante, and the latter's, ex post.

Given the impossibility of specifying in advance all the actions a manager should take and avoid on behalf of the shareholders whose resources she stewards, setting forth standards of managerial conduct may be a better means of policing agency costs within a corporation. Three questions then arise. First, who should set forth the standards – the parties (shareholders and managers) or the government? Second, what should the standards consist of? Third, how should those standards be enforced?

With respect to the first question, states have promulgated the standards of behavior rather than relying on shareholders and managers to adopt them contractually. In the United States, every corporation is organized under the law of a particular state, which need not be a state in which the business operates or owns property. (Delaware is by far the leading state for incorporations of big companies.) Under the "internal affairs" doctrine, relations between the parties to the corporate contract are governed by the law of the state of incorporation. Thus, when business planners choose to organize (or reorganize) under the law of a particular state, they are opting to have the relations between their shareholders and managers governed by the rules and standards set forth in that state's corporate law.

This system has created something of a "law market," where states vying for corporate charters (and the tax revenues they generate) compete to offer the most attractive set of rules and standards to govern the relations between managers and shareholders.[7] Among those standards are "fiduciary duties" that obligate the managers of the corporation to act in a certain way in stewarding their shareholders' resources. States, then, are the source of the standards aimed at stemming agency costs in the corporate context.

---

6   This is not to say that people cannot contract to abide by standards of behavior. They can and sometimes do. But rules are far more common in contracts.

7   Many scholars once worried that this competition for charters would lead to a "race to the bottom," where the states with the most management-friendly corporate law would attract the most incorporations. This has turned out not to be the case. Because corporations whose managers are subject to lax standards of behavior tend to be subject to high agency costs and thus offer lower returns to investors and impose higher risks on creditors, such companies have a harder time raising money to fund their operations. They ultimately must pay more to creditors and investors to induce them to provide capital. To avoid a higher cost of capital, business planners tend to seek out corporate laws that will maximize the value of the enterprise, not necessarily those that will go easiest on managers.

But the standards are *quasi*-contractual for a couple of reasons. First, the parties have some choice over what standards will govern their relations. Corporate organizers, who often end up being the initial managers, effectively choose a corporate law when they determine their state of incorporation, and managers and shareholders may always cause the corporation to be reorganized elsewhere if they become dissatisfied with that state's law. Second, because standards are fleshed out ex post, most of the work of crafting obligations is done by state courts adjudicating concrete cases. When they decide, ex post, what a manager should have done (and thus what similarly situated managers should do in the future), they often ask what managerial behavior the parties would have contracted for ex ante had they engaged in such contracting. This "hypothetical bargain" approach to crafting fiduciary duties gives the duties a contractual flavor, even though they are technically the product of the state rather than of the parties' mutual assent.

Turning to the substance of the standards, states have typically saddled corporate managers with two fiduciary duties. The first, the fiduciary duty of loyalty, obligates managers to avoid any sort of self-dealing or opportunism in stewarding shareholders' resources. Absent approval by disinterested shareholders or directors, they may not cause the company to enter any transaction that benefits them personally. Nor may they take for themselves any opportunity that could have gone to the corporation (and ultimately its shareholders). The fiduciary duty of care, then, requires managers to make reasonable decisions on behalf of the shareholders. They are obligated (1) to use reasonable care to become informed when making a decision (i.e., to engage in a reasonable decision-making process), and (2) to make substantively reasonable decisions. Under the "business judgment rule," however, courts will typically abstain from second-guessing the substance of a business judgment as long as the managers complied with the duty of loyalty and the *procedural* aspect of the duty of care. By precluding shareholder challenges claiming merely that a business decision was substantively unreasonable, the business judgment rule encourages managers to take the sorts of business risks that are necessary to maximize shareholder returns.[8]

---

[8]   The business judgment rule responds to corporate managers' tendency to be more risk averse than the shareholders whose resources they manage. There are several reasons for this discrepancy in preferences for business risk. First, shareholders have "limited liability," meaning that the most they have to lose from a bad business decision is the amount they have invested in the company. Managers, by contrast, will lose their jobs *and* their reputations (and possibly future employment opportunities) if they cause the company to take a business risk that doesn't pan out. Second, by diversifying their investments, shareholders can eliminate non-systematic (i.e., company-specific) risk from their portfolios. Managers, by contrast, cannot diversify their human capital (i.e., their labor), so they experience company-specific risks more intensely.

Enforcement of managers' fiduciary duties typically occurs through lawsuits that are brought, at least nominally, by shareholders. If a manager's violation of fiduciary duty causes the corporation to be less valuable and thereby injures shareholders, a shareholder may be able to bring a "derivative" suit. (The term reflects the fact that the shareholder's injury – a decrease in the value of her investment – is "derived" from that of the corporation.) Because derivative suits seek relief for *the corporation's* injury, they effectively aggregate the claims of all the corporation's shareholders. If the manager's breach of duty injures a shareholder apart from just reducing the value of her investment (i.e., if her injury is not wholly derived from the corporation's injury), she may bring a "direct" lawsuit against the manager. Because a direct action is not brought on behalf of the corporation itself, it does not automatically aggregate all shareholders' claims based on the same alleged misconduct. Direct shareholder suits may, however, be brought as class actions on behalf of all shareholders.

While nominally asserting shareholders' claims, lawsuits against managers for breach of fiduciary duty tend to be lawyer-driven. Because the per-share recovery in a suit against managers is usually quite small, few shareholders – only those owning a large proportion of the company's stock – have an incentive to incur the cost of bringing such a lawsuit. Plaintiffs' lawyers, by contrast, have much to gain from a shareholder suit resulting in a favorable verdict or settlement. If the lawsuit results in a monetary payment to the corporation or a class of shareholders, the lawyers may receive a sizeable chunk of the recovery as compensation for their services. Even absent a monetary recovery, courts routinely award attorney fees to plaintiffs' lawyers when the shareholder lawsuits they have brought result in managers' making changes that could benefit the shareholders. (For example, if managers settle the lawsuit by agreeing to appoint a board committee to prevent similar duty breaches in the future, the plaintiffs' lawyers may be entitled to payment from the corporation.) The theory is that the corporation has been unjustly enriched at the attorneys' expense and should therefore make restitution.

Third, shareholders, who are entitled to the profit a company earns after it has paid all other claimants (including its managers, who are entitled to their salaries), earn nothing if the company just breaks even. Managers, on the other hand, still get paid if the company just breaks even. In light of these considerations, managers tend to prefer endeavors that are low-risk, even though they earn little profit. Shareholders, by contrast, would prefer that the company take bigger risks in the hope of bigger rewards. By precluding shareholder challenges to the mere substance of business decisions, the business judgment rule helps align the incentives of managers and shareholders with respect to business risk. See generally Stephen Bainbridge, *Corporation Law and Economics* (New York: Foundation Press, 2002) 259–63.

So what should we make of a scheme that seeks to reduce unwarranted agency costs by saddling corporate managers with amorphous fiduciary duties that are fleshed out ex post and are enforced by lawsuits driven primarily by plaintiffs' lawyers? Like so many regulatory approaches, it seems to be a mixed bag. Imposing the fiduciary duties of loyalty and care is probably, on balance, a good thing. The duties would seem to prohibit most instances of managerial misbehavior, but, being standards, they retain the flexibility to account for specific circumstances that ex ante rules might not anticipate. Because the duties largely condemn the bad without prohibiting the good, they are likely the sorts of standards shareholders and managers would agree to were they to bargain over managerial conduct restrictions. Since that's the case, it seems sensible to have the state impose them as a matter of background law. Doing so prevents shareholders and managers, who would probably bargain for the duties anyway, from having to write them into their contracts.

This is not to say that the fiduciary duties that have evolved in the case law are perfect. For one thing, they may overemphasize the decision-making *process*. Providing corporate managers with the protection of the business judgment rule only if they have used procedural care to become reasonably informed encourages managers to "paper" their decision-making with costly advisers, consultants, expert reports, etc. The managers use shareholder money to pay for all this outside expertise, and it's often questionable whether the shareholders get much additional benefit from it. It's also somewhat troubling that the fiduciary duties, while flexible, are not fully contractual, such that shareholders and managers could tailor them (or perhaps even opt out of them) as needed. As we'll see when we look at insider trading, imposing inalterable fiduciary duties on corporate managers may prevent shareholders from authorizing their managers to engage in certain conduct that would enhance firm value and benefit shareholders in the long term. Despite these downsides, though, corporate law's imposition of fiduciary duties on managers seems beneficial on the whole.

The problem with using fiduciary duties to constrain agency costs in the corporate context is the enforcement mechanism – shareholder suits. Plaintiffs' lawyers, the driving force behind such suits, often have interests that diverge from those of the shareholders they represent. They want to maximize their profits from the lawsuits, not necessarily the plaintiffs' recovery. This can lead them to mismanage the shareholders' claims. If the fee arrangement calls for the lawyer to receive a portion of the shareholders' recovery, the lawyer may have an incentive to settle early, for less than the shareholders would receive in a trial, in order to avoid the costs of continued litigation. If the court awarding fees instead follows the "lodestar" method, which takes into account the hours counsel has spent on the lawsuit, the lawyer has an incentive to drag out the litigation and to reject, at least initially, reasonable settlement offers.

The shareholder–lawyer relationship, in short, is riddled with the same sorts of agency costs as the shareholder–manager relationship.[9] In each case, the agent (manager or lawyer) stewards the shareholders' assets (money or valuable legal claims) and has interests that differ from those of the shareholders. In each case, shareholder monitoring is unlikely to prevent misallocations because shareholders are informationally disadvantaged relative to their agents and, in light of rational ignorance and free-rider concerns, are likely to remain so.[10] There is thus significant irony in a system that relies on shareholder suits to enforce managers' fiduciary duties: In endeavoring to reduce agency costs, such a system produces agency costs. Indeed, the shareholder–lawyer relationship may be more susceptible to agency costs than the shareholder–manager relationship. For a publicly traded corporation, the stock price acts as a sort of running metric of managerial performance; managers who regularly misallocate shareholders' resources are exposed by ailing stock prices. No such mechanism exists to expose plaintiffs' lawyers who are mishandling shareholders' legal claims. They operate with precious little accountability.

Deploying an agency cost-ridden shareholder–lawyer relationship to combat the agency costs resulting from the shareholder–manager relationship tends to generate "strike suits" and "collusive settlements." Strike suits are meritless lawsuits filed for purposes of extracting a settlement. They create cost without benefit, destroying wealth. In the corporate context, plaintiffs' lawyers frequently file them because they know managers will face large costs in defending against even a meritless lawsuit and will often prefer just to settle quickly.

Plaintiffs' lawyers also know that the rules on who pays attorney fees in the corporate context enhance managers' willingness to settle meritless claims. The leading rule on managers' legal expenses is that the corporation must indemnify the manager if she succeeds "on the merits or otherwise."[11] She is

---

[9]   See generally Macey, supra note 5, at 136–47.
[10] Shareholders tend to be rationally ignorant of what their agents are doing because each shareholder owns such a small portion of the stock that his benefit from learning what the agent is doing is too small to justify his cost of becoming informed. Shareholder monitoring is subject to the free-rider problem because any shareholder who does monitor and thereby hold his agents in check confers benefits on all shareholders. Each shareholder may hold off on monitoring, hoping to take a free ride on some other shareholder's monitoring effort.
[11] Del. Code Ann., tit.8, § 145(c).

deemed to have done so if she is dismissed from the lawsuit without having to pay a monetary judgment. Most courts also hold that if a shareholder suit results in a substantial benefit to the corporation, the (unjustly enriched) corporation must pay the plaintiffs' lawyers for their services. Substantial benefit has been defined generously, so a mere agreement by managers to do or refrain from doing something in the future is often taken to qualify. Taken together, these rules create fertile ground for cooperation between managers and plaintiffs' lawyers: If the parties settle the lawsuit on terms that do not require managers to pay anything but do involve some sort of conduct remedy, the managers' expenses are indemnified and the plaintiffs' lawyers get paid. (Of course, not everyone wins here. The shareholders, whose money is used to pay both the plaintiffs' attorneys and managers' defense lawyers, are losers.)

Examples of strike suits followed by collusive settlements abound. One of the most famous involved Caremark, a large provider of managed health care services. Federal regulators investigated Caremark for violating a statute making it illegal for health care providers to provide any form of compensation in exchange for referrals of Medicare or Medicaid patients. The company was ultimately indicted and agreed to pay fines and damages of $250 million. Following that settlement, some shareholder plaintiffs filed a derivative action against the company's directors. The lawsuit alleged that the directors had breached their fiduciary duties not by violating the anti-referral payments law (no one contended they knew of the wrongdoing) but by failing to monitor and supervise Caremark's business appropriately. As is typical for these sorts of suits, the directors settled. Under the principal requirements of the settlement, they agreed to take steps aimed at preventing future violations of the anti-referral payments law, to advise patients in writing of any relationship between Caremark and a referring health care professional, and to create a board committee to monitor future conduct by employees. That was all the shareholders got from the litigation. For their efforts in securing the agreement, however, the plaintiffs' lawyers were awarded fees of $816,000 – paid from shareholders' money. The court approved the settlement and fees despite finding "a very low probability that it would be determined that the directors of Caremark breached any duty to appropriately monitor and supervise the enterprise."[12]

An even more egregious case of a strike suit followed by a collusive settlement occurred in the early 1990s, when securities class action lawyers brought a fraud action against Occidental Petroleum Company after its managers cut

---

[12]   In re Caremark International Inc. Derivative Litigation, 698 A.2d 959, 961 (Del. Ch. 1996).

dividends from $3 to $2 per share. The parties settled the suit for an agreement by management not to reduce dividends below $2 per share unless, "in the judgment of the company's board of directors, the dividend should be reduced." For procuring that toothless commitment, the plaintiffs' lawyers were initially awarded a whopping $2,975,000 in fees.[13] These examples suggest that, while fighting fire with fire sometimes makes sense, fighting agency costs with a relationship subject to agency costs really doesn't.

Proponents of shareholder suits as a means to constrain agency costs within the corporation respond to these sorts of criticisms by observing that settlements of derivative suits and shareholder class actions must be approved by a judge. Subjecting settlement agreements to judicial scrutiny, they say, tends to prevent the sort of collusive settlements that fuel strike suits. But there are a number of reasons to doubt that judicial supervision will provide a meaningful check on collusive settlements.[14] First, judges tend to be biased in favor of approving settlements because settlements clear crowded dockets and reduce judges' workloads. Second, judges care about their reputations and want to avoid both tardiness, which is more likely to occur the fuller the judge's docket, and reversal, which is a possibility if a case is litigated to judgment but not if it is settled. Third, judges are dependent on the parties' lawyers, who have colluded to craft the settlement under review, for the information needed to evaluate the settlement's fairness. Settlement hearings end up being bizarre rituals in which each side tries to convince the judge of the weakness of its case, the strength of the other's, and the wisdom of splitting the baby as proposed. Such hearings lack the adversarial feature typically relied upon to reveal the truth in a trial setting. Facing a barrage of voices arguing in concert for the fairness of a deal, even a well-meaning judge can be duped into approving an absurd settlement.

Mandatory Structural Rules

State corporate law's imposition of fiduciary duties may be viewed as an effort to supplement the implicit contract between corporate managers and shareholders with *standards* governing managers' *conduct*. When it comes to the structure of the corporation, as opposed to the behavior of corporate agents,

---

[13] See Lawrence W. Schonbrun, The Class Action Con Game, 20 *Regulation* 50, 54–55 (1997). The fee award was vacated on appeal, see Zucker v. Occidental Petroleum Corp., 68 F.3d 482 (9th Cir. 1995), and ultimately reduced to a still whopping (in light of the benefit to plaintiffs) $1.15 million. See Zucker v. Occidental Petroleum Corp., 968 F. Supp. 1396 (C.D. Cal. 1997).

[14] See Macey, supra note 5, at 151–53.

state corporate law has taken a largely hands-off approach. State laws do typically provide that ultimate control of the business must reside in a board of directors, that shareholders must elect those directors, and that shareholders must be allowed to vote on a small number of other matters (e.g., mergers, amendments to the articles of incorporation). Beyond that, though, there are few structural mandates. Board members need not possess special qualifications, and boards are generally free to allocate decision-making authority among their members as they choose, subject to the fiduciary duties of loyalty and care. Boards also have great leeway in determining how to monitor the officers and other managers who have been hired to run the business on a day-to-day basis. Of course, capital markets impose significant discipline on boards and prevent them from acting negligently or wielding their power in a manner that reduces the value of the enterprise; if they do so, the company's stock price will fall, and the business will find that it has to pay higher interest rates when it seeks to borrow money. State corporate law, though, has typically relied on market pressures, rather than precise legal mandates, to induce boards to structure governance mechanisms appropriately.

In recent years, this system has begun to change. In response to the corporate scandals of the early 2000s, reformers pushed for, and legislatures and regulatory bodies adopted, mandatory *rules* (not standards) concerning *corporate structure* (not managerial behavior). Some of those rules have been imposed directly by legislatures (chiefly, the US Congress); others, by regulatory agencies, primarily the SEC; still others, by theoretically private stock exchanges (e.g., the New York Stock Exchange or NASDAQ), which set listing standards for the companies whose stock is traded on the exchanges. Despite the fact that their immediate source is a private entity, such listing standards should be deemed regulation because the SEC, pursuant to congressional direction, has essentially mandated that the exchanges impose them.[15]

Prominent examples of recently implemented or proposed rules dictating corporate structure include:

---

[15]   See Macey, supra note 5, at 112 ("[T]he available evidence indicates the organized exchanges do not even act as stand-alone regulators anymore. Instead, they are better understood as conduits for the SEC, which coordinates the corporate governance regulations that ostensibly are promulgated under the exchanges' authority as self-regulatory organizations."); Roberta Todd Lang, et al., American Bar Association, Special Study on Market Structure, Listing Standards and Corporate Governance, 57 *Bus. Lawyer* 1503 (2002) ("[T]he SEC has adopted a practice of encouraging the exchanges 'voluntarily' to adopt given corporate governance listing standards and in the process has urged the exchanges' listed companies and shareholders to reach consensus on those standards.").

- Requirements that the boards of publicly traded corporations maintain, and delegate particular decisions to, various committees of directors;[16]
- Requirements that a majority of the board of directors and all members of certain required committees (compensation, nominating, and audit committees) be financially and relationally independent from the company's officers, with "independence" defined narrowly;[17]
- Requirements that shareholders be allowed to vote on certain matters (e.g., the propriety of compensation for top executives)[18] and to nominate director candidates for inclusion on management's proxy card, the main "ballot" in director elections;[19] and
- Requirements that corporations implement "internal controls" – procedures designed to detect and prevent fraud – that outside auditors deem to be effective.[20]

Imposing corporate structure rules to constrain agency costs is really a form of command-and-control. As such, it is subject to versions of command-and-control's typical pros and cons. On the pro side, the chief virtues of imposing structural rules are clarity and responsiveness.[21] Whereas state law fiduciary duties, as standards, are somewhat vague and amorphous until fleshed out in adjudication following an alleged violation, the requirements of structural rules such as those set forth above are typically clear to those governed by them. This clarity lowers decision costs by making it easier for business planners, enforcers, and adjudicators to know what is and isn't allowed.

---

[16] NYSE Listed Company Manual § 303A; NASDAQ Listing Rule 5605.

[17] NYSE Listed Company Manual § 303A.01 (independent majority for board); NASDAQ Listing Rule 5605(b)(1) (independent majority for board); NYSE Listed Company Manual §§ 303A.06, 303A.05(a), 303A.04(a) (requiring independent audit, compensation, and nominating committees); NASDAQ Listing Rules 5605(c)(2), 5605A(d), 5605(e) (requiring independent audit, compensation, and nominating committees); NYSE Listed Company Manual § 303A.02 (defining independence); NASDAQ Listing Rule 5605(a)(2) (defining independence).

[18] See, e.g., Dodd-Frank Wall Street Reform and Consumer Protection Act [hereinafter, "Dodd-Frank"], Pub. L. No. 111–203, § 951, 124 Stat. 1899 (2010).

[19] 75 Fed. Reg. 56,668, et seq. (Sept. 16, 2010) (vacated by Business Roundtable v. SEC, 647 F.3d 1144 (D.C. Cir. 2011)).

[20] Sarbanes-Oxley Act of 2002 [hereinafter "Sarbanes-Oxley"], Pub. L. No. 107–204, § 404, 116 Stat. 745 (2002), codified at 15 U.S.C. § 7262.

[21] In addition to the benefits of clarity and responsiveness, imposition of structural rules offers the perhaps specious benefit of signaling to the public and regulated entities that regulators are "doing something." I call this a potentially specious benefit because signaling that regulators are imposing rules that are toothless, that will not work, or that create greater cost than benefit is of very little, if any, social value. Still, some slight benefit may result from simply reminding corporate agents that regulators have the power to come down on them if they misstep in the future.

Because they can be designed to take immediate effect, structural rules are also able to respond more quickly to identified deficiencies in corporate governance. State corporate law's fiduciary duties may not affect the behavior of the relevant corporate parties until after shareholders have sued over an agent's conduct, the lawsuit has resulted in a judgment in the plaintiffs' favor, and the decision has been reported to similarly situated firms whose agents are engaged in the same sort of conduct. Market mechanisms (the subject of the following section) may also involve a lag. As we will see, the market mechanisms that discipline agency costs largely depend on price effects, which require that often hidden information make its way to market actors.[22] That may take some time. By contrast, imposition of a structural rule can occasion an almost immediate effect on corporate governance.

Balancing against (and probably outweighing) these upsides of imposing structural rules are some familiar downsides. For one thing, the knowledge problem exists in spades in this context. Business corporations are extraordinarily diverse, and central planners neither have nor could process the information needed to say what structures should govern all companies. For that reason, states vying for corporate charters have imposed very few mandatory structural rules. The structural rules that do exist in state corporate law are typically "default" rules that business planners may opt out of if they believe, in light of specific circumstances to which they (unlike regulators) are privy, that the rules would reduce the value of the entity. States have then relied upon capital market pressures to drive business planners to select structural rules that, given the specific needs of their businesses, are value-maximizing. An approach that addresses agency costs by instead mandating structural rules ignores government planners' informational limitations. The predictable result has been resource misallocation resulting from regulator error.

Consider the error costs stemming from recent mandates concerning internal controls. Section 404 of the 2002 Sarbanes-Oxley Act, enacted in the wake of the Enron scandal, required that public companies adopt, and that their management and outside auditors attest to the effectiveness of, internal controls designed to assure that the companies accurately report their finances.[23] These mandates proved to be quite costly, and since the fixed cost of setting up and auditing controls varies little with the size of a corporation, the burden was especially heavy on smaller companies. In 2004, for example, US companies

---

[22] Markets quickly incorporate publicly available information but not information that is hidden – the sort of information that is often most likely to reveal needed governance changes.

[23] Sarbanes-Oxley, Pub. L. No. 107–204, § 404, 116 Stat. 745 (2002), codified at 15 U.S.C. § 7262(a), (b).

with revenues exceeding \$5 billion spent an average of 0.06 percent of their revenues complying with the internal controls mandate, while the compliance cost of companies bringing in less than \$100 million averaged, on a percentage basis, nearly 43 *times* as much (2.55 percent of revenues).[24] A measure that may have been cost-justified for some companies surely wasn't for others. Yet, the rule initially applied equally to all.[25]

The recently enacted rules on director independence exemplify the same difficulty. Rules imposed by the major stock exchanges (at the behest of Congress and the SEC) require that all listed companies have a majority of independent directors.[26] Independence is then narrowly defined so that any director holding a management position or having a financial or familial relationship with anyone in management is not deemed independent.[27] Reasoning that a director may go easy on management if she is herself a manager or is in some sort of relationship with one, proponents of the majority independence rule maintain that it creates value for shareholders by enhancing the board's monitoring of management. Confident that this approach is appropriate across the board, the SEC pushed the major exchanges to require it of all listed companies.

The problem is that different corporations need different things from their directors. Traditionally, boards of directors have performed two primary functions: they have *monitored* management, and they have *managed* the business by making strategic decisions that were then largely implemented by non-director managers. When it comes to the former function, independence from management may be a virtue. With respect to the latter, it is not. To make sound management decisions, boards need all sorts of inside information about the company's business, its competitive advantages, its weaknesses, its personnel, etc. They often require the sort of "soft" information that is difficult to put into a formal report but essential to wise decision-making. Inside directors tend to know this information, often reflexively. Independent directors, by contrast, must rely on insiders to inform them of the relevant facts. Those insiders have an incentive to shade the facts in a way that promotes the decision that will benefit them personally, and even an insider who is firmly

---

[24] Final Report of the Advisory Committee on Smaller Public Companies to the US Securities and Exchange Commission 33 (Apr. 23, 2006), available at www.sec.gov/info/smallbus/acspc /acspc-finalreport.pdf.

[25] Congress ultimately amended Section 404 to exempt smaller companies (those with a market capitalization of less than \$75 million) from the most expensive part of the internal controls mandate, the outside audit requirement. Dodd-Frank, Pub. L. No. 111–203, § 989G(a) (adding section 404(c) to Sarbanes-Oxley, codified at 15 U.S.C. § 7262(c)).

[26] See supra note 17 and accompanying text.

[27] NYSE Listed Company Manual § 303A.02; NASDAQ Listing Rule 5605(a)(2).

committed to sharing information as objectively as possible may not be able to provide all the information an inside director would possess. That objective insider may not know what information to share, and may face difficulty communicating soft information, which often manifests itself as intuitions or "hunches."

In light of these facts, it should not be surprising that the empirical evidence does not support the view – an apparent assumption of the listing standards – that greater board independence enhances value for shareholders. In an exhaustive study of the empirical evidence relevant to Sarbanes-Oxley's corporate governance provisions, Professor Roberta Romano found that none of the studies, which employed a variety of accounting, market performance, and asset productivity measures, found any positive relation between board independence and corporate performance.[28] Indeed, research suggests that at some point, increased board independence is counterproductive. Professors Sanjai Baghat and Bernard Black, for example, found that companies with a "moderate number" of inside directors on an average-sized board (i.e., three to five insiders on a board of eleven) tend to be more profitable than similar companies with a lower percentage of inside directors.[29]

At the end of the day, the optimal mix of inside and independent directors depends largely on whether the corporation at issue needs for its board to provide more monitoring or more management. The central planners who crafted the majority independence requirement for public company boards could not possibly know which corporations need which sorts of boards. Their blanket, one-size-fits-all rule is sure to misallocate managerial talent in a great many cases. The losers will be the shareholders, who would prefer that their company's board be structured to provide the precise monitoring/managing balance that will maximize firm value.

In addition to the knowledge problem, public choice concerns often afflict efforts to combat agency costs with structural rules. The bodies that promulgate such rules – legislatures and administrative agencies – are more subject to such concerns than are the more politically insulated courts that fashion managerial conduct standards (i.e., fiduciary duties). Legislatures respond to well-organized interest groups, particularly those that, for whatever reason, are popular at the moment. They tend to give short shrift to the interests of widely dispersed, disorganized groups and to those that are out of favor with the

---

[28] Roberta Romano, The Sarbanes-Oxley Act and the Making of Quack Corporate Governance, 114 *Yale L. J.* 1530 (2005).

[29] Sanjai Baghat and Bernard Black, The Uncertain Relationship Between Board Composition and Firm Performance, 54 *Bus. Lawyer* 921 (1999).

public. The same goes for administrative agencies, which also tend to promote outcomes that expand their power and resources, even when those outcomes reduce net social welfare.

Public choice may offer the best explanation for the recent rules dictating board structure. As observed, when Congress and the SEC strong-armed the exchanges into requiring boards to maintain certain committees and a majority of independent directors, the empirical evidence didn't support the view that such measures would enhance firm value. What's more, those measures, ostensibly promulgated to avoid future Enrons, would have done *nothing* to prevent the actual implosion of Enron. At the time Enron went bankrupt, its board was a model of "good" corporate governance: Twelve of the fourteen directors were outsiders; the directors met frequently; and the board maintained separate audit, compensation, and nominating committees comprised exclusively of independent directors. As Professor Macey wryly observed, "if Enron survived to this day, it would not have to change its corporate governance structure at all to conform to the requirements of the Sarbanes-Oxley Act."[30]

What explains policymakers' apparent disregard of the empirical evidence – including the experience of Enron itself – in imposing on all public companies structural rules that are unlikely to achieve their purported objective? In a word, politics. As the early 2000s corporate scandals mounted and the Internet stock bubble burst, popular opinion soured on "big business," encouraging policymakers to defer to interest groups that had long desired to impose certain structural rules on corporate boards. Acting as "policy entrepreneurs," those groups exploited popular sentiments and the political climate to sell their pre-packaged corporate reforms. Interest groups that could have countered those policy entrepreneurs were out of favor with the public and therefore impotent. As Professor Romano has explained,

> That th[e] literature [on the effectiveness of the structural rules imposed] was not even cursorily addressed is indicative of the poor quality of decisionmaking that characterized the enactment of the [Sarbanes-Oxley] corporate governance mandates. The corporate governance mandates stemmed from the intricate interaction of the Senate banking committee chairman's response to suggestions of policy entrepreneurs and party politics in an election cycle coinciding with spectacular corporate scandals, a sharp stock market decline, and the consequent political collapse of the interest groups (the accounting profession and the business community) whose policy position was most consistent with the findings of the empirical literature.[31]

---

[30] Macey, supra note 5, at 81.   [31] Romano, supra note 28, at 1543–44.

When favorable political winds are behind a policy entrepreneur at a legislature or administrative agency, evidence rarely creates much of an impediment.

Rules expanding shareholder voting rights also seem to be more the result of political considerations than of any legitimate effort to reduce agency costs and enhance shareholder value. Take the SEC's now-abrogated "proxy access" rule.[32] That rule required covered corporations to allow a shareholder owning at least 3 percent of the company's stock for at least three years to nominate a director candidate for inclusion on management's proxy solicitation card. Shareholders seeking to gain control of the company were prohibited from using the rule to put forward board candidates, and the total number of shareholder nominees included on the proxy card could not exceed a quarter of the board.[33] In light of these limitations, the rule could not facilitate a change of control of a poorly managed company. Moreover, there was little reason to think many shareholder nominees would ever make it on the board; shareholder-nominated candidates who are opposed by management are almost always defeated.

So why would the SEC push so hard for a proxy access rule, downplaying the evidence against its effectiveness to such an extent that a federal appeals court ultimately invalidated the rule as arbitrary and capricious?[34] It seems the Commission was responding to the demands of two groups with which it sought to curry favor: labor unions and public pension funds. Those groups, key constituencies of the political party in control of the Commission when the rule was promulgated, have long sought proxy access not as a means of effecting board composition, but in order to secure private benefits such as board commitments not to reduce jobs. Professor Joseph Grundfest, a former SEC Commissioner, identifies three reasons labor unions and pension funds so aggressively lobbied the SEC for a mandate that would seem to create little shareholder value:

> First, proxy access generates "megaphone externalities" that are exceptionally valuable to labor unions and public pension funds. These megaphone externalities describe the additional publicity that accrues, at very little cost, to shareholder groups who run their own board nominees advocating a particular cause. To generate megaphone externalities, a candidate need not even come close to winning. The candidate need only gain publicity for

---

[32] 75 Fed. Reg. 56,668, et seq. (Sept. 16, 2010), abrogated by Business Roundtable *v.* SEC, 647 F.3d 1144 (D.C. Cir. 2011).

[33] If qualifying shareholders collectively nominated directors totaling more than 25 percent of the board, preference would be given to nominees of shareholders with the largest holdings.

[34] See *Business Roundtable*, 647 F.3d 1144.

the act of running. Second, proxy access generates "electoral leverage" by giving candidates and their supporters the ability to extract concessions from some corporations as consideration for not nominating candidates, for withdrawing candidates, or for modulating their campaign positions, even if the candidate has no credible chance of prevailing. Third, unions and public pension funds understand that if the matter were put to a shareholder vote, there is a high probability that shareholders would not support access at [stock ownership] thresholds that maximize megaphone externalities or electoral leverage. Special interest groups will therefore rationally seek to influence the Commission to adopt mandatory rules that would not be supported by a shareholder majority.[35]

Special interest manipulation similarly offers the best explanation for the recently implemented "say-on-pay" mandates. The 2010 Dodd–Frank Act dictates that most public corporations hold an advisory shareholder vote on executive compensation (a "say-on-pay") at least once every three years. It also requires that shareholders be allowed to vote to increase the frequency of say-on-pay to every year or every other year ("say-on-frequency"). And it mandates that shareholders be given an advisory vote on compensation arrangements for executives whose positions are threatened by significant corporate transactions, such as a merger or sale of the company's assets ("say-on-golden-parachutes").[36]

The value of all these mandatory votes is hardly apparent. Shareholders almost always approve compensation (e.g., 97.6 percent of the time in 2014),[37] and when they don't, the vote is non-binding. Granted, the mere possibility of shareholder disapproval and the resulting public relations fiasco could dissuade boards from authorizing excessive compensation packages. But it's hard to believe that a rule mandating an advisory vote on executive compensation is cost-justified. Indeed, before the rule was implemented, shareholders rejected the vast majority of proposals to implement say-on-pay at their corporations. Between 2008 and the implementation of the mandatory rule in early 2011, 107 say-on-pay plans were proposed, frequently by labor unions or pension funds, at Fortune 100 companies; only 14 were adopted by shareholders.[38] A rule mandating a shareholder voting right that shareholders themselves have

---

[35] Joseph Grundfest, The SEC's Proposed Proxy Access Rules: Politics, Economics, and the Law, 65 *Bus. Lawyer* 361, 379–80 (Feb. 2010).

[36] Dodd-Frank Act, Pub. L. No. 111–203, § 951, 124 Stat. 1899 (2010).

[37] See Semler Brossy, *Report update: Results for the entire 2014 proxy season; 60 companies have failed SOP* (Jan. 21, 2015) (available at www.semlerbrossy.com/say-on-pay/report-update-results-for-the-entire-2014-proxy-season-60-companies-have-failed-sop/).

[38] Labor Unions Key Drivers of Shareholder Proposals on Executive Compensation, *Proxy Monitor*, Manhattan Institute Center for Legal Policy (2011).

Government regulations should also take into account labor and other factors

almost always rejected seems curious – at least until one considers the matter from a public choice perspective.

It seems the private interests of politically powerful labor unions and public pension funds, members of Congress, and SEC bureaucrats coalesced in favor of the policy shareholders had usually rejected. Mandating a say-on-pay gives labor unions and pension funds a bargaining chip in negotiations with management (e.g., "we'll vote for the executive compensation package and won't raise a stink if you protect employees as we'd like"). Such groups also benefit from shareholder voting on "golden parachutes" – lucrative payouts to incumbent managers who lose their jobs when corporate control changes. Golden parachutes facilitate mergers by providing displaced officials with a valuable consolation prize, thereby reducing management opposition to proposed combinations. Corporate mergers, in turn, typically benefit shareholders, who usually receive a premium for their stock, but often result in job losses that labor unions and public pensions oppose. To the extent that letting shareholders weigh in on golden parachutes makes such arrangements less likely (or less generous), a mandatory say-on-golden-parachutes makes mergers more difficult to accomplish and thereby benefits labor unions and pension funds. Shareholders as a whole tend to lose out, but shareholders are widely dispersed and difficult to organize and are therefore a less effective interest group than labor unions and public pension funds. Thus, when the mandatory voting rules were under consideration, Congress and the SEC were more likely to defer to the wishes of organized labor and public pensions, especially since doing so allowed Congress to appear to be "doing something" about corporate corruption and permitted the SEC to expand its powers and enhance its budget.

Before we move on, it is worth noting one additional downside to addressing corporate agency costs by imposing mandatory structural rules. A key benefit of state corporate law is jurisdictional competition. Business planners may choose the state of incorporation, and their costs of financing the enterprise – interest charges on loans, for example – will be lower if they select a state whose rules tend to maximize the value of the business. States receive benefits (franchise fees, etc.) from incorporations, so they have an incentive to develop rules that attract them. The result of all this is a corporate law "market" in which states compete to provide the body of law that is most likely to maximize the value of incorporated businesses. In contrast to this system, the structural rules we have been considering in this section have been imposed nationally by the federal government. Competition among nations for corporate charters is far less vigorous than that within the interstate corporate law market. Relative to traditional state corporate law, then, federal structural rules are less subject to market discipline and more likely to reduce enterprise value.

mandatory structural rules are affirmative government interference

Market Mechanisms

Corporate law's fiduciary duties and the mandatory structural rules we have just considered involve affirmative government interference with the corporate contract. Several other agency cost-reducing institutions, by contrast, require no government action besides enforcing property rights and contracts. Since those institutions needn't entail governmental mandates beyond those existing in the common law, we wouldn't normally deem them to be regulation. When it comes to these mechanisms, however, policymakers have erected government barriers that reduce the mechanisms' effectiveness. Some sort of governmental fix – removal of the pertinent barriers – is therefore required for these mechanisms to achieve their promise.

We may refer to these promising but currently hobbled mechanisms as "market" mechanisms because they all involve voluntary exchanges in which property rights are defined and transferable, contracts are enforceable, and (absent the aforementioned barriers) the government puts no thumb on the scale by either encouraging or discouraging particular transactions. These market mechanisms go beyond the symptoms of agency costs to address the underlying disease, which we earlier identified as something like an externality coupled with information asymmetry. Each of the market mechanisms considered here – a non-exhaustive list – reduces agency costs by addressing the externality, the information asymmetry, or both.

The Market for Corporate Control

As the name would suggest, the market for corporate control is a market in which people who believe themselves to be good at managing businesses may purchase the right to control corporations they believe are currently mismanaged. One who buys such control rights and corrects the mismanagement so as to unlock more of the business's inherent value may then sell the business for a higher price, earning a significant profit.

A couple of key questions about this market are "Who is in it?" and "What determines prices?" The answer to the first question is simple: every corporation whose stock is publicly traded. If a company's stock is held by members of the public and is freely transferable, the right to control that company is effectively for sale. Potential managers may buy up the publicly held stock and, upon acquiring at least 50 percent of the outstanding shares, may vote out the existing directors, install their own, and thereby gain control of the business. To accomplish their objective, people seeking to gain control make "tender offers" in which they agree to pay a premium for shares that are tendered to them *as long as* a certain percentage of the shares (usually just over 50 percent) are tendered by some certain date. If the shareholders collectively express a willingness to sell enough shares by the cut-off date, the deal closes and the acquirer gains control of the company; otherwise, shareholders just keep the stock they tendered. Potential acquirers who lack the cash to buy the stock may borrow it. If they can convince lenders that their plans for the company will unlock value and generate significant profits, they should have little difficulty borrowing sufficient money to fund their stock purchase. By engaging in such a "leveraged buyout," even a cash-poor group of potential managers – as long as they're able to convince lenders to bet on their plans – may be able to gain control of a corporation.

When it comes to prices paid in the market for corporate control, the key determinants are predictions about profits. Because the primary benefit corporate stock provides to minority (i.e., non-controlling) shareholders is a pro rata share of the company's surplus, the value of a share of stock is determined by expectations about the company's future "free cash flows." If one were to take all the future dividends the share of stock would pay, discount them to present value (to account for the fact that the right to receive a sum of money in the future is worth less than receiving that same sum today), and add all those present values together, that would be the value of the share of stock. The market price of stock reflects the predictions of millions of investors – all armed with their own private knowledge and gambling with their own money – about what that value is. It's really the best estimate we have of the profit potential of a company under its current management.

When a company's stock price drops relative to where it has been in the past or where one would expect it to be given the company's assets, or perhaps relative to the price of similarly situated companies, that is a signal that the company is being poorly managed. It's also an opportunity for potential managers who believe they could do a better job than the incumbents. Those insurgents can launch a tender offer at a price in excess of the stock's current market price (depressed because of mismanagement) but below the price the stock would likely attain under the insurgents' superior management. If the offer's premium over market price is large enough, the insurgents will probably succeed in gaining control of the company. If they then correct the mismanagement, driving up the market price of the stock, they will profit.

All this makes the market for corporate control a highly effective means of constraining agency costs. Managers know that their disloyalty and laziness will reduce the company's expected profits and drive down its stock price, rendering the company a takeover target. They also know that if their company is taken over through a tender offer, they will lose their jobs, and their reputations will be tarnished. To avoid that undesirable outcome, managers will work hard and avoid disloyal acts that hurt the company's business. The market for corporate control thus internalizes the externality resulting from the separation of ownership and control in a corporation: Managers can't foist costs onto shareholders without expecting that those costs may eventually impair managers' own welfare. By internalizing the costs of mismanagement, the market for corporate control induces exactly the sorts of behavior state corporate law's imposition of fiduciary duties aims to encourage: reasonable decision-making (duty of care) and avoidance of self-dealing (duty of loyalty).[39] And it does so without all the inefficiencies of shareholder suits.

Unfortunately, legal hurdles currently hinder the operation of the market for corporate control. One such hurdle is the Williams Act, a 1968 federal statute enacted after a wave of corporate takeovers. In proposing an early version of the legislation, Senator Harrison A. Williams complained that "proud old companies" have been "reduced to corporate shells after white-collar pirates have seized control" of them.[40] The statute as ultimately enacted appropriates property rights in information from these modern-day Captain Hooks. In particular, it requires that individuals, groups, and firms planning tender offers first disclose to the public their identities, their plans for the target firm, and their sources of financing.[41] Such requirements provide an "early warning" system for incumbent managers, making it easier for them to resist a takeover attempt. Indeed, in the decade following enactment of the Williams Act, hostile takeovers declined from 14 percent to 4 percent of all mergers and acquisitions activity.[42]

A series of unfortunate court decisions dealt an even more serious blow to the hostile takeover and thus the market for corporate control. As financing innovations such as the leveraged buyout made tender offers easier to accomplish, takeover attempts began to proliferate. Incumbent managers sought ways to fight them off. In its 1985 *Unocal* decision, the Delaware Supreme Court held that managers could try to thwart takeovers – even though doing so tends to entrench managers while denying shareholders a premium for their stock – under certain circumstances. Specifically, if managers (1) reasonably

---

[39]   In addition to this ex ante benefit, which occurs even before a takeover attempt is ever made, the market for corporate control confers ex post benefits on shareholders after a tender offer is launched: Shareholders of a company that is taken over typically receive either a premium for their stock (if they sell) or shares in a more valuable company (if they hold on to the stock until after the new managers have taken control and increased the company's value in excess of the offer price).

[40]   111 Cong. Rec. 28257 (1965).   [41]   15 U.S.C. § 78m.

[42]   Henry G. Manne, Bring Back the Hostile Takeover, *Wall St. J.* A18 (June 26, 2002).

believe a takeover attempt poses a "danger to corporate policy and effectiveness," and (2) adopt a takeover defense proportionate to that threat, courts must apply the business judgment rule and abstain from second-guessing management.[43] The court concluded that the offer in that case was coercive, so there was a danger to corporate policy and effectiveness, and the defensive measure was proportionate to the threat.[44] In its *Moran* decision later the same year, the Delaware Supreme Court approved use of a "poison pill," a device put in place by corporate managers that will cause all kinds of problems for any hostile bidder that acquires more than a certain (low) percentage of the company's stock.[45] In its *Time* decision a few years later, the same court indicated that *Unocal*'s requirement that a takeover defense be based on a "danger to corporate policy and effectiveness" is easily met. The *Time* court did not require management to show that the bid it was fighting was somehow coercive of shareholders, or even particularly low, but instead credited management's self-serving claim that its own "strategic plan" for the company would ultimately benefit shareholders by more than the massive premium the bidder was offering for the company's stock.[46]

---

[43]   Unocal Corp. v. Mesa Petroleum Co., 493 A.2d 946, 955 (Del. 1985).

[44]   The bidder in *Unocal*, a corporate entity controlled by T. Boone Pickens, had made a "front-loaded, two tiered tender offer" under which shareholders who tendered their shares (to give the bidder a majority of the stock) would receive more per share than would those who held on to their shares and were "frozen out" when Pickens gained control of the company and caused it to merge into its majority shareholder. Such a tender offer is believed to be coercive because even shareholders who would prefer not to tender their shares at the offered price may do so out of fear that they will later be forced to sell their shares at a lower price if the tender offer succeeds.

[45]   Moran v. Household International, Inc., 500 A.2d 1346 (Del. 1985). With a poison pill, officially called a "shareholder rights plan," managers distribute to shareholders certain "rights" that eventually become tradeable apart from the stock and entitle their holders to engage in certain transactions upon triggering events. A right that has a "flip-in" element, for example, entitles the holder to buy newly issued stock of the target company at a very low price if a bidder manages to acquire some percentage (often 20 percent) of the target's stock. The bidder is not allowed to exercise any such purchase right, so the effect of triggering the flip-in element is to massively dilute the bidder's percentage ownership of the target company. Another common feature of a poison pill is a "flip-over" element, which entitles the right holder to buy newly issued stock of the *bidder* if it should attempt to merge the target company into itself. Triggering a flip-over dilutes the bidder's stock and angers its existing stockholders. Poison pills also usually have a feature that allows them to be redeemed at an extremely low price (e.g., a penny) by managers of the target company. Such a redemption provision gives bidders an incentive to try to win the favor of the target company's managers by making an offer those managers deem acceptable. See generally William A. Klein, J. Mark Ramseyer, and Stephen M. Bainbridge, *Business Associations: Cases and Materials on Agency, Partnerships, LLCs, and Corporations* (New York: Foundation Press, 9th edn., 2015) 731–32.

[46]   Paramount Communications, Inc. v. Time Inc., 571 A.2d 1140, 1152–53 (1989).

Taken together, *Unocal, Moran,* and *Time* make it extremely easy for incumbent managers to prevent takeovers by implementing poison pills. As Professor Macey has observed, "by judicial fiat, the Delaware courts have removed from the marketplace the hostile tender offer, which is the most powerful corporate governance device in the shareholders' corporate governance arsenal."[47]

The persistence of this unfortunate body of state corporate law may initially seem perplexing. As we have already observed, competition among states for corporate charters generally leads to substantive corporate law standards calculated to maximize firm value. But Delaware's law on takeover defenses, by thwarting what is probably the most effective corporate governance measure out there, does no such thing. On other matters, when the Delaware courts have issued decisions that have threatened to reduce enterprise value, the legislature has responded with some sort of statutory fix.[48] Why not here?

Public choice suggests an answer. While shareholders may lose when the market for corporate control is impeded, there are other winners – most notably, corporate managers (who are less likely to suffer punishment for mismanagement) and employees (whose jobs are often threatened by takeovers aimed at enhancing business efficiency). Corporate managers tend to be politically connected and are well represented by entities such as the Business Roundtable. Individual employees may lack similar political connections, but there is hardly a more effective lobbying voice than organized labor. Shareholders, by contrast, are poorly represented in the political arena. Their diversity and geographic dispersion makes them difficult to organize. Accordingly, they are in a bad position to secure a legislative fix to judicial decisions that inure to the benefit of organized groups such as corporate managers and employees. There is thus a persistent dark spot in Delaware corporate law: The doctrine on takeover defenses impairs the best mechanism for reducing agency costs in the corporate context.

Insider Trading

The notion that insider trading – stock trading on the basis of material, non-public information – could be an effective device for reducing agency costs

---

[47] Macey, supra note 5, at 126.

[48] For example, following a court opinion that imposed personal liability on corporate managers who failed to gather sufficient information before making a decision – a precedent that encouraged a perhaps excessive level of information-gathering – the Delaware legislature adopted a provision permitting corporations to exculpate their directors from the sort of liability that would encourage wasteful process. See Del. Gen. Corp. L. § 102(b)(7), adopted in response to Smith v. Van Gorkom, 488 A.2d 858 (Del. 1985).

will no doubt strike many readers as heretical. After all, popular accounts of insider trading routinely stress that it is a legal no-no that injures uninformed investors. The former part of that statement may be true, but not necessarily the latter.

The theory as to how insider trading may reduce agency costs is straightforward. No one is in as good a position to know when managers are failing to steward shareholders' resources as are corporate insiders. If they believe their company is overvalued because of secret managerial malfeasance, they may profit by trading on that information. If they own stock in their company, they may sell it at an inflated price. If they don't, they may either buy "put" options to sell their company's stock near its current price in the future (when the malfeasance has caused the market price to drop so they can first buy the stock at a lower price) or engage in "short-selling," where they borrow the stock from a broker, sell it, and then rebuy it and return it to the broker after the price has fallen. If others learn that insiders are making these sorts of trades, they will infer that those closest to the company believe it to be overvalued. Buyers will reduce the amount they're willing to pay, and sellers will lower their price demands. The end result is that the market price of the stock will quickly fall, indicating that something is wrong at the company.

This sort of price effect tends to reduce managerial malfeasance in two ways. First, it allows existing mischief to be discovered and brought to an end more quickly (an ex post benefit). Second, it reminds corporate managers that they're likely to get caught if they act disloyally, and it thereby encourages faithful management (an ex ante benefit). In the end, then, insider trading helps reduce agency costs by remedying the information asymmetry that prevents shareholder-principals from taking corrective action against their manager-agents and tempts those agents to act disloyally in the first place.

For a concrete example of insider trading's mismanagement-revealing benefits, one need look no further than *Dirks v. SEC*,[49] one of the US Supreme Court's leading insider trading decisions. In the early 1970s, insurance company Equity Funding of America, like Enron in the late 1990s, appeared to be going gangbusters. In reality, the company's appearance of success, like Enron's, was a matter of smoke and mirrors. For years, the company had been creating false insurance policies, packaging and selling them to reinsurers, and pocketing the cash. Using the fake profits to maintain the company's stock price, managers planned eventually to buy a major life insurance company and then "go straight" – much the way Enron's managers hoped their accounting manipulations would maintain the company's stock

[49]   463 U.S. 646 (1983).

price until they could come up with some way to generate enough legitimate profit to sustain it.

In March 1973, Raymond Dirks, a stock analyst at Delafield Childs, Inc., received a call from Ronald Secrist, a former controller of Equity Funding. Secrist had a bone to pick. He had recently been fired for complaining about his puny Christmas bonus, and he was determined to expose the fraud at his former employer. He had already told both the state regulatory authority and the SEC about the fraud, but each declined to follow up on his accusations. He therefore asked Dirks to help expose the fraud. Dirks first passed the information to the *Wall Street Journal*'s Los Angeles bureau chief and, in the words of the Court of Appeals, "badgered him to write a story for the *Journal* on the allegations of fraud at Equity Funding."[50] The bureau chief, though, doubted that such a massive fraud could go undetected and therefore refused to report the allegations. Dirks then passed the information to a number of his institutional investor clients who traded on the basis of the information, causing Equity Funding's stock price to plummet. The large and abrupt decline in the company's stock price led to exposure of the massive accounting fraud, whereupon the SEC – egg dripping from its face – sued Dirks for insider trading.

The federal enforcement agencies have long taken the position that all insider trading should be illegal – that the mere *possession* of material, non-public information should saddle an investor with an obligation to refrain from trading unless she first discloses her secret information. The US Supreme Court has, quite wisely, rejected that expansive, "level playing field" theory of liability, reasoning that it would disable the investor-protective securities analysis industry by preventing stock analysts from profiting on their efforts to unearth information on publicly traded companies. The Court has instead ruled that insider trading is illegal only when it amounts to fraud – a lie.

Because most instances of stock trading involve no significant affirmative statement by the trader, the fraud in an insider trading case typically consists of a *failure* to speak in the face of a *duty* to do so. Such a duty could arise when the inside trader is in some sort of trust relationship with her trading partner (e.g., a stockholder of the insider's own company) or with the source of her information, who reasonably expects her not to use the secret information for her own benefit and is "duped" if she does so.[51] If this all sounds a bit, well,

---

[50]   Dirks v. SEC, 681 F.2d 824, 831 (2nd Cir. 1982).

[51]   The "classical" theory of insider trading imposes liability if the trader is a fiduciary of her trading partner (as when an informed insider buys her own company's stock). The "misappropriation" theory imposes liability if the trader is in a relationship of trust or confidence with the source of her information and trades without first informing her source of

goofy, it is.[52] It represents the Supreme Court's attempt simultaneously to (1) ban most instances of insider trading, (2) permit investor-protective stock analysis, and (3) fit the liability rules within the federal securities laws, which prohibit fraud but not the theft or misuse of inside information.

If insider trading helps reduce corporate agency costs, what explains the enforcement agencies' relentless pursuit of the practice and the Supreme Court's willingness to stretch the securities laws' anti-fraud provisions to condemn it? Defenders of restrictions on insider trading often assert arguments based on fairness. They insist it's fundamentally unfair for an insider to have a trading advantage over her uninformed trading partner. Such purported unfairness, though, can hardly justify a government-imposed ban on insider trading. As an initial matter, banning insider trading wouldn't benefit the allegedly put-upon trading partner at all. Even if the insider hadn't traded, her trading partner would have done so on precisely the same terms as with the insider; keeping the informed insider out of the market doesn't help the uninformed trader one iota. Moreover, if a corporation has announced that its insiders may trade, any stockholder who ends up trading with an insider has assumed the risk that he might do so and can hardly claim to have been treated unfairly. The uninformed trader may even have been compensated for assuming that risk: If investors believe the risk of being matched with an insider inflicts injury, then the stock of any corporation allowing insider trading will trade at a discount. For all these reasons, it's hard to identify any real "unfairness" in permitting insider trading.

A legitimate downside of allowing insider trading, however, is that it may create perverse incentives for mismanagement. As explained above, corporate insiders who know that their company is overvalued because of undisclosed "bad news" (e.g., accounting fraud) may profit by trading on that information. But that means that insiders may profit by *creating* bad news for the company and then trading on that news before it is publicly disclosed and incorporated into the stock price. The possibility of earning profits from insider trading may also encourage managers to delay disclosures until they have had an opportunity to trade on the undisclosed information. In addition, insider trading may infringe the corporation's informational property rights, causing the disclosure of some of its legitimate secrets and thereby jeopardizing value-creating transactions that could be thwarted if those secrets were revealed.

---

her intention to do so, in effect "feigning fidelity" to the source. See United States v. O'Hagan, 521 U.S. 642, 651–54 (1997).

[52] See generally Saikrishna Prakash, Our Dysfunctional Insider Trading Regime, 99 *Colum. L. Rev.* 1491 (1999).

This last harm occurred in the famous *Texas Gulf Sulphur* case.[53] In 1959, agents of the Texas Gulf Sulphur Company (TGS) discovered a major deposit of copper and zinc ore near Timmins, Ontario. Hoping to acquire neighboring land and mineral rights at favorable prices, TGS's president instructed insiders to keep quiet about the discovery and do nothing that would tip off neighboring landowners. Disregarding that order, a number of TGS officials purchased company stock and call options (options to buy). Such trading by insiders caused the company's share price to rise from $20 when the ore discovery was chemically confirmed to $37 when it was publicly announced. That suspicious 77 percent increase in the stock price over the period of a few months might well have signaled to neighbors that the company possessed some undisclosed good news. In light of TGS's obvious activity around Timmins, neighbors could easily have inferred that they were sitting atop valuable ore. They might have demanded higher prices for their land and mineral rights, thwarting TGS's opportunity to exploit its informational advantage.

Insider trading, then, is a mixed bag: It offers a powerful tool for reducing corporate agency costs, but it may encourage mismanagement (the deliberate creation of bad news) or delayed disclosures and may usurp the corporation's informational property rights. Prevailing insider trading doctrine assumes that the bad outweighs the good, and it therefore bans nearly all informed trading by corporate insiders.

However, there may be some middle ground between the prevailing restrictive regime and one under which informed insiders may trade willy-nilly. An obvious intermediate position would be to leave the matter to corporations themselves. Each could determine whether to ban informed trading by its insiders, to permit such trading, or to allow some but not all insiders (e.g., middle managers, but not top officials) to engage in informed trading. In crafting their corporation's policy, managers would be constrained by stock market pressures. If they selected too restrictive or too permissive a policy, their stock price would suffer. To maximize the price of the stock, they would select, and implement via contract, whatever trading policy is likely to create the most value for the company. The value-maximizing policy would differ for different companies based on their specific circumstances. Such a laissez-faire, "contractarian" approach would avoid the knowledge problem inherent in any one-size-fits-all regulatory solution.

A more restrictive middle ground approach would permit corporations to authorize *disclosed* insider trading. Under that approach, which I have set

---

[53]   SEC *v.* Texas Gulf Sulphur, 401F.2d 833 (2d Cir. 1968).

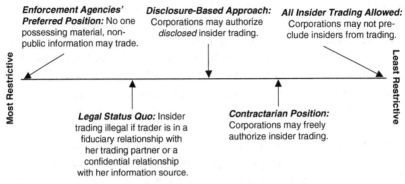

FIGURE 6.1 Potential Insider Trading Rules

forth in more detail elsewhere,[54] corporations could allow some or all of their insiders to engage in informed trading *on the condition that* the insiders first disclose their trades (but not the underlying information) to the market. The SEC could host an "Informed Trading Database" that would contain real-time information on trades by insiders. The database would be searchable by company and could be configured to send "push notifications" about insider trades in particular stocks to investors who request them. To avoid liability for insider trading, an insider at a company that had opted into the disclosed trading regime would first have to submit an electronic "Informed Insider Report" stating: (1) her identity, (2) the position she occupies at the company whose stock she is trading, (3) the nature of her trade (e.g., sale of 2,000 shares at $50 per share), and (4) the fact that she possesses material, non-public information. Once the report appeared in the SEC's database – mere seconds after its submission – the insider would be free to execute her trade.

This sort of disclosed trading regime could remedy two drawbacks to the laissez-faire, pure contractarian approach. One drawback is that insider trading affects stock prices (revealing mismanagement, etc.) only if others learn about insider trades, and most such trades occur in private. Absent leaks – e.g., insider confessions or brokers' telling others about the insider trading they have observed – insider trading may not have its salutary effect on price. A second drawback is that a pure contractarian approach does nothing to reduce insider trading's potential downsides: mismanagement, disclosure delays, and infringement of the corporation's informational

---

[54] Thomas A. Lambert, Decision Theory and the Case for an Optional, Disclosure-Based Regime for Regulating Insider Trading, in Stephen M. Bainbridge (ed.), *Research Handbook on Insider Trading* (Northampton, MA: Edward Elgar Publishing, 2013) 130.

property rights. While the approach assumes that corporate managers will account for such potential downsides and authorize insider trading only if they are outweighed by upsides, it does nothing to *reduce* those downsides.

Requiring disclosure of insider trading could assist on both fronts. First, mandating that insider trading be disclosed would ensure that other investors learn about the bets that those closest to the business are making with their own money. That would enhance insider trading's beneficial price effects. At the same time, disclosure would make it easier for managers and shareholders to police instances of corporate mismanagement, delayed disclosure, or infringement of informational property rights. Any insider who engaged in such bad behavior in an attempt to make a trading profit would likely get caught if her trading were disclosed. In the spirit of the old Johnny Mercer ditty, mandating contemporaneous disclosure of authorized insider trading would "accentuate the positive" and "eliminate the negative" aspects of such trading, allowing it to play a significant role in eliminating agency costs in the corporate context.

Activist Investment Funds

The market for corporate control, by imposing professional and reputational costs on laggard managers who become subject to takeover attempts, helps mitigate the externality resulting from the separation of ownership and control. Insider trading, by generating stock price effects that tend to reveal malfeasance, reduces the information asymmetry that prevents shareholders from holding managers accountable and tempts managers to disloyalty. Activist investment funds like private equity and hedge funds – relatively new kids on the corporate governance block – may address both aspects of the disease giving rise to agency costs.

Private equity funds are collective investment schemes in which wealthy investors pool their money to buy large percentages of the stock of underperforming companies, revamp management of those companies to unlock potential value, and ultimately sell the companies for a profit. Because turning around a business involves a hands-on approach and a significant amount of time, private equity funds typically limit their investments to a relatively small number of companies, and investors usually can't withdraw their investments for a significant period of time – often many years.

As with private equity funds, the investors in hedge funds must be wealthy. Their money is pooled and invested in a wide range of assets – stocks, commodity futures, derivatives, etc. Fund managers may also utilize investment strategies, such as short-selling stock or trading on margin (i.e., buying stock with borrowed money), that are not available to the mutual funds in which regular, non-rich folks often invest. Unlike private equity funds, hedge funds typically aim to produce the highest available returns as quickly as possible. While there are often some restrictions on investors' withdrawal of funds, the "lock-up" period is usually significantly shorter than that of the typical private equity fund (a year or so versus a decade or so).

One thing private equity and hedge funds have in common, besides the fact that both are available only to the well-off, is that both tend to be active in managing the companies in which they are invested. For private equity funds, which usually take a majority stake in their portfolio companies, that's no surprise; they buy controlling blocks of stock for the express purpose of revamping management. But even hedge funds with relatively small stakes in corporations frequently exercise significant control over those companies. Whereas mutual funds and sophisticated individual investors tend to "vote with their feet" by avoiding or selling out of poorly performing companies, hedge funds often try to dig in and turn the underperforming companies around. Unlike individual investors and mutual funds, activist investment funds such as private equity and hedge funds possess the sophistication and financial clout to exert needed control over mismanaged companies. Their involvement in a corporation thus reunites ownership and control, helping to alleviate the externality-like aspect of the agency cost disease.

One way activist investment funds have exerted control is by securing representation on boards of directors. Recent empirical studies suggest that hedge funds successfully gain board representation in around three out of four attempts.[55] Those same studies also indicate that in almost half the instances in which hedge funds have failed to secure a board seat, they have still won other concessions from managers.[56]

Even when they don't pursue board representation, activist investment funds often harness their managers' business savvy (and native assertiveness) to act as "sheriffs of the boardroom."[57] Consider, for example, the colorful letter from Dan Loeb, manager of hedge fund Third Point LLC, to Irik Sevin, CEO of Star Gas, a company in which Third Point had invested.[58] The letter

[55]   See Macey, supra note 5, at 246 (citing Jonathan R. Laing, Insiders, Look Out!, *Barrons* 1 (Feb. 19, 2007); April Klein and Emanuel Zur, *Entrepreneurial Shareholder Activism: Hedge Funds and Other Private Investors*, table 5, American Accounting Association, 2007, Financial Accounting and Reporting Session (FARS) Meeting, available at http://papers.ssrn.com/sol3/papers.cfm?abstract_id=913362).

[56]   Macey, supra note 5, at 246 (citing Laing, supra note 55).

[57]   Allan Murray, Hedge Funds are the New Sheriffs of the Boardroom, *Wall St. J.* A2 (Dec. 14, 2005).

[58]   See Jeff Gramm, *Dear Chairman: Boardroom Battles and the Rise of Shareholder Activism* (New York: Harper Collins, 2015) (reproducing Loeb letter), 234.

first questioned the appointment of Sevin's 78-year-old mother to the company's board of directors:

> We further wonder under what theory of corporate governance does one's mom sit on a Company board. Should you be found derelict in the performance of your executive duties, as we believe is the case, we do not believe your mom is the right person to fire you from your job.

The letter then offered some pointed advice:

> It is time for you to step down from your role as CEO and director so that you can do what you do best: retreat to your waterfront mansion in the Hamptons where you can play tennis and hobnob with your fellow socialites.

Sevin resigned soon after receiving the letter.[59]

Even when activist investment funds own only a small percentage of a company's stock, their enhanced abilities to monitor management and their top officials' often large public personas make them uniquely capable of "shaming" management and thereby exerting outsized control. The hedge fund managed by activist investor Carl Icahn, for example, was able to induce significant management changes at Time Warner Inc. after acquiring a mere 2.6 percent of the corporate behemoth's stock.[60] After Icahn's fund and some other activist investors procured a study of Time Warner by investment bank Lazard Freres, Icahn sent the company's shareholders a scathing letter detailing management's failures and suggesting various reforms. Following its public shaming, Time Warner management implemented a number of Icahn's suggestions, whereupon the company's laggard stock jumped in value by 12 percent. As Professor Macey observed, "Icahn used his significant minority position to add value for all shareholders by altering the corporate governance of one of the world's largest companies, achieving his long-stated goal of creating value for all shareholders and proving once again that hedge fund and private equity shareholder activism can be extremely effective."[61]

In addition to reuniting ownership and control and thereby alleviating the externality-like aspect of the agency cost disease, activist investment funds help remedy the information asymmetry that allows mismanagement to go unchecked. They are well positioned to ferret out hidden facts because they possess both the financial resources to discover obscured information and the business sophistication to analyze it. Such enhanced monitoring is often the first step to effecting change. The hedge funds led by Carl Icahn, for example,

---

[59] Macey, supra note 5, at 250.   [60] See ibid. at 258.
[61] Ibid. at 264 (quotation marks omitted).

built their case for change at Time Warner on the 371-page report they commissioned from Lazard Freres. Investors traditionally have not had the resources and sophistication to engage in that level of fact-finding.

When hedge funds discover mismanagement, they are uniquely positioned to reveal its existence to others. As observed, hedge funds are permitted to engage in certain trading strategies that are forbidden to standard mutual funds. One of those is short-selling – borrowing stock of a company believed to be overvalued, selling it, and then repurchasing and returning it to the lender once the market price has dropped. Short sales send a powerful signal that a company's stock is overpriced, and the reason for such overpricing is often some sort of secret managerial malfeasance. Hedge funds thus help to expose unfaithful managers, enabling shareholders to apply appropriate discipline.

Unfortunately, private equity and hedge funds are subject to legal impediments that hinder their ability to reduce corporate agency costs. Perhaps the most significant legal obstacle is, once again, the Williams Act. As should be obvious, the beneficial activities in which private equity and hedge funds engage aren't costless. Fund managers expend significant resources identifying underperforming companies, figuring out what's going wrong and how things can be turned around, and pressuring managers to make needed changes. They don't incur these costs for altruistic reasons; they do so to make money. They make that money by buying the subject company's stock at a low price with the goal of selling it for a higher price once they have improved the company's business operations. To make the strategy work, managers need to be able to buy up lots of a laggard company's stock while the price is depressed due to mismanagement.

With this in mind, the impediment created by the Williams Act should be apparent. That statute requires anyone launching a tender offer or purchasing more than 5 percent of the stock of a publicly traded company to disclose a good deal of information, including the source of financing for the acquisition, the acquirer's purpose in purchasing the stock, and the acquirer's plans for the company at issue.[62] When an activist fund triggers the reporting requirement, it effectively must notify shareholders that the market is undervaluing their stock relative to its potential value and that it is stepping in to correct mismanagement and alleviate the undervaluation. In response, shareholders of the company at issue are likely to increase the minimum amount they would accept for their stock. That will reduce the amount of stock the activist investor may purchase at an attractive price, which will limit the

---

[62] 15 U.S.C. § 78m(d), (e).

activist's potential upside from expending resources to identify and correct instances of mismanagement. As that potential upside shrinks, so does the activist's incentive to take agency cost-reducing actions.

Recent regulatory developments specific to private equity and hedge funds are also of concern. Traditionally, private equity and hedge funds have avoided significant substantive regulation (apart from generally applicable, and undoubtedly beneficial, provisions such as anti-fraud rules). Because they cater only to wealthy, "accredited" investors, such funds need not comply with the costly securities regulations that govern *public* offerings of stock and other investment vehicles. Nor do many of the substantive constraints on mutual funds (no short-selling, etc.) apply. The recently enacted Dodd–Frank law, however, requires that managers of private equity and hedge funds "register" with the SEC as investment advisers.[63]

This new registration requirement may ultimately limit the degree to which private equity and hedge funds constrain agency costs in the corporate context. Registration involves disclosing to the SEC and potential investors a number of items, most of which sophisticated investors – the type allowed to invest in private equity and hedge funds – would discover through the exercise of due diligence.[64] The disclosure mandate that would most likely be of interest to potential investors requires managers to "[d]escribe the methods of analysis and investment strategies you use in formulating investment advice or managing assets" and "[f]or each significant investment strategy or method of analysis ... explain the material risks involved."[65] This somewhat vague requirement creates a Catch-22 for regulators: If they allow general descriptions to suffice, the disclosures will provide little benefit to investors, but if they

---

[63] The SEC traditionally took the position that the registration requirement of the 1940 Investment Advisers Act does not apply because it covers only advisers who hold themselves out to the public as advisers or who advise at least fifteen clients. Private equity and hedge fund managers do not peddle their services to the public, and a fund, the Commission reasoned, is a single client. In 2004, the Commission revised its rules to bring hedge funds within the ambit of the registration requirement, but a federal court struck the rules as inconsistent with statutory language. See Goldstein v. SEC, 451 F.3d 873 (D.C. Cir. 2006). The 2010 Dodd–Frank Act provided new statutory authority for a registration requirement applicable to private equity and hedge fund managers. See Dodd–Frank Act, Pub. L. No. 111–203, § 403, 124 Stat. 1376, 1570 (2010).

[64] Critics of the registration requirement maintain that it provides no real protection for investors, while creating the appearance that the SEC is "doing something" to prevent malfeasance among fund managers. In the words of one fund adviser, "Any investor who feels better about me because I'm registered would just show me how ignorant they are ... I can think of 100 things more important than that." Jeff Benjamin, Hedge Fund Industry Braces for Showdown, *Investment News* (Jan. 30, 2006) (quoting Richard Van Horne).

[65] US Secs. & Exch. Comm'n, Form ADV, Items 8.A, 8.B.

require precision, fund advisers will effectively be forced to hand over valuable intellectual property. The more advisers are forced to share their money-making investment strategies with the rest of the investment community, the less likely they are to expend effort developing such strategies in the first place. Advisers may also avoid innovative investment methods because they are difficult to explain to regulators and to put into the "plain English" required by the registration rules.[66] After all, it would be awfully easy for a skilled trial lawyer to argue, after the fact, that a novel trading strategy that failed to pan out had not been adequately explained to fund investors.

Regulators may also have a difficult time limiting private equity and hedge fund regulation to *just* registration. When there is a high-profile failure of a registered fund, as is inevitable, there are sure to be calls to extend some of the substantive regulation of mutual funds to private equity and hedge funds. Resisting rules that will shackle activist investment funds and squelch the agency cost-reducing benefits they provide will require quite a bit of fortitude on the part of policymakers. In the end, then, the new registration requirement is likely to be either not worth its cost (because it provides little useful information) or downright harmful (because it stymies innovation in trading techniques and ultimately reduces the role of activist investment funds).

LESSONS FOR POLICYMAKERS

As long as people engage agents, there will be agency costs. Such costs will exist in any business organization in which investors rely on managers to steward their resources. Private ordering goes a long way toward eliminating unwarranted agency costs, and policymakers' foremost objective should be to avoid thwarting privately ordered solutions. ("First, do no harm.")

State law solutions to the problem of unwarranted agency costs are something of a mixed bag. Judicially created fiduciary duties (i.e., the duties of care and loyalty) help prevent managerial negligence and infidelity, and imposing them as a matter of background law reduces the need for costly contracting between investors and managers. Policymakers would do well, though, to make the duties

---

[66] The registration rules instruct: "Write your brochure and supplements in plain English, taking into consideration your clients' level of financial sophistication. Your brochure should be concise and direct. In drafting your brochure and brochure supplements, you should: (i) use short sentences; (ii) use definite, concrete, everyday words; (iii) use active voice; (iv) use tables or bullet lists for complex material, whenever possible; (v) avoid legal jargon or highly technical business terms unless you explain them or you believe that your clients will understand them; and (vi) avoid multiple negatives." US Secs. & Exch. Comm'n, Form ADV, General Instructions for Part 2.

fully contractual so that investors and managers may agree to reduce or remove them in certain situations. (This could, for example, make it possible to authorize certain types of insider trading that would reduce agency costs.)

The biggest problem with state law solutions to agency costs in the corporate context lies not in the fiduciary duties themselves, but in the primary means of enforcing them: shareholder lawsuits. The fundamental difficulty is that the relationship between the plaintiffs' lawyer and the shareholders is itself a source of agency costs. Policymakers should thus consider policies to minimize the agency costs resulting from shareholder suits. In particular, they should revise the rules on reimbursement for legal fees and expenses so as to discourage collusive settlement agreements between corporate managers and plaintiffs' lawyers. A promising possibility suggested by Professors Jonathan Macey and Geoffrey Miller would be for courts to auction off the right to act as lead counsel in shareholder suits, use the auction proceeds to provide immediate compensation to injured shareholders, and allow the auction-winning lawyers to keep whatever judgment they procure.[67] Such an approach offers several benefits over the status quo: It would provide an immediate benefit to shareholders, award the right to sue to the highest-quality lawyers (who should be willing to pay most), and drive attorneys' fees down to competitive levels.

Supplementing state law fiduciary duties with mandatory structural rules is generally a bad idea, especially if the rules are imposed at the federal level. Policymakers lack the information needed to set one-size-fits-all structural rules for heterogeneous companies. Moreover, government intrusion into business structure will invite special interests to seek private benefits at the expense of the public good. And federalizing corporate governance rules removes a force that has traditionally disciplined bad policymaking in the corporate context: jurisdictional competition for corporate charters.

The best thing policymakers could do to constrain agency costs in the corporate context would be to facilitate market mechanisms that punish agent malfeasance. Specifically, policymakers should (1) repeal the Williams Act provisions that hobble both the market for corporate control and the salutary activities of activist investors such as private equity and hedge funds; (2) liberalize insider trading prohibitions to allow firms to opt in to a disclosure-based regulatory regime; and (3) resist the temptation to saddle private equity and hedge funds with disclosure requirements (or other restrictions) that discourage their efforts to ferret out and expose inept managers.

---

[67]   Jonathan R. Macey and Geoffrey P. Miller, The Plaintiffs' Attorney's Role in Class Action and Derivative Litigation: Economic Analysis and Recommendations for Reform, 58 *U. Chi. L. Rev.* 1, 106–16 (1991).

7

Market Power

It's a Saturday morning, and you're on a road trip. You've decided to explore some of the tourist sites at the far end of your state, territory you've never visited. Anticipating about a three-hour drive, you get an early start and stop for a large coffee on your way out of town. About two hours into your journey, the low-fuel light illuminates on your dashboard. You know from experience that you have about 30 miles before you run out of gas. But your need to stop is a bit more urgent than usual. Your coffee has kicked in, and nature calls.

Your car's satellite navigation system indicates the location of gas stations. It shows that there is one station at the upcoming exit a mile away. Ten miles down the road is a larger town with six gas stations straddling the freeway. You've never been down this stretch of road before, so you know nothing about any of these seven stations. What do you do?

The answer, of course, depends largely on the urgency of nature's call. Absent a pressing need, though, most of us would probably be inclined to drive on to the further exit. That's because we would expect to find cheaper gas, nicer retail amenities, and cleaner restrooms at the six-station exit than at the one-station exit.

Compared to the owner of the single station at the first exit, station owners at the second exit must work harder to win business. If a second-exit station owner charged too much for gas or let his retail facilities or restrooms get too dirty, he would tend to lose business to one of the neighboring stations. The owner of the single station at the first exit, by contrast, might lose some sales to customers who were willing and able to drive the extra miles to the next exit, but he would know that many customers wouldn't incur that inconvenience and would just pay his inflated price or accept his lower-quality service. We would thus expect him to charge more or slack off on service, which is why we would expect the price-quality combination available at the second exit to be superior to that available at the first.

Our experience as participants in a market economy has taught us that competition typically enhances consumer welfare. All else being equal, firms that are in danger of losing business to actual or potential rivals tend to offer better deals – lower prices and higher quality – than those that aren't. Firms insulated from competition possess an ability that those facing vigorous rivalry lack: Unconcerned about losing sales to competitors, they may enhance their profits by raising prices from competitive levels or by skimping on quality. That ability is "market power."

SYMPTOMS/DISEASE

The foregoing example highlights the two most obvious symptoms of market power: higher prices and a reduction in the quality of available goods and services. From the standpoint of total social welfare, though, it's not obvious that higher prices and quality reductions are *adverse* effects. After all, higher prices to consumers tend to benefit the producing firms, their shareholders, and all others with an interest in their welfare. Lower standards of quality often allow for production cost reductions, which also inure to the benefit of producers and their shareholders. It's therefore impossible to say that every increase in price or decrease in quality is bad. What we'd really need to know is how the benefit to producers from market power-induced price hikes and quality reductions compares to the loss such changes occasion for consumers. When we turn our attention to the disease that gives rise to these effects, we see that it actually reduces – not just redistributes – social welfare. We also see some latent symptoms that may not be immediately apparent.

To understand the market power disease, let's return to the private ordering ideal, considered in Chapter 3. Recall from Figure 3.1 that individuals differ in their willingness-to-pay (i.e., their reservation price) for goods and services. This gives rise to a downward sloping demand curve reflecting the subjective value the marginal consumer – the one who would buy the last unit of a good if a given quantity of it were auctioned off unit-by-unit – attaches to each unit produced. The demand curve for a good or service represents the gross value (i.e., not net of costs) that results from having that good or service available in different quantities. The supply curve, depicted in Figure 3.3, shows the marginal cost of producing given quantities of a good or service. As output increases, incremental cost tends to rise as producers use less readily available, and thus costlier, inputs.

Figure 7.1 (a reproduction of Figure 3.4) illustrates how things ultimately play out in a competitive market. Absent externalities – and, as we shall see, market power – producers will supply up to, but not beyond, Q_C, and consumers will bid up the price to P_C. Producers will not stop

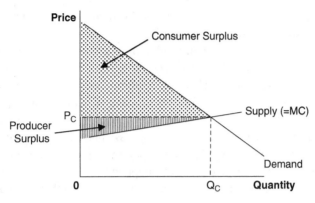

FIGURE 7.1 Competitive Market Equilibrium

shy of Q_C because they could sell each unit up to that level for more than it costs to produce. Producers will not produce units beyond Q_C because their incremental cost of producing each additional unit would exceed the price they could command for it. The shaded area (dotted and lined) in Figure 7.1 represents the wealth created from production to the equilibrium point, Q_C. The dotted area above the P_C line represents wealth going to consumers or "consumer surplus." (Consumers as a group receive value reflected in the demand curve; they must spend P_C per unit to attain that value.) The lined area below the P_C line represents wealth going to producers or "producer surplus." (Producers receive the difference between price they command for the units they sell and the marginal cost of producing those units.)

We saw in Chapter 4 how this outcome can be thwarted if there are externalities. Let's now consider what happens when a producer (or group of producers) has market power. To answer that question, we will consider two additional models: (1) the output and price decision of an individual producer in a competitive market, and (2) the output and price decision of a monopolist, a producer facing no competition from other sellers. Before examining those models, though, we need to consider two additional matters.

The first is "price discrimination": charging different prices to different consumers for the same product or service. One thing to note about price discrimination is that producers would prefer to engage in it. Look again at Figure 7.1. Total wealth (the shaded area) is divided into (lined) producer surplus and (dotted) consumer surplus, indicating that producers share the wealth their output provides. If producers could price discriminate, charging each consumer her willingness-to-pay (reflected by the demand curve), they could capture for themselves *all* the wealth their output creates; consumer surplus would become producer surplus.

Price discrimination, though, is difficult to accomplish. There are several reasons for this. One is that producers simply don't know how much each consumer values a product. That lack of information precludes "perfect" price discrimination in which each consumer is charged her reservation price. Real-world price discrimination schemes instead tend to be clumsy arrangements in which the seller makes an educated guess about how different groups of consumers vary in their willingness-to-pay for a product and then charges them accordingly. (For example, cash-strapped students and senior citizens on fixed incomes are usually charged less for a movie ticket than are working-age adults.)

Arbitrage – exploiting price differentials in different markets to earn a profit (e.g., buying at a low price in one market and reselling at a higher price in another) – constitutes another significant barrier to successful price discrimination. If different consumers are charged different prices for the same thing, favored consumers offered low prices may stockpile the product at issue and resell it to disfavored consumers, charging them a price below what the producer would charge them but above the price the favored consumer had to pay. Absent some means of preventing resales from favored to disfavored consumers, arbitrage tends to undermine price discrimination schemes.

Taken together, then, producers' ignorance of consumers' reservation prices and the threat of arbitrage make perfect price discrimination impracticable.[1] Put a pin in that point; it will be important when we consider the production and pricing decisions of a monopolist.

The second matter we must consider before turning to our next two models is "elasticity." Elasticity is a measure of price sensitivity. It assesses the degree to which a change in the price of a product will alter the quantity demanded or supplied. "Elasticity of demand" measures the price sensitivity of consumers – i.e., the extent to which they cut back their purchases in response to a price increase or buy more in response to a drop in price. "Elasticity of supply" is a parallel measure of how producers alter their supply decisions in response to price changes.

---

[1] In addition to these two price discrimination barriers, a third difficulty with price discrimination is that it's often illegal. The federal Robinson–Patman Act, 15 U.S.C. § 13 et seq., prohibits many instances of price discrimination. That statute, however, is riddled with exceptions and comprises a far less significant barrier to discriminatory pricing than do the difficulties discussed in the text.

The more elastic demand (or supply) is, the more price-sensitive consumers (or producers) are.[2]

For present purposes, there are two important things to observe about elasticity of demand. First, it is largely a function of available substitutes; the more there are, the greater elasticity of demand will be. The elasticity of demand for a particular of brand bottled water, for example, is much greater than that for a uniquely effective HIV drug. If the price of Fiji brand bottled water rises, consumers may shift to another of the many imported brands (like Evian or Vittel) or domestic spring water brands (like Crystal Geyser) or filtered waters (like Dasani) or even – heaven forbid – tap water. Even a slight increase in the price of Fiji water, then, is likely to occasion a significant reduction in quantity demanded. By contrast, if drug manufacturer AbbVie were to raise the price of its drug Norvir, which (at the time of this writing) is a uniquely effective "booster" of the protease inhibitors used to fight HIV, few buyers would shift to other drugs, which tend to be far less effective. The availability of close substitutes, then, determines elasticity of demand.

The second thing to observe about elasticity of demand is its effect on the slope of the demand curve. If a slight increase in price leads to a large decrease in quantity demanded – that is, if demand is relatively elastic, as one would expect with Fiji water – the demand curve will tend to be flatter. When rising prices are accompanied by only small reductions in sales, as one would expect for Norvir, the demand curve is steeper. (Contrast Figures 7.2 and 7.3.)

Having considered the difficulty of price discrimination and the concept of elasticity of demand, its relation to available substitutes, and its effect on the slope of the demand curve, we are ready to compare the production decision of a producer in a competitive market to that of a monopolist. Let's start with the individual producer in a competitive market. Such a producer is one of a great many sellers of a product whose characteristics do not vary from producer to producer (i.e., different brands are totally fungible). It is very easy for others to begin producing and selling the product, and each producer's capacity is so small relative to the overall volume of product available that no producer can alter the market price by varying its level of production. Markets for commodities like wheat come close to embodying these four features of an "ideal" competitive

---

[2] Mathematically, elasticity is calculated as the percent change in quantity (demanded or supplied) divided by the percent change in price ($\%\Delta Q / \%\Delta P$). For example, if 100 widgets are purchased when the price is $1 per widget, but only 80 are purchased when the price rises to $1.25, the elasticity of demand for widgets is $-20/25$, or -0.8. It is common to use the absolute value, here 0.8, when discussing elasticity. For elasticity of demand, where quantity demanded is *inversely* related to price changes, the sign will always be negative; for elasticity of supply, where quantity demanded is *directly* related to the price change, the sign will always be positive. The sign, positive or negative, is thus implicitly conveyed by indicating whether the measure is elasticity of demand (negative) or elasticity of supply (positive).

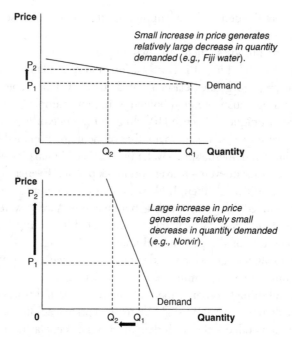

FIGURES 7.2 AND 7.3 Elastic and Inelastic Demand

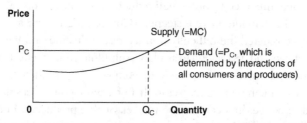

FIGURE 7.4 Output and Price of Individual Supplier in a Competitive Market

market: numerous sellers, a fungible product, easy entry, and an absence of power on the part of any producer to affect market price.

Figure 7.4 illustrates demand and supply for the individual competitive firm's product (e.g., Farmer Brown's wheat). Because that product has scads of perfect substitutes (e.g., Farmer Smith's wheat, Farmer Jones's wheat), demand is perfectly elastic, implying that the demand curve is completely flat. The curve is set at the competitive market price (P_C), which is determined by the aggregate interactions of all buyers and sellers of the product and cannot be altered by the individual producer. The flat demand curve indicates that the producer could sell *any amount it could produce* at the market price but could sell *none of the product* at a price above that level. The individual competitor's supply curve, then, reflects the producer's marginal cost and is upward sloping (to account for the fact that less readily available resources are used as production increases).

The individual competitor will produce to, but not beyond, Q_C. It will not stop short of that point because additional units would command a price (P_C) in excess of their marginal cost. It will not produce units beyond Q_C because each would cost more than the revenue it would generate (P_C). Aggregating each individual competitor's production would yield the competitive *market* output illustrated by Figure 7.1.

The perfectly monopolized market is the converse of the perfectly competitive market. In a monopoly market, there is only one seller, the product is totally unique, entry by other sellers is impossible, and – most importantly – the producer necessarily influences market price in determining how much output to produce. The situation confronting a monopolist is thus quite different from that faced by an individual producer in a competitive market.

The demand and supply curves for a monopolist's product are straightforward. Once again, the supply curve is identical to the marginal cost curve, reflecting the fact that as long as the price received for a unit at least equals its incremental cost, the monopolist will be willing to supply it. The demand curve for the monopolist's product, then, is simply the market demand curve; the monopolist, after all, is the sole supplier of the good.

A third important curve reflects the fact that the monopolist, as the only source of supply, influences the price of the product by selecting an output level. Consistent with the law of demand, as the monopolist produces more units of its product, the willingness-to-pay of the marginal consumer (the one who would buy the last unit if units were auctioned off one by one) drops. And, since price discrimination is usually impossible, the lower price required to sell the last unit produced must be charged to *all* consumers, even those that would have been willing to pay a higher price. This creates a dilemma for the monopolist: When it produces an additional unit, it may earn new revenue equal to the willingness-to-pay of the marginal consumer, but it will lose revenue equal to the amount by which it had to lower the price to sell that last unit *times* the number of units previously produced. Combining these two revenue effects – one positive and one negative – generates the "marginal revenue" resulting from production of an additional unit by a monopolist. Plotting the monopolist's marginal revenue at different levels of output yields the all-important "marginal revenue curve."

An example may help clarify these points. Suppose that if a monopolist produced one unit of its product, consumers would bid the price up to $20. If two were produced, price would be bid to only $18. Three, to $16; four, to $14; etc. Given the impracticability of price discrimination, the lower price for an additional unit would have to be charged for all units. This implies that the monopolist's marginal revenue, which accounts for lower prices on all previously produced units, would fall faster with increased production than would the market-clearing price for its product (i.e., the price at which it

TABLE 7.1. *Incremental Price and Revenue Effects of Monopolist's Production*

# Units Produced	Market-Clearing Price	Total Revenue	Marginal Revenue
1	20	20	20
2	18	36	16
3	16	48	12
4	14	56	8
5	12	60	4
6	10	60	0
7	8	56	−4
8	6	48	−8

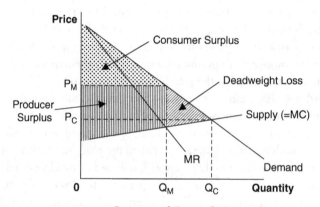

FIGURE 7.5 Output and Price of Monopolist

could sell all the units it produced, a price reflected in the demand curve). Table 7.1 summarizes the situation facing the monopolist:

Figure 7.5 illustrates the monopolist's situation by combining its demand, supply, and marginal revenue curves. As the graph makes obvious, a monopolist pursuing its own self-interest wouldn't continue production all the way to Q_C, the level of production that would attain in a competitive market. At that level of output, the monopolist's cost of producing each additional unit (illustrated by the supply curve, which reflects marginal cost) far exceeds the additional revenue the monopolist earns from supplying the unit (illustrated by the marginal revenue curve). Instead, the monopolist will produce only to point Q_M, the point at which the additional revenue it earns from the last unit produced (MR) just covers the additional cost it incurs in supplying that unit (MC). At that level of production, consumers vying for the available units will bid up the per-unit price to P_M, a level significantly above the monopolist's marginal cost.

Two effects are immediately apparent. The first is distributional: Some wealth that would have gone to consumers in a competitive market is instead transferred to the monopoly producer. To see this, compare producer surplus (the vertically lined areas) in Figures 7.1 and 7.5. Producer surplus is greater in the 7.5 monopoly market than in the 7.1 competitive market. Moreover, the gain in producer surplus in the monopoly market comes at the expense of consumer surplus, the dotted areas in Figures 7.1 and 7.5. In short, producers gain and consumers lose when there's a monopoly.

But we already knew that. The more interesting effect Figure 7.5 highlights is the *overall wealth decrease* occasioned by monopoly. That wealth reduction is illustrated by the diagonally lined triangle labeled "Deadweight Loss." Each of the units of output from Q_M to Q_C would cost less to produce than it would create in value. We can tell that from the fact that, for each of those units, the supply curve (representing the marginal cost of producing each unit) sits below the demand curve (representing the willingness-to-pay of the marginal consumer who would buy each unit if it were produced). If productive resources were allocated in a manner that would wring the greatest possible value from them, the units from Q_M to Q_C would be produced. The monopolist, though, maximizes its own profits by cutting production to Q_M, so the units go unproduced. Resources are not put to their highest and best ends, and an allocative inefficiency (a failure to allocate resources so as to secure the maximal achievable welfare) results. The upshot is that monopoly doesn't just redistribute wealth; it actually destroys it.

In fact, the wealth destruction induced by monopoly is greater than the amount reflected in the deadweight loss triangle. As a comparison of the vertically lined areas of Figures 7.1 and 7.5 reveals, producers gain from achieving monopoly power. A rational producer will thus "invest" in becoming a monopolist. In deciding whether to take a particular effort to achieve monopoly status, it will compare the cost of such effort to the incremental gain monopoly status would confer, discounted by the risk that the effort to achieve monopoly will fail. For example, if monopoly power would enhance a producer's profits by $2 million and an endeavor under consideration offered a 50 percent chance of conferring monopoly power, the producer would spend up to $1 million on that endeavor. If the endeavor were actually productive – e.g., if the producer pursued a promising course of research and development in the hopes of securing monopoly status by "building a better mousetrap" – the expenditure would be output-enhancing. Many costly efforts to achieve monopoly status, however, produce no social value. Lobbying the government for rules insulating oneself from competition, for example, creates no wealth. When a producer diverts resources away from value-creating ends (such as new product development) and toward rent-seeking, wealth is squandered. The social loss from monopoly is therefore greater than just the deadweight loss that results from the monopolist's failure to produce value-creating units. It also includes losses from misallocating resources away from productive ends and toward the pursuit of protectionist government policies.

So far, we have been speaking only of monopoly – having a single seller of a product. The same adverse effects can be generated, though, by collusion among nominal competitors. Suppose there were ten producers in a market. If they operated without coordination, each would produce and sell to the point at which its marginal cost equaled the competitive market price, a price that no single producer could control by varying its output level (see Figure 7.4). If, however, the ten producers were to coordinate, they could enhance their profits by agreeing to reduce output in an effort to raise prices. In the market depicted in Figure 7.5, for example, they would maximize their profits by collectively reducing overall market output from Q_C to Q_M, the point at which price would be driven to P_M. (As a practical matter, they might agree on minimum price, P_M, rather than on maximum output, but the effect would be identical.) If the nominal rivals so coordinated their output, market effects would be exactly the same as if there were a single monopoly producer. Perfect collusion is therefore economically equivalent to monopoly.

Fortunately, collusion is difficult to accomplish. Each producer has an incentive to "cheat" on the output limitation (or minimum price constraint) so as to enhance its own profits. But when one producer cheats by making more or lowering its own price, those remaining in the cartel will find that their potential collusive profits have dropped. Upon seeing the handsome profits the cheater is earning, the other cartel participants are even more tempted to cheat themselves. And as more and more drop out of the agreement, the temptation can become irresistible to even the most committed cartel members. Cheating, in short, tends to unravel collusive schemes.

Moreover, both collusion and monopoly are constantly threatened by the possibility of market entry. When monopolists or cartel members earn supra-competitive profits (i.e., profits in excess of those available in competitive markets), other producers or potential producers try to get in the game. New producers of the same or very similar products tend to start from scratch. Existing producers that previously sold in other areas tend to expand their production into the monopolized (or cartelized) territory. Consumers then switch to the new firms charging lower prices, and the monopolists or cartel members are forced to reduce their prices.

To summarize, then, the immediately obvious symptoms of market power are higher prices and lower quality goods and services. Other, perhaps less obvious symptoms are reduced production (deadweight loss) and wasteful expenditures on protectionist government policies. All of these symptoms result from producers' reducing their output in an effort to drive up prices and thereby enhance their profits. Producers are able to accomplish such ends if, but only if, they do not face competition from other producers. Both the temptation to cheat, in the case of collusion, and the possibility of entry, in the case of both collusion and monopoly, tend to constrain efforts to reduce output in the hopes of enhancing prices and producer profits.

AVAILABLE REMEDIES AND THEIR IMPLEMENTATION DIFFICULTIES AND SIDE EFFECTS

Treatments for the market power disease fall into two general categories. One consists of the body of law called antitrust, a set of somewhat amorphous standards that are aimed at preventing competition-reducing business practices and whose precise prohibitions are determined on a case-by-case basis. Sometimes dubbed the "residual regulator" of market power, antitrust governs potentially anticompetitive business practices *unless* it is displaced by some more tailored form of regulation. The second category of market power remedies, then, consists of direct regulation – i.e., industry-specific, ex ante rules (as opposed to antitrust's general, ex post standards[3]) designed to assure that producers do not reduce their output below, or raise prices above, the levels that would prevail in a competitive market.

The discussion that follows summarizes the basic contours of the standard-based antitrust laws and then turns to consider the alternative of direct regulation.[4] With respect to direct regulation, we will first examine its use in markets involving a "natural monopoly" (defined later in the chapter) and then assess its propriety in contexts lacking that feature. With that last inquiry, we will wade into the currently pending debate over "net neutrality."

---

[3] On the difference between rules and standards, see pp. 101–102.

[4] Given the complexity of antitrust and industry-specific regulation of market power, this chapter can do no more than describe their basic features. Readers interested in a more thorough treatment of antitrust might consult Herbert Hovenkamp, *The Antitrust Enterprise: Principle and Execution* (Cambridge, MA: Harvard University Press, 2005), or Richard A. Posner, *Antitrust Law* (Chicago: University of Chicago Press, 2nd edn., 2000). For excellent explanations of both antitrust and industry-specific market power regulation, see W. Kip Viscusi, Joseph E. Harrington, Jr., and John M. Vernon, *Economics of Antitrust and Regulation* (Cambridge, MA: MIT Press, 4th edn., 2005).

Antitrust

In the United States, the federal antitrust laws police the two situations in which competition tends to break down: monopoly (when there is a single dominant seller) and collusion (when nominal competitors agree not to compete and thus effectively act as a monopolist). Sections 1 and 2 of the 1890 Sherman Act roughly correspond to these two paradigmatic defects in competition. Section 1, which forbids any "contract, combination ... or conspiracy in restraint of trade or commerce," primarily addresses collusion. Section 2, which makes it illegal to "monopolize" a market, primarily addresses a single firm's unilateral efforts to become a monopolist.[5] The 1914 Clayton Act supplements these substantive prohibitions by empowering individuals and businesses who have been injured by an antitrust violation to sue for treble damages – i.e., three times the amount of their actual economic loss.[6]

We call antitrust a standard-based remedy for the market power disease because it sets forth only general and amorphous constraints on business behavior and evaluates the legality of specific instances of business conduct after they occur or are proposed (i.e., ex post). Although the text of Sherman Act Section 1 forbids "[e]very contract ... in restraint of trade or commerce," the Supreme Court recognized early on that such a prohibition, taken literally, would ban virtually all commercial contracts. (Anytime you agree to sell a thing to me, you "restrain" yourself from "trading" it with someone else.) The Court therefore interpreted the provision to ban only contracts that *unreasonably* restrain trade.[7] The Court later construed Section 2's

---

[5] The antitrust laws do not forbid simply *being* a monopolist or pricing as one. A firm that manages to acquire monopoly power legitimately – by, say, developing a new and unique product for which there are no good substitutes – is allowed to exist and to charge monopoly prices. Despite the harms of monopoly, it would be perverse to punish successful innovators by breaking them up or forbidding them from enjoying the spoils of their success. Indeed, the Supreme Court has recognized that the prospects of becoming a monopolist and earning monopoly profits are a key aspect of the competitive process and ultimately enhance consumer welfare by encouraging innovation. Accordingly, the antitrust laws condemn not monopoly itself but any illicit (i.e., unreasonably exclusionary) efforts to attain it. See Verizon Communications Inc. v. Law Offices of Curtis V. Trinko, LLP, 540 U.S. 398, 407 (2004) ("The opportunity to charge monopoly prices – at least for a short period – is what attracts 'business acumen' in the first place; it induces risk taking that produces innovation and economic growth. To safeguard the incentive to innovate, the possession of monopoly power will not be found unlawful unless it is accompanied by an element of anticompetitive *conduct*"; emphasis in original).

[6] The Clayton Act also forbids business mergers that would cause a substantial lessening of competition within a market. 15 U.S.C. § 18.

[7] Board of Trade of City of Chicago v. United States, 246 U.S. 231, 238–39 (1918).

prohibition of actual and attempted monopolization to preclude *unreasonably* exclusionary conduct by firms with market power.[8] Most antitrust cases thus entail an after-the-fact evaluation of the reasonableness of challenged conduct.

As antitrust law has developed, courts have come to assess the reasonableness of business practices according to their effect not on competitors but on competition itself. Competition, in turn, is understood in terms of market output, adjusted for quality. A challenged practice that enhances overall market output, benefiting consumers, is reasonable; conduct that injures consumers by reducing output is unreasonable. Most of the time, reasonableness is determined on a case-by-case basis following a "rule of reason" that takes account of market features (i.e., characteristics of the market that would make monopoly pricing harder or easier – ease of entry, for example) and assesses the actual or likely effect of the practice being challenged. For some practices, though, experience has consistently shown that the activity reduces market output, so an in-depth, case-by-case evaluation seems unnecessary. Such practices are deemed to be "per se" unreasonable and thus illegal.

While an exhaustive treatment of antitrust's prohibitions is well beyond the scope of this book, some understanding of the specific practices antitrust addresses, and how it does so, is needed in order to assess antitrust's promise and limitations as a market power remedy. Antitrust analysis usually proceeds not by finding the appropriate statutory provision and applying the rule it articulates but instead by "pigeonholing" the business practice at issue into one of the recognized categories of conduct and then applying the judicially created standard governing that category in an effort to determine if the practice is likely to benefit or injure consumers. The following discussion catalogues the main categories of conduct policed by antitrust and briefly describes the approach used to evaluate each.

Horizontal Restraints of Trade (trade-restricting agreements between economic entities at the same level in the production scheme – e.g., an agreement among retailers about how they will operate). The concern here is that such agreements may amount to or may facilitate collusion. Any horizontal agreement whose only apparent purpose is to enhance the participants' profits by raising prices and reducing output – say, a simple price-fixing agreement among rival retailers – is per se illegal. By contrast, a trade-limiting agreement that could conceivably expand output by allowing the parties to lower their costs or produce a new product or service – say, an agreement between two rival automakers to limit their competition as needed to construct and operate

---

[8]   United States *v.* Grinnell Corp., 384 U.S. 563, 570–71 (1966).

a shared factory – is evaluated under the more probing rule of reason. If market structure or the actual effects of the arrangement suggest that it will enhance market output, the agreement will pass muster.

Vertical Restraints of Trade (trade-restricting agreements between entities at different levels in the production scheme, such as a manufacturer and a distributor of its products). Vertical restraints may be "intrabrand" only, as when a manufacturer and retailer agree that the retailer will not sell the manufacturer's brand of a product below a certain price (that's "resale price maintenance"). Vertical restraints may also be "interbrand," as when a manufacturer and retailer agree that the retailer will not purchase and resell *other brands* of the product sold by the manufacturer (that's "exclusive dealing").

One concern with vertical restraints is that they may facilitate collusion. For example, retailers of a manufacturer's product may establish and police a price-fixing conspiracy among themselves by convincing the manufacturer to impose resale price maintenance on its brand. Another concern is that vertical restraints may be used to exclude rivals from a market in order to secure monopoly power. For example, if a manufacturer secures exclusive dealing arrangements with enough retailers, competing manufacturers may lose access to so many available sales outlets that they are driven out of business or forced to shrink their production so much that they become less efficient than their larger rival.

Courts used to be quite hostile to vertical restraints, deeming many types – resale price maintenance, for example – to be per se illegal. But both economic theory and empirical evidence have now shown that most vertical restraints ultimately enhance rather than reduce market output. Accordingly, with one notable and unfortunate exception, vertical restraints are now subject to a rule of reason analysis under which reviewing courts evaluate the structure of the relevant market and the terms of the challenged agreement to assess actual or likely effects on market output.[9]

Exclusionary Conduct (attempts by firms to drive their rivals from the market using unreasonable means). By excluding its rivals from the market, a firm may gain or maintain market power. Yet, most business practices that attract customers and thereby cause rivals to be "excluded" from some portion of the market are good for consumers and ought to be allowed and even encouraged. For example, if I enhance the quality of my product so

---

[9]　The exception is "tying," which involves conditioning the sale of a product over which the seller has market power (the tying product) on the buyer's purchase of another product from the seller (the tied product). Tying is governed by a quasi-per se rule under which the tying arrangement is per se illegal if (1) the defendant has market power over the tying product, (2) the tying and tied products are indeed separate products, and (3) the tie-in affects a "not insubstantial" dollar volume of commerce in the tied product market. See Fortner Enters., Inc. *v.* US Steel Corp., 394 U.S. 495, 501, 503 (1969). For an explanation of why this quasi-per se rule is so troubling, see Thomas A. Lambert, Appropriate Liability Rules for Tying and Bundled Discounting, 72 *Ohio St. L. J.* 909 (2011).

significantly that I usurp much of my competitor's business, I may cause that rival to exit the market or shrink so much that it becomes a less formidable competitor, but I've really done nothing more than compete vigorously. On the other hand, some practices tend to exclude rivals *without* offering consumer benefits that would outweigh the harms from reduced competition. Pricing below one's cost in order to drive out one's rivals and ultimately charge monopoly prices is such a practice. Such "predatory pricing" makes no business sense unless the ultimate gains to the predator from its eventual monopoly pricing will exceed the early losses it suffers while pricing below cost. That implies that even though consumers enjoy some short-term benefits from predatory pricing, the long-term harms they suffer are likely to outweigh those benefits. Predatory pricing is thus an *unreasonably* exclusionary act and is precluded.[10] Courts and commentators are divided on the precise test that should be used to identify "unreasonable" acts of exclusion, but most of the proposed tests generally lead to the same outcomes.[11]

Business Combinations (stock mergers or the acquisition of one business's assets by another). When competing firms combine (a horizontal merger), the number of competitors in the relevant market is reduced, making it easier for those rivals to form and maintain a collusive arrangement. Moreover, if the brands sold by the combining firms are particularly similar, so that one's brand is the closest substitute to the other's and vice-versa, the combined firm will be in a position to raise the price of one those brands unilaterally; it will know that any sales it loses on that brand are likely to be diverted to the closest substitute brand, which, following the merger, it also sells.

When the combining firms are vertically related, as when one firm acquires the supplier of an input it uses, it may become possible for the combined firm to injure rivals in one of the markets, either the upstream input market or the downstream output market. For example, the business providing the input might suddenly stop supplying that input to firms that compete with its merger partner in the output market.

Of course, none of these harms – greater collusion, unilateral price hikes on close substitutes, injuring rivals by cutting off supply to something they need – is likely to occur if entry into the affected markets is easy. Moreover, these

---

[10]   Not all low-pricing strategies, even if they involve some period of below-cost pricing, amount to illegal predatory pricing. Liability results only when the predator prices below its incremental cost *and* the structure of the market is such that the predator could likely recoup its losses from below-cost pricing by eventually charging monopoly prices after it has driven out its rivals. Brooke Group Ltd. *v.* Brown & Williamson Tobacco Corp., 509 U.S. 209, 222–24 (1993). Because most markets do not feature significant entry barriers, which are necessary for the recoupment of losses from below-cost pricing, predatory pricing is an exceedingly rare phenomenon.

[11]   For a discussion of the various tests courts and commentators have proposed for identifying unreasonably exclusionary conduct, see Thomas A. Lambert, Defining Unreasonably Exclusionary Conduct: The "Exclusion of a Competitive Rival" Approach, 92 *N. C. L. Rev.* 1175 (2014).

speculative harms must be balanced against the benefits a merger may occasion. Business combinations, either horizontal are vertical, routinely create all sorts of efficiencies that ultimately inure to the benefit of consumers.

To assess the legality of a merger, then, it is necessary to look hard at the markets at issue to predict (1) whether their structure could allow for any anticompetitive effects (e.g., enhanced collusion, "upward pricing pressure" on very close brands); (2) whether entry by competitors would likely prevent anticompetitive price increases; and (3) whether the efficiencies occasioned by the merger would counterbalance any potential harms. For significant business combinations, two federal agencies – the Federal Trade Commission (FTC) and the Antitrust Division of the US Department of Justice (DOJ) – take a first stab at that analysis.

With this thumbnail sketch of antitrust in mind, let's turn to consider the pros and cons of antitrust as a remedy for the market power disease. One positive feature of contemporary US antitrust law is that it is exclusively focused on competition (defined, as noted, in terms of market output) and consumer welfare. This has not always been the case. For most of the twentieth century, business practices could be condemned under the antitrust laws for reasons other than their adverse effect on market output and consumers. Most notably, courts often condemned practices simply because they threatened *competitors*. Harm to competitors, though, frequently accompanies efficient new ways of doing business, the very methods that enhance market output and benefit consumers. Contemporary doctrine therefore rejects the view that competitor harm is sufficient for liability. It maintains, at least officially, that antitrust will intervene to protect only competition itself.

A second strength of antitrust – its flexibility – is also a relatively new development. For most of the twentieth century, antitrust courts imposed all sorts of rigid per se rules of liability. Of course, per se rules are not bad *per se*. When a court is indeed confident that a business practice always or almost always reduces overall market output – as is the case with naked price-fixing, for example – per se condemnation conserves judicial resources by eliminating the need for much costly and pointless fact-finding. The problem is that courts and the economists on which they rely have often been *falsely* confident in their judgments about the adverse effects of business practices.[12] For

---

[12] As Ronald Coase observed during the heyday of per se rules, economists are often too quick to conclude that a novel business practice involves an adverse exercise of market power:

> One important result of this preoccupation with the monopoly problem is that if an economist finds something – a business practice of one sort or other – that he does not understand, he looks for a monopoly explanation. And as in this field we are very ignorant, the number of ununderstandable practices tends to be rather large, and the reliance on a monopoly explanation, frequent.

example, in the first recorded case involving a manufacturer's setting of the minimum prices retailers could charge for its product, the Supreme Court declared the practice to be per se illegal.[13] That 1911 precedent persisted for nearly a century,[14] long after economists had discovered a number of output-enhancing justifications for such resale price maintenance.[15] Fortunately, in the last few decades, the Supreme Court has abrogated all but one of the improvident per se rules of mid-twentieth century antitrust.[16] Contemporary antitrust is thus (for the most part) a flexible, evidence-driven, standard-based body of law. Those characteristics enable it both to address all sorts of diverse business practices – even those that have not yet been dreamed up – and to account for the many specific market conditions that determine how a practice is likely to affect market output and consumers.

But antitrust's flexibility – or, stated more pejoratively, its indeterminateness – also creates difficulties. As explained above, antitrust analysis usually requires some sort of reasonableness inquiry (e.g., Is the agreement an unreasonable restraint of trade? Does the conduct at issue unreasonably exclude competitors?). This inquiry is often quite costly, requiring the decisionmaker to define the market and to assess such complex matters as the ease with which competitors could enter the market and the magnitude of any efficiencies the conduct

---

Ronald H. Coase, Industrial Organization: A Proposal for Research, in *Policy Issues and Research Opportunities in Industrial Organization* (V.R. Fuchs ed.) (New York: Columbia University Press, 1972) 59, 67.

[13] Dr. Miles Med. Co. *v.* John D. Park & Sons Co., 220 U.S. 373 (1911).

[14] The per se rule against minimum resale price maintenance was abrogated in 2007. See Leegin Creative Leather Prods., Inc. *v.* PSKS, Inc., 551 U.S. 877 (2007).

[15] By the mid-twentieth century, for example, economists were well aware that manufacturers may dictate minimum resale prices for their products in order to prevent low-frills retailers from "free-riding" on rival retailers that provide retail services that enhance demand for the manufacturers' products. For example, absent resale price maintenance on a stereo manufacturer's brand, a buyer might first visit a high-end audio store to try out the stereo and receive valuable training from a sales associate, but then go to a low-service (and thus cheaper) retail rival to buy the stereo she selected at the first store. Setting minimum resale prices on the manufacturer's brand would prevent the low-service rival from engaging in such free-riding, which, were it to persist, would drive from the market the high-end retailers whose services contributed to the brand's success. See Lester G. Telser, Why Should Manufacturers Want Fair Trade?, 3 *J.L. & Econ.* 86, 90–92 (1960). This is but one of several output-enhancing justifications for resale price maintenance. See generally Thomas A. Lambert, Dr. Miles Is Dead. Now What?: Structuring a Rule of Reason for Evaluating Minimum Resale Price Maintenance, 50 *Wm. & Mary L. Rev.* 1937, 1950–60 (2009).

[16] See Continental T.V., Inc. *v.* GTE Sylvania Inc., 433 U.S. 36, 59 (1977) (abrogating per se rule against vertical non-price restraints); Tampa Elec. Co. *v.* Nashville Coal Co., 365 U.S. 320 (1961) (abrogating near-per se rule against exclusive dealing); State Oil Co. *v.* Kahn, 522 U.S. 3, 10 (1997) (abrogating per se rule against maximum resale price maintenance); Leegin, 551 U.S. 877 (abrogating per se rule against minimum resale price maintenance). The one improvident per se rule that persists is that against tying arrangements where the defendant has market power over the tying product. See supra note 9.

at issue is likely to create. Business planners must make this costly inquiry prior to embarking upon any course of conduct involving cooperation with rivals or potential harm to competitors; courts must do so if the conduct is challenged. There are thus significant ex ante and ex post costs in simply reaching a decision about the legality of novel business practices. These are antitrust's decision costs.

Significant costs are also likely to result if an adjudicator reaches the wrong liability decision. Suppose a court mistakenly fails to condemn an anticompetitive practice. The result will be an increase in market power and the allocative inefficiency it generates (deadweight loss, etc.). On the other hand, if a court wrongly condemns a procompetitive (output-enhancing) practice, consumers will lose out on the benefits greater market output would have produced. Taken together, the losses from false acquittals and false convictions are antitrust's error costs.[17]

As we discussed in Chapter 2, efforts to reduce all these costs are in tension with each other. Our long experience with misguided per se rules illustrates that courts can't simplify a liability rule to reduce decision costs without increasing the incidence of wrong decisions and thereby enhancing error costs. If a court tries to make a rule more plaintiff-friendly to reduce false acquittals, it will increase false convictions. On the other hand, if it tweaks a rule in a defendant-friendly fashion, it may reduce false convictions but will increase false acquittals. And if the court makes the liability rule more nuanced in an attempt to reduce false acquittals and false condemnations simultaneously, it will raise decision costs.

Taken together, then, the difficulty of evaluating the competitive effects of business practices (decision costs) and the inevitability of mistakes (error costs) limit what antitrust can accomplish. Perfection is impossible, and efforts to achieve it are likely to be wasteful. Of course, as Chapter 2 explains, the same can be said for all efforts to regulate mixed-bag behavior. The point is most salient with antitrust, though, because antitrust's scope is unusually broad (i.e., it is the residual regulator of *all* business behavior), and the behaviors it

---

[17] While there are harms from erring in either direction, the costs from false convictions and false acquittals under the antitrust laws are not commensurate. Whereas the market power and allocative inefficiency generated by a false acquittal will be largely constrained to the market in which the defendant participates, a false conviction of a procompetitive practice will set a precedent that tends to deter that practice in all sorts of markets. The adverse effect of a false conviction is therefore likely to reach further than that of a false conviction. Moreover, a false conviction's adverse effects will probably be more durable than those of a false acquittal. Market power, the result of a false acquittal, tends to self-correct as higher prices attract new entrants to the market. By contrast, the loss of a new business method's productive efficiency, the result of a false conviction, does not self-correct; the foregone productive efficiency can be restored only by legislation or a subsequent judicial decision reversing the mistaken conviction. See Frank H. Easterbrook, The Limits of Antitrust, 63 *Tex. L. Rev.* 1, 2 (1984).

regularly restricts – trade-restraining agreements and business methods that may injure rivals – are particularly likely to involve ambiguous welfare effects. It is especially important, then, that courts, in crafting antitrust rules and standards, eschew perfection and settle for *optimization* – that is, they should develop liability tests calculated not to catch every anticompetitive act but instead to minimize the sum of error and decision costs. Fortunately, the US Supreme Court has in recent years become far more cognizant of antitrust's inherent limits and has generally endeavored to structure antitrust's standards in a manner that will optimize the law's effectiveness.[18]

In addition to being an inherently limited body of law, a second difficulty with antitrust as a remedy for market power is that it is poorly poised to prevent harms in markets involving "natural monopolies." The discussion that follows examines natural monopoly conditions and the chief policy responses thereto.

Direct Regulation

As explained earlier, antitrust is standard-based and applies (unless displaced) to all industries. Alternative market power remedies, which we may lump together under the description "direct regulation," are generally *rule-based* and *industry-specific*. They also differ from antitrust in that they tend to be administered by expert agencies rather than by generalist courts.

Direct regulation to remedy market power is most common when there is a natural monopoly. On occasion, though, interest groups push to displace antitrust with direct regulation in markets that feature no natural monopoly. The case for direct regulation is far less persuasive in such markets. We consider below the natural monopoly problem, the types of direct regulation used to address natural monopolies, and their propriety – or lack thereof – outside the natural monopoly context.

Direct Regulation to Address Natural Monopoly

A natural monopoly exists when the total production cost of a product or service (or group of products or services) is minimized by having a single producer in the market. Natural monopolies may result from "economies of scale" or "economies of scope." Economies of scale occur when the average production cost per unit is falling as more units are being produced. This often

---

[18] See Thomas A. Lambert, The Roberts Court and the Limits of Antitrust, 52 *Boston Coll. L. Rev.* 871 (2011). Unfortunately, the federal antitrust enforcement agencies (the FTC and DOJ's Antitrust Division) have not followed the Supreme Court's lead and often fail to acknowledge antitrust's inherent limits. See Thomas A. Lambert and Alden F. Abbott, Revisiting the Limits of Antitrust: The Roberts Court Versus the Enforcement Agencies, 11 *J. Competition L. & Econ.* 791 (2015).

happens when significant upfront (or "fixed") costs must be incurred before *any* units may be produced.[19] In such circumstances, average cost will tend to fall, at least for a while, as more units are made. That's because the fixed costs – say, the cost of building a factory – can be spread out over a greater number of units.[20] Economies of scope exist when it's cheaper for a single producer to make multiple types of products than for multiple producers, each making only one type of product, to do so. Such economies often result when the same productive resource – say, a piece of equipment or an expert employee – can be used to produce different things. For example, because a seafood restaurant like Long John Silver's could use the same deep fat fryer for both fish sticks and French fries, it could probably produce both at a lower average cost than that collectively faced by two producers that each made one of the products.

Economies of scale are easier to demonstrate graphically than are economies of scope, so let's consider how the former may give rise to a natural monopoly. To do this, we will need to understand "long run average cost." Suppose Warner Widgets operates a 10,000 square foot factory. Widget production entails both fixed costs (e.g., the cost of the factory), which must be incurred up front and do not vary with the number of widgets produced, and variable costs (e.g., materials, labor), which add up as more units are made. As noted, Warner's average costs will initially decline as production increases, because all upfront, fixed costs are divided over more and more units. But as Warner exhausts its readily available non-fixed inputs (e.g., materials and labor) and eventually has to turn to costlier sources, its marginal production cost will begin to rise and will eventually surpass its diminishing average cost of production. That will then cause Warner's average cost to begin to increase. Figure 7.6 illustrates the relation between Warner's average and marginal costs of production.[21]

Widget makers of different sizes may face different average cost curves. Consider, for instance, a producer with a 15,000 square foot factory, 50 percent larger than Warner's. The larger widget maker's fixed costs would be greater

---

[19]   For example, the cost of building a widget factory is incurred before the first widget is produced, but that cost need not be incurred again as more widgets are made (at least, not until the factory needs to be replaced). The cost of the factory is "fixed," not "variable" according to the number of widgets produced.

[20]   Average total cost equals total cost (total fixed plus total variable costs) divided by the number of units produced. For example, if the fixed cost of producing *any* widgets is $1,000 and the variable cost per widget (comprised of labor and material costs) is $1, the total cost of producing 500 widgets will be $1,500 ($1,000 + $500), and the average total cost will be $3 ($1,500/500).

[21]   Note that the marginal cost curve always intersects the average cost curve at the latter's lowest point. At output levels beyond that point, marginal cost is higher than average cost and thus tends to pull average cost upward.

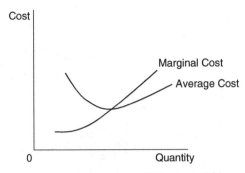

FIGURE 7.6 Average and Marginal Costs

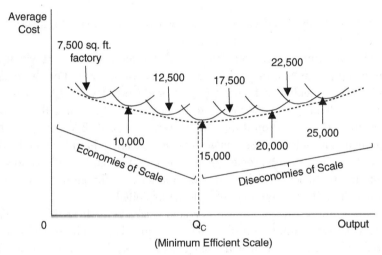

FIGURE 7.7 The Industry Long Run Average Cost Curve

than Warner's, but if the larger factory could produce and sell enough additional units over which the extra costs could be distributed, the larger firm's
minimum average cost might dip lower than Warner's. At some point, though,
a larger factory becomes unwieldy, causing the minimum achievable average
cost of production to rise.

Figure 7.7 shows the average cost curves of differently sized widget makers,
from one with a 7,500 square foot factory to one with a 25,000 square foot
factory. The dotted curve connecting the minimum average costs achievable
by the various producers indicates, for the industry at hand, how scale affects
production costs. That curve is dubbed the "industry long run average cost
curve" because it illustrates how minimum average costs correlate to

Market Power

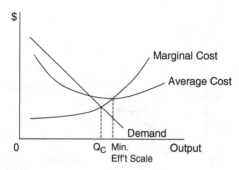

FIGURE 7.8 Natural Monopoly When There Are Economies of Scale at Optimal
Output

a producer's output *in the long run* – i.e., when even normally fixed costs such
as factory construction costs are variable.

The long run average cost curve reveals the level of output at which the
production costs within an industry may be minimized. For the widget
industry represented in Figure 7.7, that production level is Q_C. At output
levels less than Q_C, economies of scale are available, meaning that average
per-unit costs could drop if more units were produced. Beyond Q_C, widget
production is subject to *diseconomies* of scale, meaning that added production
would tend to increase average production cost. Output level Q_C is thus the
"minimum efficient scale" for widget production – the production level at
which all available economies of scale are exploited.

Now, suppose that an industry is characterized by such significant economies of scale that minimum efficient scale is quite large. (This sort of industry
would likely be one in which fixed costs are very high.) It's possible that
a single firm operating at such scale could supply enough to meet the demand
of all consumers willing to pay an above-marginal cost price for the product.
Figure 7.8 illustrates this situation.

To maximize social welfare, we would want all units that generate at least as
much benefit for the marginal consumer as they cost to produce – but no
additional units – to be produced. In Figure 7.8, that level of output is Q_C.
The long run average cost curve indicates that at that level of production, there
are economies of scale (i.e., average costs are falling with increased production).
That implies that if total output (Q_C) were divided among multiple producers,
each would produce less than Q_C and would therefore face higher average costs
than if all output were produced by a single firm.

Monopoly is "natural" under these conditions, for as the leading producer
wins business from its rivals, it gains a cost advantage that allows it to

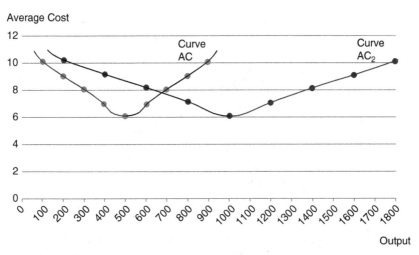

FIGURE 7.9 Average Cost of One vs. Two Maximally Efficient Producers

underprice those rivals and gain an even greater market share. That gain in market share lowers the producer's costs further, allowing it to cut prices more and win additional sales. This process will continue until there is only one producer in the market. A natural monopoly exists, then, when the competitive level of output (the intersection of the demand and marginal cost curves – the point at which all units worth their cost, but no others, are produced) is less than the level of production needed to achieve minimum efficient scale.

Suppose, though, that the competitive level of output occurs *beyond* the point at which productive costs are minimized. Does that imply there's *not* a natural monopoly? Not necessarily. Natural monopoly may exist even if the competitive level of output lies within the output range for which there are diseconomies of scale. Of course, if the competitive level of output were at least twice the minimum efficient scale, then there would be no natural monopoly; productive costs would be minimized by having at least two producers, each operating at minimum efficient scale. But what if the competitive level of output lies somewhere between minimum efficient scale and twice that level? For part of that output range, it would still be cost-minimizing to have a single producer of the good or service at issue.

To see this point, consider how average costs change when there are two maximally efficient firms in the market. Curve AC in Figure 7.9 above is the average cost curve of a single maximally efficient firm. Curve AC_2 illustrates average costs when there are two maximally efficient firms. You will note that curve AC_2 is "flatter" than curve AC. A moment's reflection reveals why that is

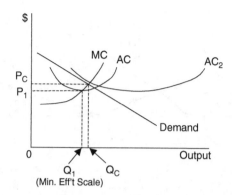

FIGURE 7.10 An Unsustainable Natural Monopoly

the case. An average cost curve correlates average production costs (the y axis) with output levels (the x axis). Adding in a second maximally efficient producer – one with the same average costs as the first (otherwise, the firms wouldn't both be maximally efficient) – will double the market output correlated with any particular level of average cost. Thus, for every unit change on the y axis (average cost), the change on the x axis (output) will be twice as great for the AC_2 curve as for the AC curve.

As Figure 7.9 reveals, there is a range of output in which a single producer would experience diseconomies of scale *and yet* productive costs are minimized by single-firm production. Curve AC shows that minimum efficient scale occurs at an output level of 500 and that diseconomies kick in beyond that point. At an output level of 600, though, it is still cheaper per unit for one firm to produce all units (average cost = 7) than for two firms to do so (average cost = 8). At an output of 800 units, by contrast, two-firm production is cheaper (average cost is 7, as opposed to single-firm average cost of 9). The point at which per-unit costs are reduced by having a second producer is the output level at which the AC and AC_2 curves intersect. Up until that point, single-firm production is cost-minimizing, even if the single producer is experiencing diseconomies of scale on the last units produced. Scale economies at the competitive level of output are thus not necessary for a natural monopoly to exist. Instead, a natural monopoly exists whenever the competitive level of output is "subadditive," meaning that "adding" a second producer and dividing total production between two firms would "subtract" from total efficiency.

Because a natural monopoly may exist even when the optimal level of output lies at a point where a single, maximally efficient producer would experience diseconomies of scale, some natural monopolies are not "sustainable." To see this point, consider Figure 7.10, where the competitive output level, Q_C, lies beyond minimum efficient scale (so within the range of diseconomies of scale) but there is still a natural monopoly (because the average cost of production is higher with two producers than with one – compare AC to AC_2).

At the competitive level of output, consumers would bid the price for the single producer's product to P_C. But that may be an unsustainable state of affairs. Under certain assumptions, we would expect another firm to enter the market, produce Q_1 or so units, sell them for a price in excess of its marginal (and average) cost (P_1) but below the price charged by the incumbent producer (P_C), and rely on that incumbent to sell units to meet residual demand (i.e., the difference between Q_1 and Q_C).[22]

Of course, if such entry were to occur, the incumbent producer would soon find its scale shrinking and its average cost rising. If it responded to sales losses by lowering its price to the level of the entrant's, then the entrant wouldn't be able to attain or sustain *its* scale and would see its average cost rise. At the end of the day, then, entry would likely result in a higher average cost – and eventually a higher price – than would exist if there were only one producer.

All this analysis suggests two problems that may exist when there is a natural monopoly. First and most importantly, when there is a single producer under natural monopoly conditions, average production costs may be minimized, but the single producer will tend to act as a monopolist. Facing no competition, the producer will seek to enhance its profits by reducing its output so that price rises. (Compare Figures 7.1 and 7.5.) The result is allocative inefficiency as units that would generate more value than they would cost to create nevertheless go unproduced. (Remember the deadweight loss triangle in Figure 7.5?) In short, the productive efficiency that comes from single-firm production in natural monopoly conditions comes at the expense of the allocative efficiency that would result from competition.

A second problem results if the natural monopoly is unsustainable, as in Figure 7.10. If a new firm enters, as may well occur if the incumbent monopolist charges a price above the minimum average cost of a firm operating at minimum efficient scale, the total quantity demanded will be split between two firms, neither of which is likely to be able to continue producing at minimum efficient scale. As the scale of the producers shrinks, their costs – and thus prices to consumers – will tend to rise. In other words, the very competition that could reduce allocative inefficiency will squander productive efficiency.

---

[22] The most important of these assumptions are (1) that the incumbent will hold its price at P_C for some period of time, and (2) that the new entrant's costs of entering the market would not be sunk because the entrant could easily redeploy its productive assets to another end or sell them to some other producer for a price near their cost.

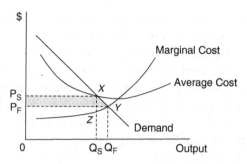

FIGURE 7.11 First- and Second-Best Outcomes in Natural Monopoly Conditions

Antitrust is ill-suited to address these two problems. With respect to the former – output reduction and price hikes by the natural monopolist – what is needed is a means by which the single seller can be induced to produce and price at the optimal level. Antitrust's amorphous standards, enforced ex post by generalist courts that lack the expertise to determine optimal prices and output and are poorly positioned to engage in continual monitoring of the monopolist's behavior, simply aren't up to the task. Nor is antitrust suited to address the problem of welfare-reducing entry. Because it generally assumes that market entry by new producers is a good thing, antitrust has no effective means of distinguishing beneficial from harmful instances of entry. In short, antitrust can't effectively address natural monopoly.

Given that the primary problems resulting from natural monopoly are excessive prices and productivity-squandering entry, regulatory responses to natural monopoly generally involve efforts to restrict producers' pricing freedom and, on occasion, to bar entry into a natural monopolist's market.

PRICE CONTROLS. The most common government intervention to alleviate problems arising from natural monopoly is some form of direct price regulation where the regulator endeavors to command the price that will create the greatest sustainable benefit for consumers. So what is that price? As we've seen a number of times now, social welfare is usually maximized with marginal cost pricing. At that price level (P_F in Figure 7.11 above), all units that consumers value at least as much as the units cost to produce – but no other units – will be made and sold. Marginal cost pricing eliminates deadweight loss, the wealth-squandering that occurs when units that are valued by more than they would cost to make and distribute nonetheless remain unproduced.

When there is a natural monopoly, though, marginal cost pricing can be problematic. Consider, for example, a producer facing the circumstances depicted in Figure 7.11 (i.e., there are economies of scale at the competitive output level, the intersection of the marginal cost and demand curves). If the producer priced at marginal cost, it would sell Q_F units and charge price P_F. While that outcome would eliminate deadweight loss, the producer couldn't stay in business because its revenues ($Q_F * P_F$) wouldn't cover all its costs ($Q_F * $ Average Cost).[23] To cover its costs and stay in business, a producer's per-unit revenue must at least equal its average cost of production. Thus, the lowest sustainable price for the producer's output would be P_S, the lowest price at which (1) all the producer's costs are covered (i.e., price is at least average cost), and (2) consumers are willing to pay for all the units produced.

Now, this outcome isn't perfect. Relative to marginal cost pricing, consumers pay more ($P_S > P_F$). As a result, their surplus shrinks by the amount of the shaded area in Figure 7.11. Of course, producers collect those higher prices, so their surplus will tend to increase with a move from marginal to average cost pricing. But the gain to producers doesn't perfectly offset the loss to consumers. With average cost pricing, the units between Q_S and Q_F will not be purchased by consumers, even though their production would cost less (Marginal Cost curve) than their value to the consumers who would purchase them (Demand curve). Average cost pricing thus entails a deadweight loss represented by the pie-shaped area, XYZ. Because it results in some dead-weight loss, average cost pricing isn't a first-best outcome. But because it creates the least deadweight loss and most consumer surplus of any *sustainable* price level (i.e., one that will generate sufficient revenue to cover the producer's costs), average cost pricing is the second-best outcome. It is the outcome a regulator seeking to achieve the best sustainable pricing strategy would pursue.[24]

So how should a regulator go about setting prices equal to the producer's average cost? One way to do so would be to cap the producer's total revenue at its total cost – including its cost of capital (the cost of raising the funds for productive facilities and other fixed costs) – and then set a schedule of prices, or price "tariff," calculated to generate that level of revenue. If costs are accurately estimated and demand accurately predicted, this approach should result in the producer's average price equaling its average cost. Such an

---

[23] The problem is that the producer's average cost at output level Q_F is higher than its marginal cost.

[24] As you may have surmised, the "F" and "S" subscripts in Figure 7.11 (e.g., Q_F, Q_S) denote "first-best" and "second-best."

approach is dubbed "rate of return" regulation because the regulator ultimately prevents monopoly pricing by restricting the rate of return the producer may earn for its financial backers.

Figuring the amount of revenue that will just cover the producer's costs (the
producer's "revenue requirement") first requires cataloguing all those costs.
They would include (1) operating expenses (e.g., the cost of supplies, labor,
and items for quick resale); (2) any taxes the producer will have to pay; and (3)
capital expenses (e.g., the cost of buildings, equipment, and other fairly
durable productive assets). That last category can be divided into two parts.
One component is the degree to which capital equipment has "worn out" –
effectively been consumed – during the relevant period of production. That's
depreciation. But even if accumulated depreciation totaled all the out-of-
pocket cost for capital equipment, that amount would not account for the
full cost of the equipment. The producer, after all, would have incurred
significant costs in raising the money to build or acquire the equipment. For
any money it borrowed, the producer would have to pay interest to lenders. For
money it raised by issuing equity (e.g., selling stock), it would need to pay
dividends to its investors. Taken together, interest charges by lenders and
dividend expectations of equity investors such as stockholders comprise
the second component of a producer's capital expenses: the "cost of capital."[25]

---

[25] Because dividends are paid to equity investors only if a firm is profitable, whereas interest on
      loans must be paid regardless of profitability, equity investments are riskier than loans.
      As a consequence, the interest rate on loans (debt) is usually lower than the dividend
      requirement of equity investors. When capital assets are financed using a mix of debt and
      equity, the cost of capital is the "weighted average cost of capital," – i.e., the interest rate on
      debt times the percentage of total financing comprised of debt, plus the expected dividend rate
      times the percentage of total financing comprised of equity.
         The interest rate on debt is, of course, a matter of express agreement between the producer
      and the lender. To determine the cost of equity financing, a regulator typically relies upon the
      "capital asset pricing model," which recognizes that equity investors need to be compensated for
      two things: the time value of money (i.e., the fact that a sum of money today is worth more than
      the same sum received in the future) and risk that the investment will not be fully repaid (the
      "risk premium"). The time value of money is equated with the interest paid on essentially riskless
      investments such as US government bonds. (That is the "risk-free rate of return.") The risk
      premium on an investment is then determined by assessing the risk premium paid to equity
      holders *generally* (i.e., the difference between the rate of return on a broad stock index like the
      S&P 500 and the risk-free rate of return) and then adjusting that "equity market premium" up or
      down, depending on how risky the particular investment is relative to equity investments overall.
      That latter adjustment is usually made by multiplying the producer's historical "beta" –
      a measure of how changes in the producer's stock price have correlated to price variance of
      the stock market as a whole (i.e., does the producer's stock price tend to swing with or against the
      market as a whole, and to what degree?) – times the equity market premium. A producer's cost of
      equity, then, is the risk-free rate of return plus the risk premium for that producer. [If, for

Having catalogued the producer's costs, we can see the basic formula for determining its revenue requirement. If operating expenses are denoted "E"; taxes, "T"; the amount of depreciation for the relevant production period, "d"; the producer's capital asset base (i.e., the value of its capital, less all previously accumulated depreciation), "B"; and the producer's cost of capital, "r," then the producer's revenue requirement ("R") should be calculated as:

$$R = (B * r) + d + E + T$$

If a natural monopolist producer's total revenue is limited to this amount, then its average price will equal its average cost, and second-best pricing will have been achieved. An example applying the revenue requirement formula appears in the text box nearby.

Once the regulatory authority has determined the natural monopolist's revenue requirement, it must set a price schedule (or "tariff") that will generate the required level of revenue but no more. In the simple but rare case in which the monopolist sells only a single product or service, average cost pricing would seem to be easy enough: To determine the unit price, simply divide the total revenue requirement by the number of units sold. Even this, though, is complicated, for the number of units sold will depend on the per-unit price, and the revenue requirement will depend on the number of units produced. The regulator would need to estimate the elasticity of demand for the producer's output (i.e., the degree to which purchases fall as price rises) and use that estimate to determine what price would maximize the number of units sold while still covering all the producer's costs.

Other pricing strategies might enhance overall market output and total surplus but will entail additional complexities. One such strategy would be to charge different prices to different buyers. If the producer lowered per-unit prices to price-sensitive customers (say, individual homeowners) and hiked up rates on purchasers with higher reservation prices (say, businesses), some consumers willing to pay at least marginal cost but not all the way up to average cost could be brought into the market. Such price discrimination would reduce deadweight loss but may raise fairness concerns.

Another way to reduce deadweight loss would be to charge a "two-part tariff" in which each consumer pays a fixed amount just to access the natural monopolist's product or service and then pays a second amount that varies

example, government bonds paid 3% interest, returns on the S&P 500 were 8%, and a producer's historical beta was 0.8 (meaning that its stock price moves in the same direction as the stock market overall – i.e., beta is positive – but tends not to vary as much as the market overall – i.e., beta is <1), the producer's cost of equity would be 3% + 0.8(5%) = 7%.]

Revenue Requirement Example

Suppose there is a brand new utility that cost $50 million to build. The owner borrowed 40% of the construction funds at an 8% interest rate. It sold stock to investors to cover the remaining construction costs. (Stock investors in similar ventures typically earn returns of about 12%.) The utility will cost $2 million per year to operate and will face a tax rate of 20%. Its annual depreciation will be around $500,000.

Because the utility faces a 20% tax rate, only 80% of its accounting profits may be used to pay dividends. That means that 80% of the utility's accounting profits must total 12% of 60% of $50 million. (Recall that stockholders, who expect to receive an annual return of 12% on their investment, provided 60% of the $50 million to build the plant.) If required accounting profits are x, then: $0.80x = (0.60)(0.12)$ $50,000,000.

Solving for x shows that the utility's required accounting profits are $4,500,000. Taxes on that amount will be $(.20)$4,500,000 = $900,000$. The interest that must be paid to lenders will be $(.08)(.40)$50,000,000 = $1,600,000.

On these facts, the utility's annual revenue requirement $[(B^*r)+ d+E+T]$ is:

Cost of capital:	($50,000,000 * [(.6)(.12) + (.4)(.08)]) = $ 5,200,000
Depreciation:	$ 500,000
Operating expenses:	$ 2,000,000
Taxes:	$ 900,000
Total	$ 8,600,000

---

with consumption. If the former amount collectively covered fixed costs and the latter were set at marginal cost, consumers that entered the market by paying the upfront fee would tend to buy more (lower-priced) units than under a single price system. This could increase total market output, but the magnitude of any increase is unclear. Some consumers who would have purchased at least some units under single-tier average price system may be unwilling to pay the two-part tariff's upfront access fee and may therefore forego all consumption.

As the foregoing discussion makes clear, setting appropriate tariffs requires a tremendous volume of information even in the "simple" and rare case in which the natural monopolist sells a single product or service. Things get even more complicated in the more common situation in which the natural monopolist sells multiple products or services.

Because most offerings by natural monopolists can be divided into component parts, each of which could be separately priced (e.g., long distance and local telephone service, basic and premium channel cable television, electricity during periods of peak and non-peak demand), there are a great many price combinations that could "just cover" all the producers' costs. If the monopolist distributed both gas and electricity, for example, it might price gas at marginal cost and raise the price of electricity to cover all its fixed costs; or it might hold electricity rates to marginal cost and hike the price of gas; or it might set price somewhat above marginal cost on each product. Price regulators need some means of determining the optimal price combination for a multiproduct natural monopolist's offerings. Specifically, they need to know how much above marginal cost each of the natural monopolist's products should be priced if the goal is to cover all the producer's costs while minimizing the deadweight loss that results when price exceeds marginal cost.

Writing in the late 1920s, economist Frank P. Ramsey addressed a similar issue involving taxation: How should the government set tax rates on different goods so as to meet its revenue goals while reducing taxpayer surplus as little as possible?[26] The tax principles Ramsey set forth can be used to determine what price combination will allow a multiproduct natural monopolist to meet its revenue requirements while preserving as much consumer surplus as possible. Although the details of so-called Ramsey pricing can quickly get complicated and are beyond the scope of our discussion here, we can at least consider the basic intuition that underlies Ramsey pricing.[27]

Raising price above marginal cost, a necessity if a natural monopolist is to recover its fixed costs, always creates some deadweight loss (i.e., some units that would create more additional benefit than additional costs are not produced). But some price increases generate more producer revenue and create less deadweight loss than others. The key consideration is the elasticity of demand for the product subject to the price increase.[28]

---

[26] Frank Ramsey, A Contribution to the Theory of Taxation, 37 *Econ. J.* 47 (Mar. 1927).

[27] For an excellent, highly readable explanation of Ramsey pricing, see Kenneth E. Train, *Optimal Regulation: The Economic Theory of Natural Monopoly* (Cambridge, MA: MIT Press 1991) 115–46.

[28] Recall that elasticity of demand, the percent change in quantity demanded divided by the percent change in price ($\%\Delta Q / \%\Delta P$), is a measure of consumers' price sensitivity. The more elastic demand is, the more consumers collectively will cut back their purchases in response to a price increase.

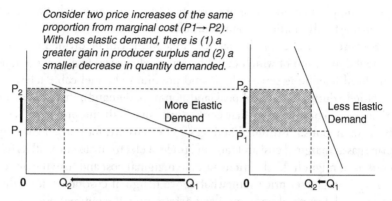

FIGURE 7.12 The Intuition Underlying Ramsey Pricing

Suppose, for example, that a natural monopolist produced two products with the same competitive price; for both, the demand curve would intersect the marginal cost curve at P_1. Imagine, then, that the monopolist raised the price of each product by the same proportion (which, because the competitive price of both was the same, would be the same absolute amount). As Figure 7.12 demonstrates, the resulting changes in both producer surplus and quantity demanded would be different for the two products, depending on the elasticity of demand for each. An increase in price of some proportion on a product with relatively inelastic demand (i.e., a product for which consumers are not very price-sensitive) will generate more producer surplus (the shaded area) and will cause consumption to fall by less $(Q_1 - Q_2)$ than a proportionately equal price increase on a product with more elastic demand.

Since the point of increasing price above marginal cost is to generate more revenue for the producer (so that it can recover fixed costs) and the downside is decreased consumption, the lesson of Figure 7.12 should be clear: Prices should be raised more on products for which demand is inelastic than on products for which demand is elastic. More specifically, to set second-best prices for a multiproduct natural monopolist, prices should be raised from competitive levels in inverse proportion to the demand elasticities of the products at issue.[29]

While rate-of-return regulation can prevent monopoly pricing by a natural monopolist, it has its drawbacks. The most obvious is the familiar knowledge

[29] For example, if the elasticity of demand for product A were 1.25 (relatively elastic) and that for product B were 0.8 (relatively inelastic), the price of product B should be raised by 1.25% for every 0.8% increase in the price of product A. This implies that the price increase on product B should be 1.5625 times the increase on product A (1.25/0.8 = 1.5625).

problem. To determine the natural monopolist's overall revenue requirement, the regulator must know the producer's expected operating expenses, the value of the producer's asset base, and what rate of return should be allowed on capital. These data are not readily available. Operating expenses change with market developments (fluctuations in fuel prices, etc.), and the best information about likely operating costs resides with the producers themselves, who are likely to be less than forthcoming with their overseers. Valuing the producer's asset base requires the regulator first to decide what metric to use (e.g., The actual amount spent on the assets? The cost of reproducing the precise technologies used? The cost of replacing the productive assets with the latest technologies?) and then to estimate the value of the assets according to that metric. Determining the allowable rate of return usually requires ascertaining the producer's cost of equity, which requires knowing quite a bit about investor expectations.[30] Moreover, even knowing the exact cost of capital is not enough. If the allowed rate of return is set right at the cost of capital, the producer may be indifferent between continuing its operations and shutting down and selling off its assets.[31] To encourage continued production, the regulator might wish to set the allowed rate of return slightly above the cost of capital. But how far above? Too much will lead to deadweight loss; too little will fail to encourage investment in the industry. In short, a vast amount of difficult-to-acquire information is needed for a regulator just to determine the producer's revenue requirement.

The information requirement becomes even more overwhelming when the regulator has to determine the natural monopolist's price tariff. Setting prices that will "just meet" the producer's revenue requirement requires the regulator to know the elasticity of demand for the producer's output. In the more common scenario in which the natural monopolist sells multiple products, information about elasticity of demand is required to implement Ramsey pricing. Even in the single-product case, however, the regulator needs to know how much consumption would occur at different price levels in order to determine what price level will maximize the number of units sold while still covering the producer's costs.

---

[30] See supra note 25 and accompanying text.

[31] If the producer continues its operations, it gets return on capital (the amount it cost to finance its capital assets) plus depreciation (the amount by which the asset is devalued by production), and it gets to keep the depreciated asset, which is worth something. If the producer instead shuts down and sells off the asset, it gets only the dollar value of the asset, but it avoids further depreciation and financing costs. Thus, if the allowed rate of return is the actual cost of capital, the producer will be in the exact same position if it shuts down or if it continues production.

One way to check the regulator's fact-finding is by employing a "yardstick" approach under which the regulatee's return rate, revenue requirement, prices, etc., are compared to those of similarly situated producers in similar markets. But this is trickier than it sounds. It can be difficult to find sufficiently analogous producers and markets. In addition, even if one is able to identify such analogues, a yardstick approach is justified only if there are good reasons for believing the regulators in the comparator markets got things right. We could otherwise end up with the blind leading the blind.

Adverse public choice concerns also tend to plague direct price regulation of natural monopolists. Charged with keeping natural monopolists' returns at competitive levels, price regulators perpetually monitor the monopolist producers and may order all sorts of changes whenever the producers' returns appear to be rising above or falling below competitive levels. A regulator that has both regular contact with its regulatees and significant discretionary authority over them is particularly susceptible to capture. The regulator's discretionary authority provides regulatees with a strong motive to win over the regulator, which has the power to hobble the regulatee's potential rivals and protect its revenue stream. The regular contact between the regulator and the regulatee provides the regulatee with better access to those in power than that available to parties with opposing interests. Moreover, the regulatee's preferred course of action is likely (1) to create concentrated benefits (to the regulatee) and diffuse costs (to consumers generally), and (2) to involve an expansion of the regulator's authority. The upshot is that those who bear the cost of the preferred policy are less likely to organize against it, and regulators, who benefit from turf expansion, are more likely to prefer it. Rate-of-return regulation thus involves the precise combination that leads to regulatory expansion at consumer expense: broad and discretionary government power, close contact between regulators and regulatees, decisions that generally involve concentrated benefits and diffuse costs, and regular opportunities to expand regulators' power and prestige.

In light of this combination of features, it should come as no surprise that the history of rate-of-return regulation is littered with instances of agency capture and regulatory expansion. Take, for instance, surface transportation. Railroads, which were the dominant means of long-distance transportation in the late 1800s, have high fixed costs (e.g., the cost of right-of-ways, track, switching stations, etc.). The result is that, for a broad range of output, their average costs decline as output increases. If the market demand curve for railroad transportation along some route intersects a railroad's average cost curve in the range in which average costs are declining (i.e., in the output range for which there are economies of scale), then marginal cost is necessarily below average cost. (Refer back to Figure 7.8 to see this point.) If competition erupts and forces prices down toward marginal cost, as competition tends to do, then the railroad will not earn enough revenue to cover its total costs. There may thus be a natural monopoly argument for price and entry regulation in the railroad industry. The Interstate Commerce Act of 1887 imposed just such regulation by creating the Interstate Commerce Commission (ICC) and empowering it to dictate the pricing, entry, and exit of railroads.[32]

The ICC, however, soon became captured by the railroads, which sought to have the price and entry rules to which they were subject imposed upon the trucking industry as well. Trucking companies, unlike railroads, are not natural monopolies. The fixed costs of trucking are far lower (no tracks, right-of-ways, etc.) so scale economies are much smaller, and market demand for trucking services can accommodate many firms operating at minimum efficient scale. If trucking firms could provide transportation services on the routes that were most profitable for railroads, then unregulated trucking firms might underprice the railroads, usurp their profits on the best routes, and make it impossible for the railroads to cover their costs while continuing to service less profitable routes. Railroad executives, who had long been in close contact with ICC officials, pressed this concern to their overseers and lobbied for regulatory expansion to cover trucking. ICC officials, who stood to benefit if the Commission's regulatory turf were expanded, pressured Congress to extend its jurisdiction to other forms of surface transportation. Congress acquiesced, extending ICC control of rates and entry to trucking with the Motor Carrier Act of 1935 and to water barges with the Transportation Act of 1940. Trucking firms and barges thus became subject to natural monopoly price controls even though they were not natural monopolists. Regulatory control of prices, it seems, is difficult to circumscribe.

A third difficulty bedeviling rate-of-return regulation is that it may generate inefficiency. As we have seen, rate-of-return regulation helps reduce allocative inefficiency – the wealth loss that occurs when productive resources are not put to the ends most highly valued by consumers – because it makes it impossible for monopolists to enhance their profits by cutting back on production and forcing prices upward. But rate-of-return regulation may induce productive inefficiency – the welfare loss that occurs when a given level of

---

[32] Prior to creation of the ICC, the railroads attempted to avoid "ruinous competition" by agreeing to charge prices at or above their average cost. They did so by establishing, in 1879, a Joint Executive Committee that would coordinate their prices. The Committee, however, was largely ineffectual, and price wars erupted in 1881, 1884, and 1885. (Collusion is difficult, remember!) Today, the Sherman Act would preclude the sort of price-fixing attempted by the Joint Executive Committee.

output is produced using more inputs than necessary to produce that output – because it weakens the regulated monopolist's incentive to cut its production costs. Recall that the monopolist's revenue requirement, which determines the prices it may charge, is determined in part by its operating expenses. When they go up, the monopolist is permitted to earn higher revenues by charging higher prices; when they go down, the monopolist's permitted prices are reduced accordingly. There's little reason, then, for a monopolist subject to rate-of-return regulation to revamp its production methods to reduce its operating expenses.[33]

Moreover, rate-of-return regulation may generate allocative inefficiency – and ultimately higher production costs – by encouraging producers to use too much capital equipment and too little labor. Under the revenue requirement formula, the producer is allowed to recover its labor costs as an operating expense. It recovers its cost of capital equipment as depreciation (to account for wear and tear) plus a return on capital (to account for its financing costs). In practice, however, regulators typically set the allowable rate of return on capital slightly in excess of producers' true cost of capital. (As noted, they do this to encourage continued production rather than liquidation.[34]) The upshot is that a producer earns more if it substitutes capital equipment, on which it may earn a "bonus," for labor, for which it recovers only its actual costs. As implemented, then, rate-of-return regulation may encourage an allocative inefficiency – an inefficiently high level of capital relative to labor – which causes production costs to be higher than necessary. Named after the economists who first identified this tendency of rate-of-return regulation, this inefficiency is often dubbed the "Averch–Johnson Effect."[35]

An alternative form of price regulation may mitigate some of the inefficiencies of rate-of-return regulation. Recall that rate-of-return regulation controls prices as a means of controlling the producer's profits – i.e., of limiting them to levels that would persist in a competitive market and would minimize deadweight loss. Since the objective is to prevent supracompetitive profits, any reduction in the monopolist's costs should result in an immediate lowering of permitted prices (otherwise, profits would spike). But if monopolists know that

---

[33] The reduction in the prices the monopolist may charge will not occur until the next "rate case" (i.e., the proceeding in which the regulator determines the monopolist's revenue requirement and price tariff). "Regulatory lag" – a delay between a monopolist's reduction in operating expenses and a reduction in its allowed prices – may thus create some incentive for the monopolist to reduce its operating expenses.

[34] See supra note 31 and accompanying text.

[35] Harvey Averch and Leland L. Johnson, Behavior of the Firm Under Regulatory Constraint, 52 Am. Econ. Rev. 1052 (1962).

cutting production costs won't create any benefit for them, then why cut costs at all? In light of the disincentive to cut one's costs when one's profits are capped, many natural monopoly regulators have transitioned to a system that caps prices rather than profits.

Under price cap regulation, the government sets the maximum prices natural monopolists may charge and commits not to lower those price caps for some set period of time, after which they will be adjusted. During the time in which the price caps cannot be lowered, the natural monopolist has an incentive to reduce its costs: It gets to keep the incremental profits it earns by enhancing its productive efficiency, and it need not worry that its efficiency gain will result in lower maximum prices. Price cap regulation therefore mitigates rate-of-return regulation's tendency to discourage investment in more efficient means of production.

But a price cap approach creates its own difficulties. By allowing natural monopolists that enhance their efficiency to charge prices in excess of their average costs, price cap regulation creates some deadweight loss that wouldn't exist if prices were reduced to average cost (i.e., some units that would be consumed if priced at average cost won't be purchased). This allocative inefficiency offsets some of the productive efficiency a price cap approach generates.

In addition, effective price cap regulation requires certain information that isn't needed for traditional rate-of-return regulation. Because productive efficiency tends to increase with technological development, we expect a natural monopolist's costs to fall over time. In a competitive market, prices would follow suit. If the goal is to bring prices as close as possible to competitive levels, then price caps should be set to account for the efficiency gains that would ordinarily be achieved in a competitive market. Price caps should fall a little every year so that the natural monopolist producer gets to keep only the cost-savings that result from its extraordinary efforts to rein in costs.

But figuring the amount by which maximum prices should fall to account for ordinary efficiency gains – an amount sometimes called the "X factor" – is difficult. Setting the X factor too low will result in prices that are too high relative to cost and will produce deadweight loss; setting it too high may result in prices that are insufficient to cover the producer's costs. Using historical productivity growth rates to estimate the X factor is problematic when the monopolist was previously subject to rate-of-return regulation and therefore had little incentive to enhance its productive efficiency. Regulators transitioning to price caps therefore typically set the X factor by taking the historical productivity growth rate and adding a "stretch factor" aimed to account for past disincentives toward productivity. There's quite a bit of guesswork here.

Despite its heightened informational requirement and its potential to permit prices above average cost, the salutary incentives created by price cap regulation may make it superior to traditional rate-of-return regulation. Indeed, empirical evidence suggests that price caps are associated with lower consumer prices than those persisting under rate-of-return regulation.[36]

FRANCHISE BIDDING. The stated justification for price controls on natural monopolists is a lack of competition: Since there is (and should be) only one producer in a natural monopoly market, consumers can't turn to a rival to get a better deal, so the natural monopolist will hike up prices unless constrained by government edict. But even if competition is undesirable once a natural monopolist is up and running, couldn't consumers be protected by competition before the monopolist is in operation? A system of franchise bidding substitutes competition *to be* the natural monopolist producer in place of top-down price regulation. The government sets up a competition for the right to supply the natural monopoly product in some area and provides that the winner will be the producer that commits to charge the lowest price while maintaining certain quality standards. If competition is vigorous, price will be driven to a point near the most efficient producer's average cost. (If, as is common, the competition is organized as a reverse auction in which progressively lower potential prices are announced and producers bow out when the price gets too low for them, then price should be driven to a point just below the second-most efficient producer's average cost.) Rights to operate cable television systems in particular communities, for example, are often allocated via franchise bidding.

Franchise bidding may alleviate the primary difficulties of a price control approach: the knowledge problem, agency capture, and, with rate-of-return regulation, productive inefficiencies resulting from both the disincentive to cut operating costs and the incentive to over-invest in capital (the Averch–Johnson Effect). Franchise bidding involves a lower informational requirement because the government need not determine what any producer's average cost is; competing producers reveal as much through their bidding behavior. Franchise bidding also entails a lower risk of agency capture because regulators, who need not continually sign off on prices, have less contact with their regulatees and, since prices are set out in advance, less discretionary control over them. Relative to rate-of-return regulation, franchise

[36] See Viscusi, et al., supra note 4, at 441; Alan D. Mathios and Robert P. Rogers, The Impact of Alternative Forms of State Regulation of AT&T on Direct-Dial, Long-Distance Telephone Rates, 20 *Rand J. Econ.* 437 (1989).

bidding may lead to greater productive efficiencies because once the franchise is awarded and fees are capped at the low-bid rates, the producer has every incentive to minimize operating costs and to select the optimal combination of capital and labor.

But franchise bidding poses its own difficulties. As an initial matter, for franchise bidding to serve as an effective substitute for price regulation, there must be sufficient competition at the bidding stage. If potential producers engage in bid-rigging (i.e., if they agree among themselves to divvy up available franchises and not bid vigorously), then price will not be driven down to (near) average cost. And, because the price of the winning bidder is likely to be just below the average cost of the second-most efficient producer, it is crucial that the pool of bidders include multiple highly efficient firms.

Moreover, even when there's vigorous competition at the bidding stage, a franchise bidding system may ultimately come to resemble traditional price regulation. Because the winning bidder commits to charge certain prices and to adhere to specified standards of quality, some government body must monitor the quality of the producer's offering and, if necessary, order price reductions or rebates to account for quality deficiencies. Moreover, because unanticipated changes (increased costs of inputs, etc.) may render the winning bidder's commitments impossible to keep, that same government body must have power to adjust the winner's obligations. But if an agency is empowered to monitor the natural monopolist producer, control its quality, and make price adjustments, we are an awfully long way back toward traditional price regulation.

A third difficulty with a franchise bidding approach is that it may reduce tax transparency and thus political accountability. Always searching for new sources of revenue, local governments have often charged franchise fees to natural monopolist producers that have acquired their right to operate through franchise bidding. Because the franchisees (local cable systems operators, for example) incorporate anticipated fees into their bids and pass them along to consumers, the fees are effectively taxes. But they tend to be less visible than income or property taxes, or even than the taxes imposed on utilities that did not secure their monopolist status via franchise bidding. Taxes on those utilities are typically imposed after the producers are established in business, and the taxes are usually listed as a separate line item on the bill sent to consumers. Because franchise fees are incorporated into a franchise bidder's base price, they remain hidden and are less susceptible to political discipline.

PUBLIC ENTERPRISE. Under both the price control and franchise bidding approaches to regulating natural monopolies, the product or service at issue is provided by a privately owned producer. A price control approach employs governmental entry and price constraints to ensure that the producer is able to maintain minimum efficient scale and doesn't charge supracompetitive prices. Franchise bidding similarly restricts entry but employs competition for the right to produce, rather than price regulation, as the primary means of preventing monopolistic pricing. With both approaches, though, the producer is owned and (primarily) controlled by a private entity.

A third approach to the natural monopoly problem is to have a government-owned entity provide the product or service at issue. For example, Amtrak (a provider of passenger rail service) and the Tennessee Valley Authority (an electricity provider) are both publicly owned participants in industries exhibiting some natural monopoly characteristics.[37] The theory underlying this approach is that a publicly owned producer – one not beholden to its investors – would not seek profit-maximization, the objective that leads privately owned monopolists to reduce output and hike price (see Figure 7.5), but would instead respond to the demand of voters, who are both the owners and the customers of the producer. If the producer were run in a manner that failed to maximize productive efficiencies, voters, as the producer's owners, would punish those in control of the entity. But, wearing their consumer hats, voters would also punish supracompetitive pricing.[38] Public accountability, then, could lead the controllers of the public enterprise to manage it so as to minimize productive and allocative inefficiency.

The chief problem with public ownership is that political accountability is far less effective than market discipline as a means of promoting productive efficiency. A publicly owned producer's prices may be salient to voters; its costs almost never are. Moreover, whereas a privately owned producer must constrain its costs in order to raise capital and will fold if its costs consistently exceed its revenues, a public entity can almost always access the public fisc and can never really fail. (Consider, for example, the perpetually in-the-red US Postal Service.) The incentive for public firm managers, then, is to hold prices down while largely ignoring costs.

---

[37] Public ownership is far more common abroad. For example, whereas most of the non-passenger railroad transporters and all domestic commercial airlines are privately owned in the United States, both industries are almost entirely government-owned in most European countries.

[38] Supracompetitive pricing would provide some benefit to voters by increasing the publicly owned firm's profits, but the increase in profit would be less than the decrease in consumer welfare resulting from the supracompetitive pricing (see Figure 7.5). Accordingly, such pricing would entail a net loss for voters.

Not only do public entities escape the cost-constraining discipline that comes from having to access the capital markets and worry about failure, they also avoid the disciplining effect of the market for corporate control. As explained in Chapter 6, the threat of a takeover is a powerful force for constraining agency costs in a private corporation. If private managers slack off or act opportunistically to the detriment of company business, their firms' stock prices will fall, and they may lose their jobs in a takeover. Recognition of that possibility encourages them to be both diligent and loyal. This requires, though, that ownership interests in the firm be transferable. Voluntary sales and purchases of such interests (e.g., stock) produce an entity's market price, the metric of managerial performance, and enable the ouster of poorly performing managers. Ownership interests in publicly owned (government) firms, however, are not transferable. For such firms, there is neither a market-based measure of managerial performance (i.e., a stock price) nor a political mechanism for punishing bad managers. Not surprisingly, then, publicly owned natural monopolies tend to be less efficient than their privately owned counterparts.[39]

Direct Regulation of Market Power in the Absence of Natural Monopoly: The Case of Net Neutrality Rules

A key question for policymakers confronting potential market power is whether to leave the matter to antitrust or instead to impose some form of direct regulation. As we have seen, antitrust is poorly positioned to address natural monopoly conditions, which often call for ex ante, industry-specific regulation. But what if there's not a natural monopoly? Might direct regulation still be the better way to address potential exercises of market power?

That question has recently arisen in the debate over whether and how to regulate the Internet. Proponents of so-called net neutrality maintain that the entities controlling data transmission across the Internet – primarily Internet Service Providers (ISPs), such as cable and telephone companies – should not be allowed to treat different data packets differently. In particular, ISPs should be prohibited from providing faster transmission of the data from some content, or "edge," provider (e.g., Netflix) in exchange for money or some other benefit. Nor should ISPs be allowed to slow down data from content providers that haven't paid for a fast lane.

So far, ISPs have generally refrained from blocking or "throttling" Internet content. Indeed, the FCC, which has come down firmly in favor of net neutrality, could identify only four troubling instances of non-neutral network

---

[39] See Viscusi, et al., supra note 4, at 515–16 (discussing empirical evidence).

management over the entire history of the commercial Internet.[40] Nevertheless, proponents of net neutrality (including, at the time of this writing, a majority of the sitting FCC commissioners) point to a parade of horribles that could occur if non-neutral transmission practices were to proliferate. Those adverse effects include degraded Internet performance (as ISPs disfavor edge providers that refuse to pay for fast lanes), reduced innovation by edge providers (which will have less money for R&D if they must pay for priority transmission), and higher prices for Internet content (as edge providers pass on prioritization charges to consumers).

Market power is the disease that could produce these adverse symptoms. If they faced vigorous competition, ISPs would seek to win business by managing network traffic in accordance with consumer preferences. Unfortunately, competition among broadband service providers is somewhat anemic in many parts of the country. Absent the threat of losing business to rivals, ISPs might decide to transport data in a manner that fails to optimize the end-user experience. In particular, they may favor content providers with which they have a relationship or disfavor those that somehow compete with them or their affiliates. ISP and cable provider Comcast, for example, could opt to speed up content from the Internet video service HULU, which streams the television programming of Comcast's NBC subsidiary, or might slow down content from Netflix, whose streaming video competes with Comcast's own cable programming.

The existing statutory landscape offers several options for addressing potentially anticompetitive instances of non-neutral network management. The simplest approach would be to leave the matter to antitrust, which applies in the absence of more focused direct regulation. ISPs' network management practices are the sort of "vertical restraints of trade" with which antitrust tribunals are quite familiar. In recent decades, courts have revised the standards governing such restraints so that antitrust, which used to treat vertical restraints in a ham-fisted fashion, now does a pretty good job separating pro-consumer restraints from anti-consumer ones. There is no natural monopoly rationale for eschewing an antitrust approach; most regions of the country are served by multiple ISPs, all of which appear to be wholly sustainable, and the explosion of wireless broadband service suggests that competition among broadband providers will only grow. Taking no further regulatory action and relying on antitrust, then, could be the best way to address competitive concerns arising from non-neutral network management practices.

---

[40] See Gerald R. Faulhaber, The Economics of Network Neutrality, 34 *Regulation* 18 (Winter 2011–2012) (detailing instances).

That is not the tack the FCC has taken. Instead, the Commission has sought to impose ex ante rules forbidding the blocking, throttling, or paid prioritization of Internet traffic. The Commission first tried to impose such rules in 2010, but a federal appeals court invalidated them because the Commission had not cited an adequate statutory basis for its rulemaking.[41] The Commission tried again in 2014. That time, it claimed authority under Section 706 of the 1996 Telecommunications Act, which directs the FCC to "encourage the deployment on a reasonable and timely basis of advanced telecommunications capability to all Americans."[42] Prohibiting the blocking, throttling, and paid prioritization of data, the Commission contended, would encourage innovation by edge providers (e.g., Netflix, Facebook), which would stimulate consumer demand for high-speed Internet access, which would encourage greater investment in broadband networks.

The appeals court accepted the purported statutory basis for the rules, but it identified another problem with them: They effectively transformed ISPs into "common carriers."[43] Title II of the 1934 Communications Act subjects common carriers to a host of obligations. Among other things, they must "furnish . . . communication service upon reasonable request," avoid "unjust or unreasonable discrimination in charges, practices, classifications, regulations, facilities, or services," and charge only "just and reasonable" rates.[44] But the statute provides that entities providing only "information services," not "telecommunications services," may not be subjected to such intrusive common carrier rules.[45] Because the FCC had previously characterized the provision of broadband Internet access as an information service, ISPs couldn't be regulated as common carriers. And since the Commission's bans on blocking, throttling, and paid prioritization of Internet traffic constituted common carrier regulation, the court reasoned, they exceeded the FCC's authority. Notably, the court suggested ways the rules might be tweaked so that they wouldn't constitute common carrier regulation and could thus be sustained under Section 706.[46]

Using the court's second opinion as a roadmap, the FCC set about revising its net neutrality rules to avoid transforming broadband providers into common carriers. Reclassifying ISPs as providers of telecommunications services and subjecting them to full Title II regulation, the Commission maintained, was far too draconian for such a dynamic industry – one that had achieved astonishing success with little ex ante regulation.

---

[41] See Comcast Corp. v. FCC, 600 F.3d 642 (D.C. Cir. 2010).   [42] 47 U.S.C. § 1302(a).
[43] Verizon v. FCC, 740 F.3d 623, 649–59 (D.C. Cir. 2014).
[44] 47 U.S.C. §§ 201(a), (b); 202(a).   [45] 47 U.S.C. § 153(51).
[46] Verizon, 740 F.3d at 655–59.

Things changed when President Barack Obama, seizing the opportunity to weigh in on an issue of interest to his core base of political supporters, posted a YouTube video encouraging the FCC to abandon its targeted rulemaking and subject broadband providers to Title II regulation.[47] That same day, activists picketed the home of FCC Chairman Tom Wheeler, demanding full Title II regulation of Internet broadband. Soon afterwards, the FCC abruptly changed its position: Title II reclassification went from being too draconian to being the preferred policy option. The nominally independent commissioners voted 3–2 along party lines to reclassify ISPs as telecommunications services and subject them to net neutrality obligations. It promised, however, to "forebear" from forcing them to comply with a number of Title II rules, including all rate regulation.[48]

At the time of this writing, then, network management by ISPs is policed not by antitrust but by direct, ex ante regulation imposed by the FCC. Moreover, because the Commission abandoned its Section 706 rules and acceded to President Obama's demand that ISPs be reclassified as common carriers, the regulation does not consist merely of the targeted rules previously promulgated but potentially entails the full panoply of Title II rules and standards.

This is not the optimal remedy for potentially anticompetitive instances of non-neutral network management. Relying on antitrust would have been superior to either form of direct regulation. And between the two types of direct regulation – targeted rules under Section 706 or full common carrier regulation under Title II – the former would have been better than the latter.

The choice between antitrust and direct regulation generally (under either Section 706 or Title II) involves a trade-off between flexibility and determinacy. Antitrust is flexible but somewhat indeterminate; it would condemn non-neutral network management practices that are likely to injure consumers, but it would permit such practices if they would lower costs, improve quality, or otherwise enhance consumer welfare. The direct regulatory approaches are rigid but clearer; they declare all instances of non-neutral network management to be illegal per se.

Determinacy and flexibility influence decision and error costs. Because they are more determinate, ex ante rules should impose lower decision costs than would antitrust. But direct regulation's inflexibility – automatic condemnation, no questions asked – will generate higher error costs. That's because

---

[47] See Brian Fung, Obama to the FCC: Adopt "the strongest possible rules" on net neutrality, including Title II, *Wash. Post* (Nov. 10, 2014).

[48] Federal Communications Commission, *In the Matter of Protecting and Promoting the Open Internet*, Report and Order on Remand, Declaratory Ruling, and Order, GN Dock. No. 14–28 (Mar. 12, 2015).

non-neutral network management is often good for end users. For example, speeding up the transmission of content for which delivery lags are particularly detrimental to the end-user experience (e.g., an Internet telephone call, streaming video) at the expense of content that is less lag-sensitive (e.g., digital photographs downloaded from a photo-sharing website) can create a net consumer benefit and should probably be allowed. A per se rule against non-neutral network management would therefore err fairly frequently. Antitrust's flexible approach, informed by a century of economic learning on the output effects of contractual restraints between vertically related firms (like content producers and distributors), would probably generate lower error costs.

Although both antitrust and direct regulation offer advantages vis-à-vis each other, this isn't simply a wash. The error cost advantage antitrust holds over direct regulation likely swamps direct regulation's decision cost advantage. Extensive experience with vertical restraints on distribution have shown that they are usually good for consumers. For that reason, antitrust courts in recent decades have discarded their old per se rules against such practices – rules that resemble the FCC's direct regulatory approach – in favor of structured rules of reason that assess liability based on specific features of the market and the restraint at issue.[49] While these rules of reason (standards, really) may be less determinate than the old, error-prone per se rules, they are not *in*determinate. By relying on past precedents and the overarching principle that legality turns on consumer welfare effects, business planners and adjudicators ought to be able to determine fairly easily whether a non-neutral network management practice passes muster. Indeed, the fact that the FCC has uncovered only four instances of anticompetitive network management over the commercial Internet's entire history – a period in which antitrust, but not direct regulation, has governed ISPs – suggests that business planners are capable of determining what behavior is off-limits. Direct regulation's per se rule against non-neutral network management is thus likely to add error costs that exceed any reduction in decision costs. It is probably not the remedy that would be selected under this book's recommended approach.

In any event, direct regulation *under Title II*, the currently prevailing approach, is certainly not the optimal way to address potentially anticompetitive instances of non-neutral network management by ISPs. Whereas any ex ante regulation of network management will confront the familiar knowledge problem, opting for direct regulation under Title II, rather than the more cabined approach under Section 706, adds adverse public choice concerns to the mix.

---

[49]   See supra note 16 and accompanying text.

As explained earlier, reclassifying ISPs to bring them under Title II empowers the FCC to scrutinize the "justice" and "reasonableness" of nearly every aspect of every arrangement between content providers, ISPs, and consumers. Granted, the current commissioners have pledged not to exercise their Title II authority beyond mandating network neutrality, but public choice insights suggest that this promised forbearance is unlikely to endure. FCC officials, who remain self-interest maximizers even when acting in their official capacities, benefit from expanding their regulatory turf; they gain increased power and prestige, larger budgets to manage, a greater ability to "make or break" businesses, and thus more opportunity to take actions that may enhance their future career opportunities. They will therefore face constant temptation to exercise the Title II authority that they have committed, as of now, to leave fallow. Regulated businesses, knowing that FCC decisions are key to their success, will expend significant resources lobbying for outcomes that benefit them or impair their rivals. If they don't get what they want because of the commissioners' voluntary forbearance, they may bring legal challenges asserting that the Commission has failed to assure just and reasonable practices as Title II demands. Many of the decisions at issue will involve the familiar concentrated benefits/diffused costs dynamic that tends to result in under-representation by those who are adversely affected by a contemplated decision. Taken together, these considerations make it unlikely that the current commissioners' promised restraint will endure. Reclassification of ISPs so that they are subject to Title II regulation will probably lead to additional constraints on edge providers and ISPs.

Indeed, in the first few months following the FCC's reclassification of ISPs into common carriers subject to Title II, the Commission received thousands of requests to regulate Internet pricing, business practices, and products. The producer of the struggling Blackberry smartphone, for example, demanded that Netflix be forced to stream its video content on Blackberry's unpopular phones. Organizations representing heavy Internet users have pushed for the elimination of policies charging higher fees to subscribers who exceed broadband data limits, a development that would require consumers who use the Internet for only email and casual web browsing to subsidize round-the-clock video gamers and those who watch hours of movies and television on their smartphones. In the face of continual requests for expanded regulation, maintaining their forbearance policy will require significant fortitude on the part of the commissioners, particularly new ones who were not part of the original forbearance arrangement.

The recent experience of telecommunications provider T-Mobile suggests how fragile the FCC's promised forbearance is likely to be. In November 2015, the FCC's chairman praised as "innovative" T-Mobile's "Binge On" service, which offered cost-conscious subscribers unlimited access to Netflix, ESPN, HBO, and several other popular streaming video providers. Ridiculing the notion that Title II regulation would chill innovative offerings like T-Mobile's, he remarked:

> I also kind of chuckle at the fact that as we were debating the open Internet, everybody was saying, "Oh, this is going to thwart innovation, it's going to be terrible. People are going to have to come to the FCC to say, 'Mother, may I?' before they do anything in the market." Well that certainly didn't happen here.[50]

It seems the chairman spoke too soon. Within a few weeks of his remarks, complaints by a number of well-organized interest groups led the FCC to demand that T-Mobile appear before Commission staff to defend offering service packages that discriminate among content providers.[51] The company was, in fact, ordered to seek permission to offer a service its cost-conscious consumers have demanded.

Implicitly acknowledging that Title II regulation does effectively require FCC permission for virtually all innovation by ISPs, edge providers, and other Internet businesses, the Commission recently established a system for obtaining non-binding pre-approval of innovations. Unfortunately, the pre-approval mechanism will do little to alleviate business planners' concerns.

According to the rules implementing the FCC's Internet innovation pre-approval program,

> A proposed course of conduct for which an advisory opinion is sought must be sufficiently concrete and detailed so as to be more than merely hypothetical; it must be sufficiently defined to enable the Bureau to conduct an in-depth evaluation of the proposal. In addition, the Bureau will not respond to requests for opinions that relate to ongoing or prior conduct.[52]

The set of innovations that are not "hypothetical" but yet remain unimplemented so that they are not "ongoing" would seem to be small indeed. Presumably, the Commission means that the innovator must have developed

---

[50] See L. Gordon Crovitz, Obamanet Goes to Court, *Wall St. J.* (Nov. 29, 2015).

[51] See Letter from Roger C. Sherman, Wireless Telecommunication Bureau Chief, Federal Communications Commission to Kathleen Ham, Senior Vice President of Government Affairs, T-Mobile (Dec. 16, 2015), available at www.documentcloud.org/documents/2648554-Letter-to-Kathleen-Ham.html.

[52] Federal Communications Commission Public Notice, *Open Internet Advisory Opinion Procedures*, Protecting and Promoting the Open Internet, GN Dock. No. 14–28 (July 2, 2015), available at https://apps.fcc.gov/edocs_public/attachmatch/DA-15-692A1.pdf.

the proposed course of conduct to the point of launch but not yet pulled the trigger. But if that is so, then the pre-approval mechanism can offer innovators no assurance of legality before they expend the considerable quantum of resources required to get an innovation to the launching point. Moreover, because both the FCC's advisory opinions and the detailed requests to which they are responding will be public, innovators will be reluctant to seek advice on product or service developments involving proprietary information and strategies. In the end, the FCC's pre-approval system is unlikely to mitigate the innovation-chilling that results from the extreme breadth of potential restrictions under Title II.

Not surprisingly, private investment in Internet infrastructure has fallen substantially since the FCC revealed its Title II strategy.[53] In the first half of 2015, as the Commission was formulating its new Title II approach, spending by the major ISPs on capital equipment fell by an average of 12 percent, with the overall industry average falling by 8 percent. At AT&T and Charter Communications, capital spending was down 29 percent. It fell 10 percent at Cablevision and 4 percent at Verizon. While it would be fallacious reasoning to conclude that this decrease in investment was due entirely to looming Title II regulation, it is notable that this was only the third time in the history of the commercial Internet that infrastructure investment fell from the previous year. The other two times were in 2001, following the dot.com bust, and 2009, after the 2008 financial crash and ensuing recession. Such historical evidence lends support to the common sense view that regulatory uncertainty – a persistent force when nearly all agreements are subject to review for "justice" and "reasonableness" – threatens innovation and investment among ISPs.

It seems, then, that mandating net neutrality under Title II of the 1934 Communications Act is the least desirable of the three statutorily available approaches to addressing anticompetitive network management practices. The Title II approach combines the inflexibility and ensuing error costs of the Section 706 direct regulation approach with the indeterminacy and higher decision costs of an antitrust approach. Indeed, the indeterminacy under Title II is significantly greater than that under antitrust because the "just and reasonable" requirements of the Communications Act, unlike antitrust's reasonableness requirements (no unreasonable restraint of trade, no unreasonably exclusionary conduct) are not constrained by the consumer welfare principle. Whereas antitrust always protects consumers, not competitors, the FCC may well decide that business practices in the Internet space are unjust

---

[53] See L. Gordon Crovitz, Obamanet Is Hurting Broadband, *Wall St. J.* (Sept. 13, 2015); Hal Singer, How the FCC Will Wreck the Internet, *Wall St. J.* (May 28, 2015).

or unreasonable solely because they make things harder for the perpetrator's rivals. Business planners are thus really "at sea" when it comes to assessing the legality of novel practices.

All this implies that Internet businesses regulated by Title II need to court the FCC's favor, that FCC officials have more ability than ever to manipulate government power to private ends, that organized interest groups are well-poised to secure their preferences when the costs are great but widely dispersed, and that the regulators' dictated outcomes – immune from market pressures reflecting consumers' preferences – are less likely to maximize net social welfare. In opting for a Title II solution to what is essentially a market power problem, the powers that be gave short shrift to an antitrust approach, even though there was no natural monopoly justification for direct regulation. They paid little heed to the adverse consequences likely to result from rigid per se rules adopted under a highly discretionary (and politically manipulable) standard. They should have gone back to basics, assessing the disease to be remedied (market power), the full range of available remedies (including antitrust), and the potential side effects of each. In other words, they could have used this book.

LESSONS FOR POLICYMAKERS

Available remedies for the market power disease divide into standards that are fleshed out ex post (i.e., antitrust: "don't unreasonably restrain trade or engage in unreasonably exclusionary conduct") and rules whose strictures are specified ex ante (i.e., price regulation: "don't charge more than x"; franchise bidding: "don't sell in this market unless you were the lowest-priced bidder, and in that case, charge only your bid price"; and public ownership: "don't compete against the government in this market"). The first thing policymakers confronting potential market power must decide, then, is whether to rely on antitrust, the residual regulator, or to impose some form of direct regulation.

Because both the knowledge problem and public choice concerns are more severe for rigid rules than for flexible standards, antitrust should be used unless there is some reason to believe it would be ineffective. That will usually be the case with natural monopolies, but not otherwise. As experience under the FCC's politically motivated net neutrality rules is showing, direct regulation is a poor response to market power concerns in markets not involving natural monopoly. Relying on antitrust would be a better approach.

As for the substance of antitrust, policymakers should continue the US Supreme Court's approach of construing substantive liability standards to minimize the sum of error and decision costs.[54] In particular, the federal enforcement agencies – the FTC and the DOJ's Antitrust Division – should recognize that their relentless efforts to stamp out every instance of anticompetitive conduct chills procompetitive business behavior. They should stop trying to maximize deterrence and instead seek to optimize antitrust's effectiveness.[55] (Never forget Voltaire's prudent maxim, "The enemy is the perfect of the good.") For its part, the US Supreme Court should finish the job of eliminating improvident per se rules that result in the condemnation of many instances of procompetitive conduct: It should treat tying like other "mixed bag" business practices – exclusive dealing, resale price maintenance, vertical non-price restraints – and evaluate its legality under the rule of reason.

When there is a natural monopoly, so that some form of direct regulation is appropriate, franchise bidding should be the preferred option. Such an approach minimizes the knowledge problem (competition determines rates) and reduces regulators' discretionary authority and, with it, the risk of agency capture and other public choice concerns. When there are not enough potential producers for a competitive auction, some form of price regulation may be appropriate. In such cases, a price cap approach, which preserves the regulatee's incentive to achieve productive efficiencies, will usually trump traditional rate-of-return regulation. Public ownership is rarely appropriate.

---

[54] See Lambert, supra note 18. [55] See Lambert and Abbott, supra note 18.

8

Information Asymmetry

On-campus interviews are a rite of passage for American law students. Each fall, law firms from around the country send representatives to campuses to interview students beginning their second year of the three-year JD program. Successful candidates are invited for callback interviews. If they nail those, they land "summer associate" jobs for the following summer. Most law firms do the bulk of their permanent hiring from their summer associate programs.

This means that for law students at all but the most elite schools, first-year grades really matter. Those grades strongly influence what summer job a student will get, which typically determines where he or she will work after graduation. Summer associate jobs at the top national firms lead to permanent positions with salaries that start near $200,000 and rise quickly with seniority. At the other end of the spectrum, salaries start in the $40,000 range and grow slowly.

The upshot is that people heading to most law schools are taking a significant gamble. If they dominate the first year, their prospects will be bright. If they tank, they will have spent lots of money (or, more likely, incurred a good bit of debt) earning a degree that isn't worth much.

So here's an idea: Why not sell bad grade insurance to entering first-year law students? Most people are risk-averse, so they value having someone else bear some of the downside of their risky activity. If the value they attach to such risk-shifting exceeds the cost the other person incurs in taking on that additional risk, there's an opportunity for a wealth-creating trade.

Suppose, for example, that an incoming law student believes that any job she could obtain if her grades end up in the bottom quarter of her class would not be worth the cost of tuition. She therefore wants to be paid an amount sufficient to cover the first year's tuition – $20,000 at her state law school – in the event her first-year grade point average is below the 25th percentile. Assuming that the purchasers of bad grade insurance (the insureds) are evenly distributed among the class, the expected cost of an insurer's promise to pay $20,000 if an insured's grades are below the 25th percentile should be around $5,000. There are probably some risk-averse entering law students who would be willing to pay that amount to have their first year's tuition effectively refunded if their first-year grades are poor.

So why don't we see bad grade insurance? As we discussed in Chapter 3, private ordering tends to make available all goods and services that create more value than they cost to produce. Bad grade insurance seems to be one of those things. Isn't there an opportunity here for some enterprising entrepreneur to create social value – and earn profits for himself – by offering this product? Should you set this book aside and start drawing up a business plan?

Probably not. Bad grade insurance is a non-starter. That's not because there aren't people out there who would be willing to pay more than the cost of creating and selling the product. There probably are. The problem is instead "information asymmetry." Compared to the insureds buying its product, the bad grade insurer would know less about buyers' characteristics (e.g., their native intelligence) and post-purchase behavior (e.g., their exam preparation efforts). As we'll soon see, when buyer and seller have significantly different levels of information about each other's offerings and conduct, markets may not emerge even for products and services that create greater value than they cost to produce and sell.

SYMPTOMS/DISEASE

As the foregoing discussion suggests, the primary symptom of information asymmetry between buyers and sellers is product unavailability: Goods and services that people would like to have are not made available even when they cost less to produce than the value they generate. Understanding why this unhappy situation emerges requires examining more closely what happens when the parties to a transaction face an informational imbalance. As it turns out, the general asymmetric information disease manifests itself in two more specific maladies.

To understand the first malady, consider a classic market in which buyers and sellers have significantly different levels of information about the thing being sold: the used car market. It's hard for most used car buyers to tell the difference between a reliable used car (a "peach") and one with latent mechanical problems (a "lemon"). Lemons often look like good cars even though they're mechanical disasters. Used car sellers, on the other hand, usually have a good sense of what their car is really worth. They know if it's really a lemon or a peach or something in between (a kumquat?).

So suppose a community contains 100 peach-looking used cars ranging in value from $10,000 at the high end down to $100. Suppose further that each car's value is unique and that the values are evenly distributed throughout the range (e.g., $10,000, $9,900, $9,800, . . . $300, $200, $100). Each seller knows her car's true worth; potential buyers, on the other hand, know only that each car is worth *up to* $10,000, the value of a perfect peach.

If you were a buyer in this community, how much would you be willing to pay for a used car offered for sale? Assuming you can't tell whether you're buying a lemon or a peach, it would make little sense to pay more than $5,000, the average value of a car in this community. If you offer that amount, you stand a 50% chance of getting a bargain (i.e., of paying less than the car's value) and a 50% chance of overpaying.

But wait a minute. If car owners figure out that buyers are unlikely to pay more than $5,000 for a used automobile, any owner of a car worth more than that amount, a peach, would be unlikely to offer it for sale. That means the range of value of cars for sale would be not $100 to $10,000 but $100 to $5,000. And that suggests your offer price shouldn't exceed $2,500, the average value of a car *likely to be offered for sale*.

But car owners who *really* think this situation through will realize that they're unlikely to collect more than $2,500 for any car they sell, so they'll pull from the market all cars worth more than that amount. The range of value of used cars for sale would thus be $100 to $2,500, making $1,250 the maximum rational offer price for a buyer. You know what would happen next.

What we have just considered is the famous "lemons problem" first identified by Nobel Prize winning economist George Akerlof.[1] Akerlof's primary point was that asymmetric information between buyers and sellers may lead to "adverse selection," which may cause a market to unravel. Adverse selection occurs when something causes "bad" market participants – those offering below-average value to their trading partners – to be overrepresented in a pool of buyers or sellers; that pool has been "selected adversely."

Asymmetric information between buyers and sellers may give rise to adverse selection because the informationally advantaged parties (e.g., used car sellers), knowing their less informed trading partners will make offers based on average value assumptions, will withdraw from the market when they know they are offering higher-than-average value. Trading partners respond by changing some term of their offer – usually the price – to account for the lower value they are likely to receive. But that change tends to make the pool even worse by driving

---

[1] George Akerlof, The Market for "Lemons": Quality Uncertainty and the Market Mechanism, 84 *Q. J. Econ.* 488 (1970).

the participants offering the most value out of the pool. In other words, selection becomes even more adverse. Eventually, the only participants left in the pool will be those offering very low value. And this means transactions involving participants offering *high* value become impossible, even when there are trading partners out there who would be willing to pay for that high value.[2]

Markets for durable goods such as used cars involve informationally advantaged sellers. Adverse selection may also occur, though, when *buyers* possess the informational advantage. That's often the situation with insurance. Relative to insurers, the insureds who purchase policies usually know more about the likelihood that the insured-against event – sickness, property damage, etc. – will occur. Insurers price their policies so as to cover their expected payouts (the magnitude of losses times their likelihood of occurrence) plus their administrative costs. If insurers calculate expected payouts, and thus policy prices, on the basis of the average likelihood that a claim will be made, their policies will be unattractive to purchasers posing lower risks. Their pool of insureds will therefore be riskier than average, so their revenues (from prices that assumed only average risk) won't cover their costs (from payouts to relatively high-risk policyholders). Of course, if insurers set prices on the assumption that their insureds pose a higher-than-average risk, their policies will become unattractive to insureds whose risk of making a claim is just average. As long as insureds know the magnitude of risk they pose better than does the insurer, selection into the pool of insureds is likely to be somewhat adverse.

---

[2] Adverse selection of the sort Akerlof predicted occurred a few years back in the market for used versions of Microsoft's Xbox 360 home video console. In November 2009, Microsoft banned users of modified ("modded") consoles from its online gaming service. (Users often physically modify their consoles to enable use of non-Microsoft software and other components.) Modded machines were not "bricked," meaning that they could still be used to play games offline, but their users couldn't gain access to the gaming system's Internet features. Thousands of users responded by offering their units for sale on eBay and Craigslist.

This created a huge problem for people trying to resell *unmodded* consoles. Microsoft's new policy created a significant disparity in the value of a modded versus an unmodded Xbox, and web purchasers couldn't tell which type of used machine they were buying. Consistent with Akerlof's predictions, the immediate result was a drop in prices for used Xbox 360s as buyers took account of the risk that the machine would turn out to be a modded lemon. That, in turn, led to the withdrawal of unmodded consoles (peaches) from the market. EBay responded by posting a warning in its guide section: "If you are looking to buy an Xbox 360 on eBay in the near future, ask the seller if it has been banned from Xbox Live and be sure to pay by PayPal in case they lie. If you do get a banned console, start a PayPal claim." See Dan Steinberg, *EBay Flooded with Net-Banned Xbox Consoles*, CBC News (Nov. 13, 2009) (available at www.cbc.ca /news/technology/ebay-flooded-with-net-banned-xbox-consoles-1.833289). Pretty soon, the market stabilized – and unmodded Xbox 360s again became available – as buyers and sellers developed ways to level the informational playing field. (We consider this sort of privately ordered solution to adverse selection later in this chapter.)

This is one of the problems with bad grade insurance: Since potential buyers know better than the insurer whether they're likely to score poorly on exams, they'll tend to buy bad grade insurance only if it constitutes a "bargain" for them in that its expected benefit (magnitude of payout times likelihood of bad grades) exceeds its price. Absent some means to avoid the adverse selection that would result from information asymmetry, the bad grade insurer's business would be doomed to failure.

Of course, information asymmetry must not be an insurmountable barrier to the provision of insurance; private insurance does exist. But that's because insurers have figured out ways to mitigate the adverse selection that tends to result from information asymmetry. With health insurance, for example, insurers traditionally accomplished that objective by creating incentives for lower-risk insureds – young, healthy people – to purchase insurance. Insurers often refused to sell policies to people after they had become sick, and, when insurers did sell to such folks, they typically charged higher rates to account for the higher likelihood of claims. They also refused to cover claims based on "pre-existing conditions" (i.e., ailments that were in existence when the policy was purchased). In light of these common practices, young, healthy people purchased insurance coverage even during periods in which they didn't expect to make claims because they didn't want to lose the ability to procure coverage at affordable rates if they did develop an adverse medical condition. Driving young, healthy people – health insurance peaches – into the pool of insureds mitigated adverse selection and allowed health insurance markets to stabilize.[3]

The Patient Protection and Affordable Care Act of 2010 (the ACA, known colloquially as "Obamacare") disrupted this scheme. The ACA mandated both "guaranteed issue" (an insurer must sell to anyone who seeks to buy coverage) and "community rating" (prices may not be based on an individual buyer's illnesses or risk factors). It also barred insurers from refusing to pay for claims arising from pre-existing conditions. Taken together, these three restrictions on insurers' contractual freedom drastically reduced the incentive for young, healthy people to purchase insurance; why buy it before you need it? This is the reason for the ACA's much-maligned "individual mandate," which

---

[3] There were, of course, some unfortunate victims of these otherwise salutary practices. Many responsible people who, for no fault of their own, had failed to procure insurance coverage found that it was not obtainable when they developed adverse conditions. The Patient Protection and Affordable Care Act, discussed next in the text, was intended to address that problem. Unfortunately, it may have created even bigger problems. Remember, there are side effects to nearly every regulatory intervention.

requires individuals to purchase health insurance or else pay a penalty (or, according to the US Supreme Court, a "tax").[4]

As of the time of this writing, it is unclear whether the ACA's non-coverage tax will be sufficient to prevent widespread adverse selection in health insurance markets. In recent months, a number of major health insurers have stopped participating in the Obamacare exchanges.[5] Selling individual policies through the exchanges, they say, is unprofitable because young, healthy people are opting to forego insurance, causing exchange purchasers to be relatively old and sick. That's adverse selection.

Adverse selection results when buyers and sellers possess asymmetric information about each other's *characteristics* (or, more precisely, about the characteristics of each other's offerings). A second malady may result when buyers and sellers have asymmetric information about each other's *actions*.

In many transactions, the value to one party depends largely on how the other party acts after the transaction is executed. Whether you got a good deal or a raw deal in hiring me to provide some service depends largely on what I do after we have entered into our employment relationship. An insurer that sells health coverage to a young, fit person may find its peach has soured if the insured subsequently becomes a methamphetamine addict, a coal miner, or a professional pie-eater.

What's more, when one party knows that she can capture the value of a transaction even if she performs poorly (as in the case of a service provider who is paid in advance) or that the other party will cover the cost of her bad behavior (as in the case of an insured deciding what level of risk to incur), she may be tempted to act badly. If the put-upon party could monitor his contracting partner's activities and respond to bad behavior by imposing previously agreed-upon penalties (e.g., wage cuts for poor performance, premium increases for risky behavior), there would be little problem. But if the badly behaving party can keep her conduct a secret, the put-upon party can't engage in such self-help. The upshot is that one possessing an informational advantage over her contracting partner with respect to her post-contract conduct will be tempted to succumb to bad behavior. Information asymmetry concerning contracting parties' actions thus begets "moral

---

[4]   See National Fed'n of Independent Businesses v. Sebelius, 567 U.S. 519, 231 S.Ct. 2566 (2012).
[5]   See Reed Abelson, UnitedHealth to Pull Back from Insurance Exchanges, Citing Losses, N.Y. *Times* (Apr. 19, 2016); Anna Wilde Mathews and Stephanie Armour, Insurance Options Dwindle in Some Rural Regions, *Wall St. J.* (May 16, 2016); Reed Abelson and Margot Sanger-Katz, Obamacare Options? In Many Parts of the Country, Only One Insurer Will Remain, N.Y. *Times* (Aug. 19, 2016).

hazard" – a temptation to engage in inefficient, but obscurable, conduct for which another must pay.

Moral hazard is quite common. It exists to some degree in nearly all long-term and "relational" contracts such as employment agreements.[6] Given that people enter such contracts all the time, we know moral hazard isn't an insuperable barrier for contracting parties. But when the party who is likely to be a victim of moral hazard has no practicable means of protecting himself (say, by monitoring his contracting partner's behavior), he may be better off avoiding the contract altogether. A potential seller of bad grade insurance, for example, will know that students who buy his product have less incentive to study. If, as is likely, he could not practicably monitor his insureds' study efforts or otherwise ensure their diligence, the insurer would likely choose to forego selling bad grade insurance.

Bad grade insurance thus exemplifies both of the maladies information asymmetry tends to generate, as well as the resulting symptom. An informational imbalance with respect to students' characteristics (aptitude, etc.) leads to adverse selection: The only students likely to buy bad grade insurance are relatively bad students, i.e., those most likely to impose high costs on the insurer. Asymmetric information about insured students' post-contract actions generates moral hazard: Procuring bad grade insurances reduces one's incentive to study hard, and the insurer has no good means to monitor effort and punish shirking. Taken together, those two maladies produce information asymmetry's standard symptom: product unavailability. Bad grade insurance doesn't exist, even though some consumers would likely value it at more than it costs to produce and sell.

AVAILABLE REMEDIES AND THEIR IMPLEMENTATION
DIFFICULTIES AND SIDE EFFECTS

Moral Hazard

As the foregoing discussion suggests, moral hazard is typically addressed by monitoring the behavior of the party that may be tempted to act badly and imposing agreed-upon penalties for malfeasance. The difficulty lies in implementing an effective monitoring system. On that matter, the government usually has no comparative advantage over the party that stands to be harmed by the other's bad behavior. Indeed, government officials tend to be further

---

[6]   Indeed, agency costs are really a result of moral hazard. As Chapter 6 explained, the agency cost disease involves aspects of both externalities and information asymmetry. The asymmetrically distributed information concerns the agent's actions.

removed from the activity to be monitored and thus face a comparative disadvantage relative to the potential victim. Accordingly, moral hazard is rarely addressed via regulation, and we will thus focus here on the other malady arising from information asymmetry: adverse selection.

There are, however, a couple of important things to note about the government's role with respect to moral hazard. One is that government intervention often causes it. Any time private actors believe government officials will rescue them from the adverse consequences of their choices, they are more likely to take inefficient risks. For example, when the US government during the 2008 financial crisis bailed out institutions that had taken significant financial gambles, it sent a moral hazard-inducing signal, one strengthened by the provision in the 2010 Dodd–Frank Financial Reform Act calling for some financial institutions to be officially designated "systemically important" (a.k.a., too big to fail).[7] This is not to say that the bank bailouts were wrong or that Dodd–Frank is altogether misguided; the point here is simply that moral hazard is an inevitable cost of any government action suggesting that private actors will not have to live with the consequences of their decisions. That cost may be worth incurring, but it should be properly accounted for when crafting public policy. Given the ubiquity of governmental rescue efforts, moral hazard is as much a government failure as a market failure.

Not only may government interventions create moral hazard, they may also thwart private efforts to constrain it. Potential victims of moral hazard typically try to limit their exposure by carefully selecting the parties with whom they transact, monitoring their partners' post-transaction behavior, and imposing previously agreed penalties for bad conduct. Candidates who get screened out as bad risks often complain of unfair discrimination. Parties who make it through the screening process sometimes contend that the monitoring of their behavior constitutes an invasion of their privacy. In the face of these complaints, especially when amplified through news media that focus disproportionately on the "victims" of efforts to constrain moral hazard, government officials may face significant pressure to enact anti-discrimination, privacy protection, and other rules that prevent private efforts to reduce moral hazard.

Consider, for example, the reaction to recent efforts by employers to contain their healthcare expenditures. Employer-provided health insurance reduces employees' incentives to make healthful choices that will keep the doctor

---

[7] See Michael S. Gibson, Director, Division of Banking Supervision and Regulation, *Systemically important financial institutions and the Dodd-Frank Act,* Testimony Before the Subcommittee on Financial Institutions and Consumer Credit, Committee on Financial Services, US House of Representatives (May 16, 2012) (describing Dodd–Frank provisions).

away. In recent years, employers have implemented a number of policies to reduce such moral hazard. For example, businesses as diverse as Alaska Airlines, the Cleveland Clinic, and Scotts Miracle-Gro have refused to hire smokers.[8] Other employers have begun actively monitoring their employees' exercise patterns and other lifestyle choices.[9] Both practices have come under attack – the hiring policy as discriminatory, the monitoring as a privacy invasion. If regulators decide to restrict such practices, moral hazard will grow. Again, that's not to say that the practices should go unregulated.[10] Regulators should understand, though, that a cost of tying employers' hands will be an increase in both moral hazard and the inefficiency it generates.

Adverse Selection

We turn, then, to remedies for the other information asymmetry malady, which has more often been the subject of regulation. Recall that adverse selection may occur when the parties to a transaction possess significantly different levels of information about the quality of one party's offering. That situation frequently exists. A doctor, for example, knows more about her skills and the depth of her medical knowledge than her patients do. Managers of a corporation issuing stock know more about the company's prospects than do potential investors. Manufacturers of processed foods know what ingredients their products contain; consumers don't. Food producers also know, unlike consumers, whether their products are organically produced, kosher, or free of genetically modified (GM) ingredients.

A number of remedies are available for alleviating adverse selection resulting from information asymmetry. Some are regulatory, some privately ordered. And some of the privately ordered remedies entail a degree of government intervention, though not what we'd call regulation. To survey

---

[8] See Steve Wartenberg, More employers demand applicants quit smoking, *Columbus Dispatch* (Nov. 25, 2012) (available at www.dispatch.com/content/stories/business/2012/11/25/more-employers-demand-applicants-quit-smoking.html#).

[9] See Elizabeth Dunbar, Employer health monitoring raises privacy concerns, *MPR News* (Nov. 20, 2012) (available at www.mprnews.org/story/2012/11/20/health-monitoring-raises-privacy-concerns).

[10] Nor is it to approve of the typical American practice of having employees receive their health insurance from their employers. The tying of health insurance to employment, which stems from anomalies in the US Tax Code, creates a number of problems in health care and health insurance markets. See Thomas A. Lambert, How the Supreme Court Doomed the ACA to Failure, 35 *Regulation* 32, 36–37 (Winter 2012–2013) (explaining how tax code encourages overly generous health insurance benefits that discourage price competition among health care providers).

the spectrum of available remedies for adverse selection-inducing information asymmetry, consider the different ways the lemons problem is avoided in the markets for the products and services catalogued in the previous paragraph: physician services, corporate stock, processed foodstuffs, organic products, and kosher and non-GM foods.

Licensure

To prevent a lemons problem in markets for the services of doctors, lawyers, and other professionals, governments have generally imposed licensing regimes that endeavor to ensure a minimum level of quality. A person typically may not practice medicine without first graduating from an accredited four-year medical school, completing a multi-year residency program, and passing a series of examinations designed to assess medical competence. Attorneys must successfully complete three years of law school, pass a state bar examination, and demonstrate their "character and fitness" for the practice of law. Service providers as diverse as interior decorators, African hair braiders, and funeral directors are subject to similar licensing regimes, all of which are ostensibly aimed at guaranteeing that service providers won't be duds.[11]

Such licensing requirements (or, in the context of goods, minimum quality standards) prevent a spiral of adverse selection: If consumers expect decent quality, they won't reduce their willingness-to-pay, and higher-quality service providers will remain in the market. That, at least, is the official justification for licensing requirements and minimum quality standards (collectively, licensure regimes). As we'll see, there are also other, less sunny reasons for their prevalence.

Licensure regimes are "palliative" remedies in that they mitigate the symptom of adverse selection – an absence of high-quality offerings – but don't address the underlying disease – information asymmetry between sellers and buyers. They are also highly restrictive, prophylactic remedies in that they ban certain transactions even if the informationally advantaged party has brought the other up to speed. Suppose, for example, that you have a cousin who completed law school and interned for a law firm but never took the bar exam. Even if she told you everything about her training and experience in contract law, and you still believed her fully competent to review a simple contract for you, she could not legally accept payment for doing so. In states requiring that interior decorators hold a license, an acquaintance with impeccable taste

---

[11] See Dick M. Carpenter, II, et al., *License to Work: A National Study of Burdens from Occupational Licensing* 10–11 (Institute for Justice, May 2012) (available at http://ij.org/repor t/license-to-work/).

licensure imposes a ban

couldn't take money for helping you select window treatments, even if you knew every detail about his decorating experience. At the end of the day, a licensure regime imposes a ban, the most restrictive form of regulation.

In light of their restrictiveness, licensure regimes are particularly susceptible to the familiar difficulties that tend to beset regulation generally. First, there is the knowledge problem. How is a government official in Nashville to know that he is enhancing welfare when he bans an experienced but untrained hair shampooer from selling her services to a willing buyer? (Tennessee requires that any "shampoo technician," defined as a "person who brushes, combs, shampoos, rinses and conditions upon the hair and scalp," first complete at least 300 hours of education on the "practice and theory" of shampooing.[12]) Could a bureaucrat in Baton Rouge be sure she was making the world a better place when she banned aspiring florists who had not passed performance examinations graded by incumbent florists from selling their services to willing buyers? It's certainly possible – a near certainty, in fact – that Tennessee's ban on unlicensed shampoo technicians and Louisiana's (now-liberalized) licensing requirements for florists[13] have thwarted transactions that would have left both parties better off.

The knowledge problem exists even for more traditional licensing requirements. Plenty of people might prefer to pay less to have their wills prepared by individuals who have developed expertise in will-drafting but haven't completed law school or mastered unrelated bar-tested subjects such as criminal procedure or commercial paper. Not everyone needs or wants a fully loaded Cadillac all the time; sometimes a Chevy will do. In requiring that will-preparers be qualified to practice any area of law, regulators presume to know potential clients' preferences. When they're wrong, they destroy wealth by thwarting win–win transactions.

Public choice concerns present an even bigger problem for licensure regimes. Because the costs of securing a license or meeting minimum quality standards are usually lower for incumbent providers than for new entrants, licensure regimes tend to create entry barriers that benefit established firms. Accordingly, incumbents often lobby for license restrictions that will insulate them from competition. Following the old "bootleggers and Baptists" playbook, they frequently enlist politically sympathetic "quality advocates" to make a public interest case for the restrictions. While consumers often suffer

[12] See Tennessee Dep't of Comm. & Ins., Shampoo Technician Frequently Asked Questions (available at www.tn.gov/commerce/article/cosmo-shampoo-technician).

[13] See Robert Travis Scott, Florists bill delivered to Gov. Bobby Jindal's desk, *New Orleans Times-Picayune* (June 16, 2010).

a net harm from the reduction in competition, the costs they bear are so widely dispersed that no one has an incentive to incur the expense of counter-lobbying. The result of this familiar pattern of concentrated benefits and diffuse costs is that licensure regimes are regularly imposed, and prove remarkably durable, even when they aren't cost-justified.

Examination of actual licensing patterns suggests that this "malign" public choice account explains more instances of licensure than does the "benign" public interest theory. If licensure were really needed to avoid a lemons problem, as the public interest account holds, then the failure to license an occupation (or otherwise regulate it to avoid adverse selection) would prevent markets from including high-quality offerings. Yet, the vast majority of non-professional occupations that are subject to licensure somewhere in the country are practiced in other areas without any noticeable difference in available quality. Indeed, a recent study of non-professional occupational licensing (i.e., not doctors, lawyers, and the like) found that only 15 of 102 licensed, non-professional occupations were subject to licensing requirements in 40 or more states.[14] On average, a licensed occupation was subject to licensing in only 22 states.[15] The fact that licensed occupations were successfully practiced on an unlicensed basis elsewhere suggests that much occupational licensing is driven by something other than the need to avoid a lemons problem.

The public interest account is also inconsistent with the degree to which licensing burdens vary across states. For example, while ten states require at least 120 days of training for manicurists, Iowa requires just 9 and Alaska only 4.[16] The widespread availability of high-quality manicurist services in Des Moines and Anchorage suggests that the more burdensome requirements in other states have little to do with avoiding adverse selection.

The lack of correlation between the burdensomeness of licensing requirements and the likelihood of adverse selection or any other social harm further undermines the public interest account of occupational licensing. For example, the public interest case for licensing interior decorators, who make few decisions affecting public safety and are generally hired on the basis of reputation,[17] would seem to be far weaker than the case for licensing either emergency medical technicians (who make life-or-death decisions) or locksmiths (whom people typically engage when they are in a jam and can't investigate the service provider's reputation). Yet, the average number of days of education and experience required of interior decorators – 2,190 – swamps that required of emergency medical technicians (33) and locksmiths

---

[14] See License to Work, supra note 11, at 5.   [15] Ibid.   [16] Ibid.

[17] As we'll see, reputation provides a means for avoiding adverse selection.

(77).[18] Something besides a concern for the public interest appears to be driving licensing requirements. <u>The most likely candidate is the self-interest of incumbent licensees.</u>[19]

Mandatory Disclosure *Addresses the underlying disease*

Whereas licensure regimes are palliative remedies that seek to alleviate the symptom of adverse selection, mandatory disclosure regimes address the underlying disease: unbalanced information about one party's offering. Mandatory disclosure approaches are also less restrictive than licensure regimes and, for that reason, entail fewer difficulties resulting from the knowledge problem and public choice concerns.

Under a mandatory disclosure approach, government officials seek to prevent adverse selection by requiring informationally advantaged parties to share specified information with their counterparties. The federal securities laws, for example, require that companies selling ("issuing") securities such as corporate stock first provide potential investors with certain otherwise hidden information about the underlying company and the class of securities being sold. Rules from the US Department of Agriculture (USDA) require that manufacturers of processed foods disclose what ingredients they use, as well as certain nutritional information (calories per serving, etc.). The theory underlying mandatory disclosure approaches, which have been imposed across a host of industries, is that if the informationally disadvantaged party (e.g., the investor) is brought up to speed about the characteristics of the other's offering (e.g., the issuer's stock), she won't reduce her willingness-to-pay to the level of average value, thereby driving high-quality offerings from the market.

In implementing a mandatory disclosure regime, the regulator must decide whether the information at issue must be disclosed from one of

---

[18]   License to Work, supra note 11, at 16–17.

[19]   This is particularly pernicious given that non-professional licensing requirements disproportionately disadvantage the less fortunate. The people seeking to enter non-professional occupations subject to licensing tend to be poorer and less educated than the general population. See License to Work, supra note 11, at 11. It seems perverse to create regulatory barriers to a vocation for such individuals, especially when the barriers appear to be designed to protect incumbent providers from competition.

     Consider, for example, Tennessee's requirement that shampoo technicians complete 300 hours of study. The Cleveland, Tennessee-based Franklin Academy charges $2,700 for its shampoo tech program, not including the $400 required book and kit or the $100 registration fee. Franklin Academy 2015 Catalog 21 (available at www.franklinacademy.edu/consumer-information/downloads/Franklin-Academy-Catalog.pdf). Where is the sense in requiring that individuals seeking to better themselves by becoming shampoo technicians first shell out this sort of money?

the transacting parties directly to each of its partners (direct disclosure), or whether the party making disclosure must do so only once, to some centralized authority (centralized disclosure). USDA's nutritional labeling rules embrace the former approach: Hershey must tell every buyer what's in its chocolate bar. The federal securities laws, by contrast, sometimes require direct disclosure but sometimes follow the centralized disclosure approach: When stock is sold for the first time, the issuer must provide each buyer with an informative prospectus, but after the stock has been sold and is outstanding, the issuer may constructively inform subsequent buyers of company-specific information by making centralized filings with the SEC. Centralized disclosure, which is often less costly than direct disclosure, will generally suffice if the sole purpose of disclosure is to avoid a lemons problem and there are enough "searching" consumers (i.e., buyers who will seek out the information) or intermediaries (e.g., stock analysts) to ensure that market prices reflect the disclosed information. When there are other reasons for mandating disclosure – say, ensuring that people with food allergies can easily learn what they're eating – a direct disclosure regime such as that mandated by the USDA may be warranted.

Being less restrictive than licensure, mandatory disclosure typically entails a less serious knowledge problem and fewer public choice difficulties. The knowledge problem tends to be less severe because regulators are not *banning* offerings they believe to be of low quality, and they therefore need not know how consumers actually value the offerings. Federal securities regulators, for example, do not preclude the sale of securities they presume to be too risky for investors whose risk preferences they do not know. Instead, they require disclosure of risk-relevant information so that investors, who alone are privy to their risk preferences, may know what they're buying. States that have gone beyond mandating disclosure and have instead imposed minimum quality standards for securities under their "blue sky" laws have often destroyed wealth because the officials performing the so-called merits review lacked sufficient information to know what investors would consider a good deal. Regulators in Massachusetts, for example, banned in-state sales of the stock of Apple Inc., currently the world's most valuable company, during the corporation's initial public offering.[20] Apple stock, they decided, was too risky for residents of the commonwealth. Oops.

---

[20] See Shira Ovide and James Oberman, Flashback to Apple's 1980 IPO, *Wall St. J.* (*Deal Journal*, Oct. 6, 2011) (available at http://blogs.wsj.com/deals/2011/10/06/flashback-to-apples-1 980-ipo/).

With respect to public choice concerns, mandatory disclosure is less problematic than licensure because it imposes less significant barriers to entry. It is the difficulty of procuring a license or meeting minimum quality standards that makes licensure so attractive to established firms. Incumbents know that a licensure regime will thwart entry, and they are therefore willing to expend significant resources to have one imposed or maintained. Because the burden mandatory disclosure places on entrants is much less significant, incumbent providers typically will not invest as heavily to procure such regulation. Regulatory capture and other special interest manipulation is thus less likely under a mandatory disclosure approach than under a licensure regime.

This is not to suggest that mandatory disclosure entails *no* knowledge problem or public choice concerns. Any time the government requires someone to do something, it needs to know that the activity it's ordering is value-enhancing (the knowledge problem), and it invites private interests to manipulate the rules to secure advantages for themselves (public choice concerns). Because mandatory disclosure involves mandates, it will inevitably entail some degree of knowledge problem and some public choice concerns.

A knowledge problem exists because regulators must set forth which specific pieces of information must be disclosed. That requires that they know what information is both material to and unknown by the informationally disadvantaged party. Requiring too much disclosure – disclosure of facts that are either known or immaterial – will raise compliance costs unnecessarily. Requiring too little disclosure will fail to alleviate the information asymmetry.

In the end, though, these potential errors may not create that much concern. Disclosure tends to be fairly cheap, so overdoing it shouldn't create too much unwarranted cost.[21] And if mandated disclosure isn't extensive enough, voluntary disclosure, discussed next, may fill the gaps. The knowledge problem is thus a relatively minor issue for most mandatory disclosure regimes that are truly aimed at alleviating adverse-selection-inducing information asymmetries.[22]

---

[21] This is not to suggest that mandatory disclosure is always cheap or ever costless. The cost of complying with disclosure mandates can be significant. For example, the SEC's recent "conflict minerals" and "pay ratio" disclosure requirements, discussed later in the text, were estimated to create initial compliance costs of $3–4 billion and $1.3 billion, respectively. See Ken Tysiac, Conflict Minerals Rule Poses Compliance Challenge, *Journal of Accountancy* (Apr. 1, 2013); Victoria McGrane and Joann S. Lublin, SEC Approval of Pay Gap Rule Sparks Concerns, *Wall St. J.* (Aug. 5, 2015).

[22] When mandatory disclosure regimes venture beyond efforts to alleviate information asymmetry, they frequently create unintended consequences. See infra note 26. The difficulty of anticipating the unintended consequences of a rule is an aspect of the knowledge problem.

Public choice concerns may be a more significant matter for mandatory disclosure approaches. While disclosure mandates create smaller entry barriers than do licensure regimes, such requirements may still invite political manipulation. In recent years, for example, well-organized interest groups have successfully lobbied Congress and the SEC to require corporations to make certain disclosures that have nothing to do with the value of their securities but are instead designed to "shame" the companies into making substantive business decisions that proponents of the disclosure rules favor.

One such rule mandates that companies disclose the degree to which they utilize certain minerals (gold, tin, tantalum, and tungsten) that are produced in war-torn regions of Africa.[23] The SEC itself admitted that the objective of its "conflict minerals" rule is "quite different from the economic or investor protection benefits that [the Commission's] rules ordinarily strive to achieve."[24] The rule's proponents, mainly humanitarian groups, wanted to discourage public companies from buying minerals whose sale could help finance oppressive warlords.

A similar mandate is the SEC's recent rule requiring a covered corporation to disclose, in ratio form, how its workforce's median pay compares to that of its CEO.[25] That "pay ratio" rule isn't aimed at avoiding adverse selection, facilitating capital formation, or protecting investors, but is instead designed to "name and shame" companies whose pay practices contribute to income inequality. The labor unions that lobbied for the rule hoped that it would result in higher wages for their members.

What the conflict minerals and pay ratio rules have in common is that each is the product of efforts by well-organized interest groups to use disclosure mandates to secure concentrated benefits for themselves while imposing costs broadly.[26] Both rules demonstrate that mandatory disclosure, while less restrictive than licensure, is hardly immune to public choice concerns.

---

[23] 17 CFR 240.13p-1 ("Requirement of report regarding disclosure of registrant's supply chain information regarding conflict minerals").

[24] Conflict Minerals, 77 Fed. Reg. 56,274, 56,335 (Sept. 12, 2012).

[25] 17 CFR 222, 249 ("Pay ratio disclosure").

[26] Another thing these two disclosure mandates have in common is that each has had unintended consequences. The conflict minerals rule has increased poverty and violence in Africa's war-torn areas as the mining industry has dried up, eliminating jobs for local residents and driving warlords, who once financed their operations by shaking down miners, to increase their looting of local villages. See David Aronson, How Congress Devastated Congo, *N.Y. Times* (Aug. 7, 2011); Dominic P. Parker and Bryan Vadheim, Resource Cursed or Policy Cursed? US Regulation of Conflict Minerals and Violence in the Congo, 4 *J. of Ass'n of Envtl. & Resource Economists* 1(2017). The pay ratio rule has created a perverse disincentive against hiring low-wage workers and has encouraged firms to outsource low-wage work to foreign

Voluntary Disclosure

As we discussed earlier, the classic example of a market beset by adverse selection-inducing information asymmetry is the used car market. But here's something interesting: There are now, and always have been, thriving markets for used cars. If asymmetric information about the characteristics of offerings causes lemons problems, and if sellers of used cars know significantly more about them than do prospective buyers, why is it so easy to find a decent used car for sale?

The answer, of course, is that sellers of good used cars have discovered credible ways to signal the quality of their offerings. Such signals cause buyers to offer high enough prices to keep good cars in the market. And all this occurs without government mandates. *Voluntary* disclosure thus enables markets for used cars – and for scads of other products and services involving an asymmetry of information between buyers and sellers – to flourish. It is far and away the most common and least problematic remedy for adverse selection-inducing information asymmetry.

Voluntary disclosure that prevents adverse selection may come in many forms. Sellers of high-quality products and services *advertise* their superiority. They *brand* their offerings and invest in developing *reputations* for providing good value. Many producers obtain a *quality certification* from a reputable, third-party evaluator. Others provide *inspection periods* or *free trials* during which buyers may personally assess the quality of the offerings. A *money-back guarantee* informs buyers that the seller is so certain of its offering's quality that it will accept the risk that a buyer may be dissatisfied and rescind the transaction. Prospective employees, who are informationally advantaged about their own skills and abilities, obtain *educational degrees* that signal their aptitude to potential employers. The common thread running through these disparate devices is that the informationally advantaged party is willingly disclosing its high quality to potential transaction partners. And, in markets in which voluntary disclosure is rampant, a provider's failure to send a credible signal of high quality gives rise to a negative inference: that the non-signaling provider's offering is of relatively low quality. Voluntary disclosure, then, can signal both high *and low* quality.

By definition, voluntary disclosure involves no government coercion or threat thereof. It is therefore not "regulation" as this book defines the term.

---

contractors whose working conditions the outsourcing firms cannot control. See Glenn G. Lammi, Conflict Minerals and Pay Ratio: SEC Rules of Unintended Consequences, *Forbes.com* (Nov. 13, 2015) (available at www.forbes.com/sites/wlf/2015/11/13/conflict-minerals-and-pay-ratio-sec-rules-of-unintended-consequences/#4a95ef12ce9b).

But voluntary disclosure regimes sometimes require non-regulatory action by the government. Consider, for example, how voluntary disclosure has been used, with some government help, to address the asymmetry of information between sellers and buyers of three types of food products: organic, kosher, and non-GM foods.

GOVERNMENT SETS VOLUNTARY STANDARDS (E.G., ORGANICS). Despite a paucity of evidence that organically produced food is healthier or less risky than conventionally grown products,[27] many people prefer to consume organic food. This means that sellers can generally charge higher prices for organic than for conventional food products. Consumers, though, have no way of determining on their own whether the peaches on the grocery store shelf are "peach"-peaches (organic) or "lemon"-peaches (conventionally grown). Accordingly, producers of organic foods have looked to voluntary disclosure to prevent a lemons problem: Producers of organic foods have labeled their products as such, and consumers have generally assumed that food products not labeled organic have been conventionally produced.

A problem with this system is that there is no universally accepted understanding of what makes food "organic." Some within the organic community employ strict standards that account for things like the treatment of farm workers and the transportation required to get the product to market. Others employ a more lenient definition that disregards such non-food concerns and would even permit the use of some chemical pesticides. In the 1980s, the use of such divergent organic standards led many consumers to discount claims that products had been "organically" produced. That was troubling because voluntary disclosure requires *credible* signaling by providers of high-quality products.

Congress eventually intervened to facilitate a voluntary disclosure system for organic products. The Organic Foods Production Act of 1990 directed USDA to set forth national organic standards and establish an organic certification program based on recommendations from an expert panel.[28] Standards were first proposed in 1997 and ultimately finalized in 2002.[29] Although the standard-setting process was contentious and many have been dissatisfied with the content of USDA's organic standards (more about that later), having a label with a consistent meaning enabled producers to send credible signals about the latent characteristics of their offerings.

---

[27] Crystal Smith-Spangler, et al., Are Organic Foods Safer or Healthier Than Conventional Alternatives?: A Systematic Review, 157(5) *Annals of Internal Medicine* 348 (Sept. 2012).
[28] 7 U.S.C. § 6501 et seq.   [29] National Organic Program, 7 CFR Part 205 (2002).

The government's creation of a voluntary quality standard thus helped avert a lemons problem in the organic food market.[30]

GOVERNMENT PROTECTS INTELLECTUAL PROPERTY RIGHTS (E.G., KOSHER). Kosher status is similar to organic status in several respects. It's a characteristic for which many consumers are willing to pay a premium. It's generally known by sellers but not buyers. The information asymmetry between sellers and buyers has been addressed through voluntary disclosure (i.e., kosher labeling). Moreover, the term "kosher," like "organic," means different things to different people. Just as members of the organic community disagree on the wages required of farm workers and the permissibility of certain pesticides, groups of observant Jews have diverged in their interpretation of Jewish food laws. (For example, must gelatin be derived from properly slaughtered, non-forbidden animals? Jewish groups are split on that question.[31])

With kosher, however, the government has not intervened to set any kind of common standard. Instead, standard-setting has been left to market competition. Different Jewish groups have crafted different marks, such as the Orthodox Union's iconic "O" encircling a smaller "U." (Look for it.) Each group's mark indicates that the designated product is kosher under the relevant group's unique standard. Competing certification agencies currently utilize more than 200 registered kosher symbols in the United States.[32] This decentralized voluntary disclosure system prevents a lemons problem in the market for kosher foods and enables consumers with different understandings of what the Jewish food laws require to satisfy their heterogeneous preferences. The government's only role is to provide a system for protecting intellectual property rights (i.e., the competing certifiers' trademarks).

---

[30] Government creation of voluntary quality standards has similarly helped prevent adverse selection in meat markets. Under USDA's voluntary meat grading program, producers of meat and poultry may have federal inspectors certify the quality of their products. See US Dep't of Agriculture, Agriculture Marketing Service, *United States Standards for Grades of Slaughter Cattle* (Gov't Printing Office 1996). Utilizing a government-provided standard, inspectors assess the expected tastiness of the meat at issue. Beef, for example, is graded (from most to least tasty) as prime, choice, select, standard, commercial, utility, cutter, or canner. Informationally disadvantaged buyers may rely on the USDA grades in determining the amount they are willing to pay for a particular piece of meat. Sellers of high quality meat can thus be assured that buyers won't reduce their willingness-to-pay out of concern that they'll end up with "lemony" meat.

[31] See Benjamin Gutman, Ethical Eating: Applying the Kosher Food Regulatory Regime to Organic Food, 108 *Yale L. J.* 2351, 2366 (1999).

[32] Ibid. at 2376.

GOVERNMENT JUST REMOVES REGULATORY BARRIERS (E.G., NON-GM FOODS). Sometimes, the only thing the government needs to do to facilitate voluntary disclosure is to step out of the way. That was the case with non-GM foods.

Like organic and kosher status, non-GM status is appealing to many consumers and may allow a seller to charge a premium price. The same basic information asymmetry exists, for sellers know their products' GM status while prospective buyers don't. Given the success of voluntary disclosure in averting lemons problems and enabling thriving markets for organic and kosher products, we would expect that similar labeling would allow markets for non-GM products to flourish. While a trip down the aisle of an American supermarket reveals that such labeling is now occurring, widespread non-GM labeling has been a long time coming. That's largely because of hurdles imposed by the government.

In a 2001 document entitled *Draft Guidance for Industry: Voluntary Labeling Indicating Whether Foods Have or Have Not Been Developed Using Bioengineering*, the US Food and Drug Administration (FDA) created a virtual minefield for producers hoping to advertise their products' non-GM status. FDA directed such producers to:

- Steer clear of acronyms such as "GM" and "GMO" (because consumers purportedly don't know what they mean);
- Avoid claiming that a product is not genetically modified (because products containing any traditionally hybridized ingredient, even products containing no ingredient subject to modern bioengineering, have technically been "genetically modified");
- Eschew references to being free of GM "organisms" or "GMOs" (because they falsely imply that other products contain "organisms" – i.e., living things);
- Refrain from claiming to be "GM-free" (because virtually no food product is 100% "free" of all GM products); and
- Avoid any suggestion that the labeled item is superior to a non-GM version of the product (because there is no scientific proof that GM products are less healthy or riskier than their non-GM counterparts).

These governmental directives made it difficult for producers to advertise their products as non-GM. Indeed, the challenge the *Draft Guidance* created was similar to that presented in the board game *Taboo*, in which players must provide clues to get their teammates to identify a particular word (e.g., kangaroo) but are forbidden to speak any of the words one would most naturally use in conveying those clues (e.g., pouch, hop, animal, Australia, captain). Faced with implicit threats of fraud charges for using the aforementioned "taboo" terms in describing their products, producers of non-GM foods largely avoided voluntary disclosure of their products' status. Had non-GM labeling become widespread, it would have given rise to a negative inference that products not labeled non-GM did, in fact, contain GM ingredients.[33]

In the years since 2001, it has become apparent that government officials are unlikely to enforce the specific principles set forth in the Draft Guidance.[34] Given the widespread consumer demand for information on GM status, FDA would face a significant backlash if it took action against a producer that transgressed one of the agency's highly restrictive guidelines on non-GM labeling. As producers have realized that FDA's guidance is mainly an effort to achieve an *in terrorem* effect, non-GM labeling has proliferated. This has enabled interested consumers to know which products are non-GM and, by negative inference, which products *do* contain GM ingredients. Such information asymmetry-reducing voluntary disclosure likely would have occurred years earlier had FDA not taken action to prevent it.

So why did the agency act as it did? While we can never know for certain, the anomalous substance of the non-GM labeling guidance is suggestive. The guidance is far harder on the (typically small) producers that would like to engage in non-GM labeling than FDA normally is on the large food companies with which it regularly interacts. For example, while giant food companies are allowed to label products "fat free" even when they contain

---

[33] The negative inference from widespread labeling of non-GM foods would render unnecessary any mandatory labeling of GM products, something a number of consumer groups have demanded and one state now requires. See, e.g., Stephanie Strom, Vermont Will Require Labeling of Genetically Altered Foods, N.Y. Times (Apr. 23, 2014). A voluntary negative labeling regime for non-GM products is superior to a mandatory positive labeling system for at least four reasons. First, mandatory labeling of GM products will involve more labeling and thus higher administrative costs. (An estimated 70 percent of foods on the shelves of American grocery stores contain GM ingredients.) Second, voluntary negative labeling requires those who demand the information at issue – consumers who prefer non-GM products – to bear the cost of the information they are demanding. Third, mandating GM labeling gives the false impression that the government has reason to believe consumption of GM products is harmful; there is no credible evidence that GM foods pose health risks. Finally, to the extent a mandatory labeling rule stokes irrational fears of GM products, it may cause producers to remove them from their offerings, reducing consumer choice. These points are developed in greater detail in Thomas A. Lambert and Philip G. Peters, Regulatory Barriers to Consumer Information About Genetically Modified Foods, in *Labeling Genetically Modified Food: The Philosophical and Legal Debate* 158–60, Paul Weirich, ed. (Oxford: Oxford University Press 2007).

[34] In the recently finalized version of the Guidance, FDA clarified that it did not intend to take enforcement action against producers using taboo terms, though it still recommended that they not be used. *Guidance for Industry: Voluntary Labeling Indicating Whether Foods Have or Have Not Been Derived from Genetically Engineered Plants* (Nov. 2015) (available at www.fda .gov/Food/GuidanceRegulation/GuidanceDocumentsRegulatoryInformation/ucm059098 .htm#top).

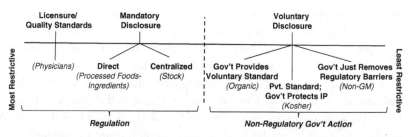

FIGURE 8.1 Available Remedies for Adverse Selection-Inducing
Information Asymmetry

small quantities of fat, "GM-free" labeling is forbidden because of the likelihood of trace amounts of non-GM ingredients. Similarly, Big Food is
permitted to label foods as being free of artificial colors and flavors, despite
the lack of evidence that such additives are harmful, but "non-GM" labels are
forbidden if they "misleadingly" suggest nutritional superiority or reduced
risk. The disparate treatment of smaller upstart businesses versus giant repeat
players suggests that FDA has been captured by its most powerful regulatees.[35]

The takeaway lesson from the non-GM labeling experience is that government restrictions, often the product of agency capture or some other public
choice malady, may thwart the sort of voluntary disclosure that prevents
adverse selection. That is not to say that all regulation of voluntary disclosure
is illicit or undesirable as a policy matter; truly misleading "disclosure" should
be forbidden. But consumers aren't nitwits, as the non-GM guidance
appeared to assume. Wise policymakers will ask whether the purported con-
sumer-protective benefits of a disclosure restriction outweigh the harms of
denying consumers valuable information. In a close case, government should
stay its hand and permit voluntary disclosure.

Figure 8.1 summarizes the range of available remedies for adverse selection-
inducing information asymmetry. In terms of restrictiveness, the remedies vary

---

[35] Agency capture resulting in similar regulatory barriers to voluntary disclosure has occurred in
the past. One example involves FDA's first foray into labels concerning bioengineering: its
1994 rules on the labeling of milk from cows that had not been treated with rBST (a genetically
engineered enzyme). Those rules discouraged "no rBST" labeling by requiring that any such
labels refer only to the process of milk production, not the milk itself, and include an
affirmative disclaimer that treating cows with rBST does not affect their milk. US Food &
Drug Admin., Interim Guidance on the Voluntary Labeling of Milk and Milk Products from
Cows That Have Not Been Treated with Recombinant Bovine Somatotropin, 59 Fed. Reg.
6279 (Feb. 10, 1994). It turns out the rules were drafted by a lawyer who had represented
Monsanto, the manufacturer of rBST, before becoming FDA's Deputy Commissioner for
Policy. Soon after leaving FDA, he became head of Monsanto's Washington, D.C. office. See
Lambert and Peters, supra note 33, at 173.

from highly restrictive licensure, where the government bans offerings that do not meet minimum quality standards, to lenient policies where the only government involvement is to remove regulatory barriers to voluntary disclosure. Remedies to the left of the dotted vertical line constitute regulation as this book defines it (i.e., threat-backed commands aimed at alleviating a defect in private ordering). Remedies to the right of the dotted line may involve some government action, but of a non-regulatory variety.

Having set forth the range of available remedies for treating adverse selection-inducing information asymmetry, we turn to consider how policymakers should go about selecting among them.

Choosing a Remedy

THE PRESUMPTIVE REMEDY. Unlike both licensure and mandatory disclosure, voluntary disclosure involves no threat-backed governmental commands. Accordingly, voluntary disclosure regimes avoid the two chief side effects of governmental fiat: the knowledge problem and public choice concerns. Because regulators neither mandate minimum quality standards nor specify what information must be disclosed, they need not know consumer preferences. Because they do not order producers to do anything, they do not inspire lobbying aimed at securing some competitive advantage. Voluntary disclosure, then, should be the *presumptive* remedy for adverse selection-inducing information asymmetry.

We will consider in a moment how the presumption in favor of a voluntary disclosure regime might be rebutted – i.e., when does it make sense to impose a more restrictive mandatory disclosure or licensure regime? Before turning to that matter, though, we should consider the appropriate degree of government involvement when voluntary disclosure is indeed the optimal remedy for information asymmetry. Specifically, when should policymakers move beyond simply removing unwarranted regulatory barriers to voluntary disclosure (as with non-GM labeling) and protecting intellectual property rights (as with kosher marks) and actually develop a voluntary standard (as with organic certification)?

In general, governmental setting of voluntary standards is more appropriate the fewer the number of criteria in the standard and the less subjective or "value-laden" they are. Even putting aside issues related to the establishment of religion, it would be a bad idea for the government to set kosher standards. There are a great many criteria involved in determining the kosher status of a product, and they are closely tied to diverse individuals' subjective beliefs and personal values. Defining kosher should be left entirely to private ordering. By contrast, there are few criteria in grading the quality of beef – primarily

the maturity of the slaughtered animal and the degree of fat marbling throughout the meat. Moreover, those matters do not relate to most people's (save
perhaps some Texans') closely held beliefs and values. There's little downside
to having a government-provided standard for grading beef, and such
a standard does facilitate voluntary disclosure by producers.
The government's setting of a voluntary standard thus seems appropriate
here, even if privately developed standards could have emerged.

Organic status falls somewhere between these two examples, though perhaps closer to kosher than to beef grades. Although there are numerous criteria
involved in determining whether food is organic, the specific rules seem less
value-laden than the kosher rules. (They are not, at least, a religious matter.)
For many people, however, consuming organically produced food is a matter
of ethical significance.

Not surprisingly, then, the government's involvement in setting organic
standards has been controversial. USDA took a dozen years (from 1990 to
2002) to create the standards Congress ordered. The agency abandoned its first
set of standards after they garnered more than 275,000 written comments – the
most USDA had ever received on a proposed rule. The ink had hardly dried on
the finalized 2002 standards before dissatisfied members of the organic community began seeking private alternatives. Just two-and-a-half years after the
government's organic standard was implemented, the *Wall Street Journal*
reported a proliferation of alternative private labels such as "biodynamic,"
"Food Alliance Certified," "beyond organic," and "tairwa" (derived from the
French word *terroir*, which translates loosely to "the essence of the land").[36]

On the one hand, the organic experience demonstrates how difficult it can
be for government officials to set voluntary standards on a multi-dimensional
matter with ethical implications. On the other hand, the experience suggests
that, as long as the government's standard is not exclusive, creation of even
a "bad" voluntary standard is unlikely to cause much harm; private certifiers
can step in with alternatives if the government-provided standard proves
unsatisfactory.[37] An additional lesson for policymakers, then, is that their
promulgation of a voluntary standard should not impose barriers to the creation of competing private standards.

---

[36] Katy McLaughlin, Is Your Tofu Biodynamic? Making Sense of the Latest Organic Food
      Terminology, *Wall St. J.* D1 (Apr. 19, 2005).
[37] Indeed, even with the uncontroversial beef grading standards, private certifiers have supple-
      mented the government-provided standards. For example, Certified Angus Beef LLC provides
      a certification over-and-above USDA's prime grade. Certified Angus Beef® must pass ten
      exacting specifications, including "less than 1-inch fat thickness," "no neck hump exceeding
      two inches," and "practically free of capillary ruptures."

THE CASE FOR MANDATORY DISCLOSURE. Mandatory disclosure, which involves greater side effects than voluntary disclosure but less than licensure, may be appropriate when voluntary disclosure is unlikely to occur.[38] That may be the case in at least four circumstances.

First, if there is little competition in the market at issue, providers may be insufficiently motivated to tout the quality of their offerings in order to win sales from rivals. If providers with high-quality offerings choose not to incur the cost of disclosing information about their superior quality (thereby implicitly impugning the quality of rivals who do not engage in similar disclosure), consumers may have a hard time distinguishing high- from low-quality offerings. Mandatory disclosure may then be needed to correct the sort of information asymmetry that generates adverse selection.

Second, producers may be loath to disclose even *good* information on some topic if merely raising the topic is likely to turn off a significant number of buyers. The safest airlines, for example, almost never advertise their exemplary safety records because simply bringing up crash risk is likely to dissuade some consumers from flying altogether. In the 1930s, automobile manufacturers advertised the comparative safety of their vehicles, but such advertising subsequently disappeared because automakers believed that calling attention to potential safety problems would hurt them, by scaring people off cars altogether, more than it would help them.[39] The same dynamic has prevented producers of safer tobacco products from disclosing their relative safety and thereby exposing the relative riskiness of rival products. As Professor Cass Sunstein has observed, "[c]ompetition over the extent of danger may decrease total purchases of [a risky] product, rather than help any manufacturer to obtain greater sales."[40] In such circumstances, disclosure mandates may be warranted.

Third, when the quality concern relates to some trait that is both negative and uncommon, voluntary disclosure may prove anemic. Voluntary disclosure corrects information asymmetry when producers possessing positive traits

---

[38] An oft-asserted, but ultimately specious, ground for mandating disclosure is to ensure apples-to-apples comparisons among providers. It is true that mandatory disclosure leads to standardization of the disclosed information if the regulator mandates that each provider disclose information on the same matters and in the same fashion. Such consistency could be achieved less restrictively, however, by having the government establish a voluntary certification system like the organic standard. The need for a consistent disclosure format, then, is not sufficient to justify a mandatory disclosure regime.

[39] Stephen Breyer, *Regulation and Its Reform* (Cambridge, MA: Harvard University Press, 1982) 28.

[40] Cass R. Sunstein, Informing America: Risk, Disclosure, and the First Amendment, 20 *Fla. St. L. Rev.* 653, 656 (1993).

or lacking negative ones willingly proclaim their status, creating an adverse inference that those remaining silent lack the positive traits or possess the negative ones. Sometimes, though, a negative trait is so rare that advertising "negative trait-free" becomes worthless since everyone else is making the same claim. Those much-maligned (but oh-so-delicious) trans fats may fall into this category. When Krispy Kreme and Dunkin' Donuts proclaim that their products contain zero grams of trans fat (as the companies now do), consumers begin to wonder if *anything* really contains trans fats, and they pay no mind to "no trans fats" labeling. Mandatory disclosure of trans fats (positive labeling) may provide a better means of correcting the information asymmetry between producers and consumers.[41]

Finally, firms may fail to make voluntary disclosures because they know that doing so could confer benefits on their rivals. This seems to be the strongest argument in favor of the mandatory disclosure provisions of the securities laws.

Even without government mandates, companies issuing securities like corporate stock have strong incentives to disclose all sorts of information about themselves and the securities they're offering. Disclosing good news increases the desirability, and thus the price, of the securities. And once an issuer starts disclosing good news, it's hard to keep mum about bad news. If the news on some issue were *fairly* bad, an issuer that typically disclosed good news would still reveal it, knowing that investors assume the worst about matters on which an otherwise vocal issuer is silent.[42] If the news were *really* bad – the worst – an issuer might remain silent, but then investors would be correct in assuming the worst.

Of course, an issuer's disclosures are of little value if investors don't believe them. But common law prohibitions on fraud, which have been enshrined and expanded in the securities laws, lend credence to stock issuers' claims. Moreover, firms regularly vouch for their disclosures by utilizing a number of verification and certification devices. For example, firms regularly hire auditors – outside accountants whose livelihoods depend on their reputations for trustworthiness – to certify their financial statements. Issuers also typically sell their securities through investment bankers who investigate the issuer, buy the

---

[41] Note, however, that when a negative trait is uncommon, the possibility that a product or service possesses it may generate little adverse selection. If consumers recognize the rarity of the negative trait, they will discount their willingness-to-pay for the product or service at issue by only a small amount, which should drive only a few producers from the market. If consumers don't make subsequent adjustments to their willingness-to-pay on the assumption that top-quality offerings will exit the market, an adverse selection "death spiral" is unlikely.

[42] See Frank H. Easterbrook and Daniel R. Fischel, *The Economic Structure of Corporate Law* (Cambridge, MA: Harvard University Press, rev. edn., 1996,) 289.

new securities for resale, and earn reputations with the customers to whom they resell the securities. (Indeed, "banker-vouching" may explain why securities are usually underwritten by syndicates of investment banks rather than by single banks; while a lone bank could usually handle the offering at issue, distributing securities through a group of banks increases the reputational capital supporting the offering.)

Firms may also enhance the credibility of their voluntary disclosures by compensating their managers, at least in part, in firm stock and by issuing debt. Equity-based compensation signals that management believes the firm to be fairly valued on the basis of its public disclosures. Debt financing requires the firm to make regular interest payments, which will force it to return to capital markets where it will be "punished" for any past misrepresentations or material omissions.[43]

Given that stock issuers have both a motive to reveal hidden information and means for doing so credibly, it should not be surprising that corporations made extensive disclosures of the sort now mandated even before the securities laws demanded them. As Judge Frank Easterbrook and Prof. Daniel Fischel have explained, "[b]y 1934, when Congress first required annual disclosure by some companies, every firm traded on the national markets made voluminous public disclosures certified by independent auditors."[44] From 1934 to 1964, when firms could avoid annual disclosure by not listing their stock on a national exchange, firms eagerly opted-in to the disclosure regime, and even firms that were not listed disclosed substantial amounts of information. Today, the securities of state and local governments are exempt from mandatory disclosure rules, but issuing states and localities still supply extensive information to investors. Both theory and experience, then, suggest that mandates aren't necessary to generate a great deal of disclosure by securities issuers.

But the degree of voluntary disclosure by securities issuers may not be *optimal* because of third-party effects – primarily positive externalities that benefit a disclosing firm's rivals and those rivals' stockholders.[45] For example, disclosure of industry facts that are not firm-specific may assist the shareholders of rivals within the industry. Disclosure of some firm-specific information – e.g., a new product in the works – could provide a competitive benefit to

---

[43]   Ibid. at 282 ("Compulsory payouts ensure that managers return to the capital market for funds, and investors then may check up on their performance before recommitting funds").

[44]   Ibid. at 289. Easterbrook and Fischel further observe that the use of auditors, whose chief function is to certify the veracity of firms' financial claims, can be traced back to the beginning of the corporation. Ibid.

[45]   Recall from Chapter 4 that when conduct generates positive externalities, people will tend to do too little of it.

rivals. Disclosure of comparative information – how disclosing firm A's prospects compare to rival B's – tells shareholders of rivals (B investors) something
they'd like to know. Rivals and their shareholders are also benefited if
a disclosing firm develops a particularly effective disclosure format that rivals
can mimic.

These potential positive externalities create a collective action problem:
Firms would benefit if they *and their rivals* all disclosed the sorts of information described above (i.e., in addition to the gain from its own disclosures,
each firm would capture some benefit from its rivals' disclosures), but each
individual firm benefits even more if it remains silent on the matters while its
rivals disclose. Under such circumstances, most firms may decide to keep
quiet on the matters at issue, and the value-maximizing outcome won't occur.
What is needed is some kind of coordinator that can induce all firms to
disclose in concert. The government may play that role by imposing mandatory disclosure rules.

But governmental mandates may not be necessary to correct the collective
action problem described above; private entities may be able to induce the
required coordination. Consider, for example, the role played by organized
stock exchanges like the New York Stock Exchange (NYSE) and the NASDAQ.
Such exchanges greatly reduce transaction costs, making stock more attractive
to investors. Issuing corporations thus have an incentive to list their shares on an
organized exchange. Each exchange, in turn, has a motivation to adopt rules
(listing standards) that enhance the attractiveness of listed stock and thereby
increase the volume of trading on the exchange. Because investors would prefer
to avoid risks resulting from the non-disclosure of important matters, stock
exchanges have an incentive to require listed companies to disclose material
facts, including those whose disclosure entails the sort of positive externalities
discussed above. Thus, as Easterbrook and Fischel explain,

> Organized exchanges offer the firms a way to cope with the collective action
> problem [identified above]. The firms can agree to be bound by the rules set
> by the exchange, and these rules can come closer to requiring optimal
> disclosure because they will "internalize" many of the third-party effects.
> Firms that bind themselves to follow the exchange's rules will have
> a competitive advantage in attracting capital.[46]

For these reasons, it should come as no surprise that private stock exchanges
traditionally required the sort of disclosures the government now mandates.
For example, even before the securities laws were enacted, the NYSE required

---

[46]   Easterbrook and Fischel, supra note 42, at 295.

extensive disclosures when a listed stock was issued and annually thereafter, regardless of whether the issuing firm had sold new securities.[47]

It seems, then, that even when disclosure may create positive externalities so that some sort of coordination is required to overcome a collective action problem, *government* mandates may not be needed or appropriate. A wise regulator will compare the downsides of imposing a government-mandated disclosure system (e.g., knowledge and public choice problems like those revealed by the SEC's conflict minerals rule) against the costs of relying on private ordering (e.g., potentially suboptimal disclosure).

THE CASE FOR LICENSURE. Finally, under what circumstances should regulators proceed beyond mandatory disclosure and impose a licensure regime to remedy adverse selection-inducing information asymmetry? Answering that question requires recognizing that such a move is fundamentally paternalistic: The government essentially says that *even if* the informationally disadvantaged party in a transaction is brought up to speed about the quality of an offering – a result that could be obtained with some sort of mandatory disclosure – she should still be barred from transacting for the offering if the government deems it to be of insufficient quality. When is such paternalism justified?

The short answer is, rarely. A paternalist strategy of this sort involves a nearly intractable knowledge problem: How can government officials, who are not privy to individuals' preferences, know they're improving welfare when they bar someone from entering a transaction she believes is in her interest? Because the strategy ultimately entails a ban, it also invites manipulation by special interests seeking a competitive advantage and will thus create substantial public choice concerns. In light of such serious side effects, moving from mandatory disclosure to licensure requires a compelling justification.

There are two possible grounds for such a move. First, a paternalistic licensure strategy might be appropriate if there are convincing reasons to believe (1) that people who transact for low-quality offerings are systematically making mistakes they will later regret, (2) that government officials can identify the minimum quality standards that will prevent such regret without thwarting too many mutually beneficial exchanges, and (3) that empowering officials to impose those standards won't invite an abuse of power by private interests. The next chapter considers this "systematic mistakes" rationale for paternalist regulation, so we'll skip it for now.

---

[47] Ibid.

Licensure might also be warranted where people's voluntary selection of low-quality offerings threatens to impose costs on others. If you choose to purchase surgery (at a bargain price) from a provider who you know has little education and experience, you will not be the only one facing a risk; your family members and friends – and probably numerous strangers who will have to intervene – will be adversely effected if you experience a bad outcome. If you save money by hiring an amateur pilot off Craigslist to fly you and your friends down to Mexico for the weekend, you impose risks on lots of people who won't be on the plane and haven't consented to those risks. When a transaction involving a low-quality offering threatens to harm people who are not parties to the transaction, government imposition of minimum quality standards (licensure) may be appropriate even if the parties to the transaction are fully informed as to the quality of the offering.

There are two things to note about this ground for licensure. First, it's not based on asymmetric information. The objective here is not to prevent adverse selection that could preclude a market for high-quality offerings; rather, it is to prevent a spillover of costs. Licensure in this instance is just a version of the command-and-control remedy for negative externalities, the subject of Chapter 4. Its propriety should be analyzed under the principles set forth there.

A second thing to note about the negative externalities justification for licensure is that it should be narrowly construed. With a little creativity, one can hypothesize adverse third-party effects to justify minimum quality standards or licensure for just about any product or service. "Prissy Aunt Margaret might faint or develop heartburn if the flowers are too tacky at your wedding. Louisiana was right – florists *should* be licensed!" "If your hair is over-conditioned, it will be flat tonight and your date will suffer embarrassment. Thank goodness Tennessee licenses shampoo technicians!"

These are absurd examples, of course, but the special interests clamoring for licensure and the competitive advantage it confers are a wily lot; they've managed to procure protectionist licensure regimes on the basis of some pretty far-fetched theories of third-party harm. The wise regulator will allow potential negative externalities to justify licensure only if the expected third-party effects are *significant*. Specifically, she will insist that the likely gain to overall welfare from preventing those externalities exceed the expected welfare loss from thwarting transactions involving lower-quality offerings. That condition may be satisfied for the services of doctors, pilots, emergency medical technicians, and school bus drivers. It almost certainly is not for the services of makeup artists (subject to licensing in 36 states), auctioneers (33 states), taxidermists

(26 states), travel guides (21 states), travel agents (8 states), upholsterers (7 states), and interior designers (4 states).[48]

Information Asymmetry and Opportunity

Before we close, one final observation on selecting a remedy for adverse selection-inducing information asymmetry. This chapter has described information asymmetry as a problem, and indeed it is one. But it can also present an opportunity for profit. Entrepreneurs have long sought to make money – and create social value – by developing ways to correct informational imbalances and thereby facilitate transactions that wouldn't otherwise occur. For example, Carfax, a web-based business that provides buyers with vehicle history reports on used automobiles, has made loads of money addressing Akerlof's original lemons problem.[49] As technology advances, entrepreneurs discover new ways to profit by alleviating information asymmetry.

Just a few years back, most people wouldn't have dreamt of paying a (possibly deranged) stranger for the opportunity to sleep in his (possibly filthy) guestroom or take a (possibly unsafe) ride in his car. Most of us would have transacted for such services only if the price were extremely low to account for the risks we were taking. People possessing nice spare bedrooms, clean and comfortable back seats, and superior driving skills would never have peddled their services because they would have known that buyers, expecting average or below quality, would pay little. Information asymmetry thus generated a lemons problem that precluded the emergence of markets for spare bedrooms and unlicensed rides around town.

We all know what happened. Some enterprising entrepreneurs, pursuing profit for themselves, figured out how to create Internet platforms where sellers of spare bedroom spaces and rides around town could connect with potential buyers, *and* (this is the crucial part) each could learn about the quality of the other's offering from that person's previous transaction partners. Uber, Airbnb, and other so-called sharing economy companies employ a reciprocal rating system where buyer and seller evaluate each other following a transaction, and the rating each receives is then incorporated into an average that is disclosed to subsequent transaction partners. These businesses thrive precisely because of information asymmetry. By offering privately ordered solutions to the problem, they allow previously under-utilized assets to generate heretofore unrealized value. And they enrich the people who created and financed them. It's a marvelous thing.

---

[48] See License to Work, supra note 11, at 10–11.
[49] See About Carfax, www.carfax.com/company/about.

Activists critical of intellectual property laws have long proclaimed that information "wants to be free." The history of entrepreneurs who have turned lemons problems into lemonade teaches us something else about information: It doesn't want to remain asymmetrically distributed. To the extent information asymmetry precludes value-creating transactions, it invites entrepreneurs to discover ways to unlock the squandered value. As information technology develops, innovators are increasingly able to do so. Policymakers should keep this in mind when selecting a remedy for information asymmetry. They should not erect barriers to information asymmetry-reducing innovations, and they should avoid locking in costly mandatory disclosure and licensure regimes that could destroy the incentive to innovate.

LESSONS FOR POLICYMAKERS

Information asymmetry, the disease generating the sorts of moral hazard and adverse selection that may prevent markets from producing goods and services that would provide more value than they would cost to produce, is ubiquitous. Yet it rarely warrants a regulatory fix. When the government steps out of the way, private ordering usually provides the optimal remedy to the maladies caused by serious information asymmetries.

When it comes to asymmetric information about contracting parties' post-contract conduct, the source of moral hazard, "far-from-the-action" governmental authorities are usually less able than the put-upon contracting party to ferret out and punish the other party's malfeasance. Accordingly, policymakers' primary responses to moral hazard should be (1) not to create it (as with government bailouts following excessive risk-taking by private businesses), and (2) not to thwart privately ordered efforts to reduce it (as with overly strict privacy and non-discrimination rules that make it hard to identify high-risk contracting parties and to sanction bad post-contract behavior).

With respect to information asymmetry about the quality of contracting parties' offerings, the source of adverse selection, voluntary disclosure usually corrects serious informational imbalances. Most of the time, the government needs only to (1) get out of the way (as it failed to do with GM labeling) and (2) protect the intellectual property rights (trademarked labels, etc.) of parties making voluntary disclosures. Beyond those two things, policymakers may seek to facilitate adverse selection-reducing voluntary disclosure by creating voluntary quality standards. Such standard-setting is generally inappropriate, however, when the matter at issue is value-laden and involves assessment along a large number of dimensions. (So governmental standards for beef grades are appropriate, while a governmental kosher standard wouldn't be).

Mandating disclosure of offering quality may be appropriate if there is reason to believe voluntary disclosure will be anemic. That may be the case if either (1) there is little competition among the providers in a market, (2) the topic on which disclosure is needed is one whose very invocation may dissuade potential contracting partners (e.g., tobacco risk), (3) the quality concern at issue is both negative and rare (e.g., the use of trans fats), or (4) there is a significant potential that voluntary disclosure will inure to the benefit of the disclosing firm's rivals (e.g., the situation facing issuers of corporate securities).

Licensure, which entails both a serious knowledge problem and considerable public choice concerns, seems an appropriate response to adverse selection-inducing information asymmetry only when people's voluntary selection of low-quality offerings threatens to impose significant costs on others. In that case, however, the primary concern is negative externalities, so policymakers should assess the propriety of a licensing regime – a form of command-and-control – in light of the principles set forth in Chapter 4.

9

Cognitive Limitations and Behavioral Quirks

He is the bane of every economics professor's existence. If you've taken a college-level economics course, you've encountered him or someone like him. His name, for our purposes, is Gadfly. He majors in something liberal artsy (philosophy, English?) or maybe another of the social sciences (psychology, sociology?). He's not a back-row student; he sits toward the front of the lecture hall, and he's an active participant in class discussion. But he is assuredly *not* buying what his economics professor is selling. Whenever the professor suggests that the government should do x to induce people to do y, or that well-meaning policy a is bad because it will just lead people to take undesirable action b, Gadfly's hand shoots up. "Real people don't behave that way," he says. "You're assuming people always act rationally. They often don't."

The economics professor has generally given Gadfly's remarks short shrift. "Yeah, yeah. People sometimes act irrationally," she has replied. "But most people act rationally most of the time. And we can't build a predictive theory of human behavior if we assume people just dart around making irrational, unpredictable decisions."

It turns out both Gadfly and his professor are right. Gadfly is correct in observing that people often act irrationally. The professor is right that people *usually* act rationally and that economists might as well close up shop if people act in unpredictable ways.

But what if people are, to borrow the title of economist Dan Ariely's bestselling book, *predictably* irrational?[1] That is, what if they generally act rationally but, in certain identifiable contexts, make the same sorts of mistakes over and over again?

---

[1] Dan Ariely, *Predictably Irrational: The Hidden Forces That Shape Our Decisions* (New York: HarperCollins, 2008).

In recent years, many social scientists – including scores of economists – have come to believe that this is indeed how humans behave.[2] Numerous studies purporting to document people's systematically irrational behavior have led many scholars to jettison the so-called rational choice model of human behavior, under which humans are assumed to act as rational, self-interest maximizers. In its place, they have adopted a "behavioral" model under which people usually act rationally but occasionally – in systematic ways – make irrational decisions. Key questions for policymakers are whether the government should intervene to protect people from irrational decisions (or somehow exploit those irrationalities to achieve "good" outcomes), and if so, how.

Before we delve into things, it is worth noting that the interventions considered in this chapter, unlike those previously examined, are not aimed at a *market* failure. A true market failure exists when the interaction of free individuals who are rationally pursuing their own best interests and not violating the well-established rights of others systematically fails to maximize social welfare. Externalities, public goods, market power, and information asymmetry generate genuine market failures; agency costs are the result of a couple of market failures (externalities and information asymmetry). Our concern in this chapter is not some welfare-reducing defect in *the system itself* but instead a collection of deficiencies that purportedly inhere in the *individual players* that operate within the system. Although there is no genuine market failure here, the deficiencies we will consider may generate predictable welfare losses that threat-backed governmental directives could conceivably lessen.

SYMPTOMS/DISEASE

Regret happens. People regularly make decisions that they later wish they'd never made. Often, that's because, well, other stuff happens. Changed circumstances may render a previously chosen course of action undesirable. Regret may also occur when people rationally fail to gather all available facts before selecting a path. Because information is costly, rational decisionmakers will gather only those pieces of information that appear to offer greater marginal benefit than their marginal cost. Sometimes, even optimally informed decisionmakers – those who have investigated the matter at issue to the point at which the incremental cost of additional study would exceed

---

[2] See generally Richard H. Thaler, *Misbehaving: The Making of Behavioral Economics* (New York: W.W. Norton, 2015).

the expected incremental benefit – will miss a crucial but buried piece of information and will make a decision that, in light of perfect information, seems improvident.

There's really nothing the government can – or should – do about these sorts of regret. Obviously, the government can't prevent the occurrence of change (the first source of regret), and if acquiring some information isn't cost-justified (the second source), it hardly seems wise for the government to mandate the collection or production of that information. The sorts of regret mentioned here result from two immutable facts about the fallen world in which we live: change is a constant, and resources, including investigatory resources, are scarce.

Regret may also occur, though, because of defects inherent in individual humans. Making "good" decisions – those reasonably calculated to maximize the decisionmaker's individual welfare – requires that the chooser *know* what is good (according to her own values and subjective preferences) and *be willing to incur the cost* of obtaining it. In other words, good decision-making involves both a rational and a volitional component. If people have problems with their reasoning or if their willpower is defective, they may make decisions that do not further their welfare as they themselves would define it. And since individual action, unlike change and scarcity, may be subject to government control, this sort of regret could conceivably be the subject of a regulatory fix.

The sort of regret at issue here frequently manifests itself in "why didn't I?" queries. "Why didn't I pass on that second piece of cake?" "Why didn't I save more when I was younger?" "Why didn't I pick the fixed rate mortgage instead of this interest-only, adjustable rate thingy with a balloon payment?" To the extent "why didn't I?" regret results not from change or scarcity, about which governments can do little, but from an individual's choices, which are subject to government control, some sort of regulatory intervention could conceivably enhance overall welfare. Thus, the symptoms we're concerned with here are decisionmakers' welfare losses and resulting regrets that stem not from post-decision changes or from choosers' failure to acquire unduly costly information but from decisionmakers' own frailties.

Those frailties, then, collectively comprise the disease that gives rise to the symptoms we'd like to eliminate. Of course, different people have different frailties, and it would make little sense to impose generally applicable policies to correct for rational and volitional impediments that afflict relatively few people. The disease with which we're concerned, then, is the collection of *systematic* frailties, those rational and volitional limitations that most people appear to exhibit.

So what are those limitations? Building on the work of cognitive psychologists, so-called behavioral economists claim to have identified a number of ways in which people regularly depart from the rational choice model of human behavior. We can group those predictable departures into three categories: imperfect optimization, bounded self-control, and non-standard preferences.[3]

Imperfect Optimization

Imperfect optimization refers to people's purported tendencies to make systematic mistakes in choosing among alternative courses of action. The rational choice model assumes that people make choices that maximize their welfare given their resource constraints. To say that people are prone to imperfect optimization is to say that even when they have fixed preferences and plenty of willpower, they tend to make decisions that don't wring the greatest possible value (as judged by them) from their resources. People make these mistakes, behavioral economists say, because they are "boundedly" rational, inclined to use "heuristics," and subject to systematic biases.

Bounded Rationality

Coined by Nobel Prize-winning economist Herbert Simon, the term "bounded rationality" refers to the fact that humans face limits on their memories, computational skills, and other mental abilities. Those limits, in turn, restrict their capacity to gather and process information.[4] To say that people are boundedly rational is not to say that they are *irrational*; it is simply to acknowledge that humans aren't computers. Even non-behavioral economists concede that fact. The notion of bounded rationality is, however, the launching pad for behavioral economics, which has purported to demonstrate what people do *in light of the fact* that they're not computers.

Heuristics

One thing they do, behavioralists say, is employ mental shortcuts or "heuristics." People frequently need to make quick judgments about things and don't have

[3] This categorization is taken from William J. Congdon, Jeffrey R. Kling, and Sendhil Mullainathan, *Policy and Choice: Public Finance Through the Lens of Behavioral Economics* 7 (Washington, D.C.: Brookings Institution, 2011). We cannot, of course, delve deeply into all the quirks and limitations behavioral economists purport to observe. For a more exhaustive overview, see *Behavioral Law and Economics*, Cass R. Sunstein, ed. (Cambridge, UK: Cambridge University Press, 2000); Thaler, supra note 2.

[4] Herbert A. Simon, Rational Choice and the Structure of the Environment, in Herbert Simon, *Models of Man: Social and Rational* (New York: Wiley, 1957) 261, 271.

the time or mental resources to gather all available information or even to process carefully all the facts they already know. To use the terminology employed by Nobel laureate Daniel Kahneman,[5] they must rely on their reflexive "system one" method of thinking (an approach that is fast, instinctive, subconscious, and often emotional – the sort of thinking one uses when he dodges an object hurtling toward him). They can't engage in reflective "system two" thinking (an approach that is slower, effortful, conscious, and logical – the approach one uses when she's buying a new car). People therefore tend to use rules of thumb or other mental shortcuts to help them make quick decisions.

One such mental shortcut, dubbed the "availability heuristic," assesses the probability of an occurrence based on how easily instances of the event may be called to mind; the more "available" past instances of the event are in one's recollection, the more probable one will deem the event to be.[6] On first glance, this seems like a sensible mental strategy. The more memories you have of past events occurring, the more probable it is that the event will recur, right?

Not always. Some events, though quite common, don't stick in our memories and thus aren't available to us when we're assessing probabilities. This can lead us to make irrational judgments. For example, people asked to estimate how many words in a document end in "ing" give higher numbers than those asked to estimate how many of the writing's words have "n" as the next-to-last letter. As a logical matter, the number of words with "n" as the penultimate letter must exceed (or equal) the number of words ending in "ing." But it's easier to call to mind "ing" words than words with a penultimate "n." It's also easier to call to mind "Detroit murders" than "Michigan murders." Not surprisingly, then, people tend to estimate that there were more murders in Detroit during some time period than there were in the state of Michigan – a logical impossibility.

Closely related to the availability heuristic is something behavioralists call "salience bias." Big, dramatic events command notice. They stick in our minds and are therefore more available to us than are regular, day-to-day events, especially when they engage our emotions. That implies that when the availability heuristic is operating, people will tend to overestimate the likelihood of noticeable (salient) events relative to occurrences that are less noteworthy but perhaps more common. Consistent with this theory, people tend to think that deaths from vehicle accidents are more common than deaths from lung cancer and that more people die from homicide than from emphysema, when in fact

---

[5] Daniel Kahneman, *Thinking, Fast and Slow* (New York: Farrar, Straus and Giroux, 2011) 19–30.
[6] Amos Tversky and Daniel Kahneman, Availability: A Heuristic for Judging Frequency and Probability, 5 *Cognitive Pyschol.* 207, 208 (1973).

more people die from lung cancer than from vehicle accidents and from emphysema than from homicide. Car wrecks and shootings are bloody and newsworthy (hence the old newspaper adage, "If it bleeds, it leads."). Lung cancer and emphysema are awful, but they're usually neither gory (eliciting a visceral reaction) nor widely reported. Instances of them are less available.

A second well-documented heuristic involves what Kahneman and his longtime co-author, Amos Tversky, called "anchoring and adjustment." When people are called upon to reach some conclusion – say, the number of pennies in a jar or the amount they're willing to pay for a new gadget – they tend to form an initial judgment based on some simple feature and then adjust that estimate, dubbed an "anchor," to reach a final conclusion. The adjustment is often quite conservative, causing the final judgment to be biased toward the anchor. In addition, the anchor frequently has little or nothing to do with the subject matter of the judgment. The result can be some bizarre patterns of judgment.

For example, Kahneman and Tversky once asked people to estimate what percentage of the countries in the United Nations (UN) were located in Africa. Before they did so, though, they had respondents spin a wheel of fortune that was secretly rigged to land on either 10 or 65. They first asked whether the percentage of African UN members was above or below that number, a relative question, and then proceeded to ask the absolute question (i.e., What precise percentage of UN members are African?). The result of the wheel spin was, of course, wholly unrelated to the matter under consideration, but it still appeared to affect respondents' answers: For subjects who spun a 10, the median answer to the latter question was 25 percent; for those spinning a 65, it was 45 percent.[7] The spin result, the researchers suggested, served as an anchor used by respondents in answering the absolute question.

Kahneman and Tversky observed a similar result when they had two groups quickly solve the same math problem but phrased the problem differently for each group. One group was asked to solve the equation, $8x7x6x5x4x3x2x1=?$; the other, $1x2x3x4x5x7x8=?$ The former group's median answer (2,250) was more than four times as large as the latter's (512).[8] Both were way off the actual answer of 40,320, but Kahneman and Tversky focused on the marked difference between the two sets of answers. They contended that respondents, required to make a quick (non-reflective, "system one") judgment, anchored on the first numbers in the problem when forming their estimates.

---

[7] Amos Tversky and Daniel Kahneman, Judgment under Uncertainty: Heuristics and Biases, 185 *Science* 1124, 1128 (1974).
[8] Ibid.

Experimental evidence suggests that anchoring and adjustment may also be at play when people form reservation prices – i.e., when they determine how much they're willing to pay for something. In an experiment with students at MIT, economists Dan Ariely, Drazen Prelac, and George Loewenstein held up various items – a bottle of wine, a cordless trackball, a textbook – and described each. They then had the MIT students say whether they would purchase each item at a price equal to the last two digits of their social security numbers. Having considered a pretend price (the social security digits), the subjects were then invited to bid on the items. Consistent with behavioralists' claims about anchoring and adjustment, the wholly irrelevant social security numbers appeared to influence the prices bid. People with high social security numbers bid substantially more than those with low numbers. For example, subjects whose last two digits were between 80 and 99 paid an average of $26 for the cordless trackball, whereas those with numbers from 00 to 19 paid an average of $9.[9] This hardly seems rational.

A third mental shortcut, the "representativeness heuristic," involves something that looks like stereotyping. When asked to judge how likely it is that *x* belongs to category *y*, people tend to ignore evidence about the magnitude of category *y* (i.e., how common it is for something to fall within that category) and rely more heavily on the degree to which *x* resembles a prototypical member of category *y*. Such thinking leads to what statisticians call "base rate neglect."[10]

For example, in an experiment by Kahneman and Tversky, respondents were lumped into three categories. One, the "base rate" group, was asked to estimate the percentages of graduate students enrolled in nine different fields of study (business administration, computer science, engineering, humanities and education, law, library science, medicine, physical and life sciences, and social science and social work). The second, the "similarity" group, was given a detailed description of a young man, Tom W., and was asked to rank the nine fields of study in terms of how prototypical Tom was of a graduate student in

---

[9] Dan Ariely, George Loewenstein, and Drazen Prelac, "Coherent Arbitrariness": Stable Demand Curves Without Stable Preferences, 118 *Q. J. Econ.* 73, 75–76 (2003).

[10] Suppose, for example, that a disease afflicts one in a thousand people. A test for the disease correctly detects every instance of infection and is 95 percent accurate when the person doesn't have the disease. If you test positive for the disease, what is the chance that you actually have it? Most people say something like 95 percent, reflecting the test's high degree of accuracy. In reality, your chance of having the disease is less than 2 percent. Out of 1,000 people tested, 51 would test positive – 1 accurately, and 50 falsely. A positive test result, then, would reflect infection in only 1 of 51 cases (1.96 percent of the time). People tend to err here because they focus only on the test's high accuracy rate and ignore the low base rate of infection.

each field. The third group, the "prediction" group, was given the same description of Tom W., told that it was written in Tom's senior year of high school by a psychologist who had subjected Tom to projective tests, and asked to rank the nine fields of graduate study in terms of the likelihood that Tom is now a student specializing in that area.

One might expect that the prediction group's judgments about the likelihood that Tom would pursue a particular course of study would reflect the estimated popularity of that course of study. But that's not how things turned out. Instead, the prediction group's judgments of likelihood were much closer to the similarity group's rankings of representativeness than to the base rate group's rankings of overall popularity of academic concentrations. For example, 95 percent of respondents said Tom was more likely a computer science student than an education or humanities student, even though the base rate group had estimated that far more graduate students concentrate in education and the humanities than in computer science.[11] The findings are consistent with the claim that people make predictions based on how representative (similar) something is, and not so much on what relative base rates are.

The representativeness heuristic misleads people when similarity and frequency diverge, and it may lead to absurd judgments. Consider, for example, an experiment involving a hypothetical woman named Linda. Subjects were told the following: "Linda is thirty-one years old, single, outspoken, and very bright. She majored in philosophy. As a student, she was deeply concerned with issues of discrimination and social justice and also participated in anti-nuclear demonstrations." Subjects were then asked to rank, in order of likelihood, possible futures for Linda, including "bank teller" and "bank teller and active in the feminist movement." In multiple iterations of this experiment, large majorities of respondents have said that the latter option (bank teller and feminist) is more probable than the former (bank teller).[12] But that logically cannot be! Any *feminist* bank teller is also a bank teller, so there's no way that it could be more likely that Linda would end up as a feminist bank teller than as a bank teller. This is another example, behavioralists claim, of humans' reflexive, system one mode of thinking overwhelming their rational, system two mode.

[11] Daniel Kahneman and Amos Tversky, On the Psychology of Prediction, 80 *Psych. Rev.* 237 (1973) (reprinted in *Judgment under Uncertainty: Heuristics and Biases*, Daniel Kahneman, Paul Slovic, and Amos Tversky, eds. (Cambridge, UK: Cambridge University Press, 1982)).

[12] See, e.g., Amos Tversky and Daniel Kahneman, Judgments Of and By Representativeness, in *Judgment Under Uncertainty*, supra note 11, at 91–96.

Biases

In addition to using heuristics, behavioralists say, people tend to suffer from biases that may lead them to make suboptimal decisions. Perhaps the most important of these is the optimism bias. Most humans, it seems, think they are more likely than average to experience good outcomes and less likely than average to suffer bad ones. For example, about 90 percent of drivers rate themselves as above-average behind the wheel. Similarly, while about half of all marriages fail, most new brides and grooms estimate their chances of divorcing as very low. Entrepreneurs routinely think they are especially likely to succeed. In a recent survey of people starting new businesses, the most common answer to the question, "What do you think is the chance of success for a new business like yours?," was 50 percent; the most common response to "What is your chance of success?" was 90 percent.[13] It seems most of us believe we're children living in Lake Wobegon. And that, behavioralists say, affects our decisions: We are more likely to take risks if we (irrationally) believe we're particularly unlikely to experience a bad outcome.

Bounded Self Control

The cognitive frailties discussed above prevent people from knowing what, given their preferences, are their best courses of action. Behavioralists also maintain that people face volitional constraints – i.e., limits on their will-power. We know from common experience how hard it can be to forego current consumption in order to secure something better in the future. Indeed, many of us are so aware of our limited willpower that we voluntarily restrict our options so as not to succumb to temptation. (Your author, for example, strictly limits the number of roasted almonds he carries to his easy chair when he's reading the newspaper before dinner. Even though he knows he'll ultimately experience more pleasure if he eats just a few nuts and saves room for a well-balanced supper, experience has taught him that he simply *cannot* avoid eating too many nuts if he takes the whole can to the lounger.) What is wrong with us?

According to behavioralists, many of our volitional frailties stem from our tendency to engage in "hyperbolic discounting." To understand what that is, consider how people trade off present consumption opportunities against opportunities to consume in the future. In general, people prefer to consume stuff sooner rather than later. Economists have thus long understood that

---

[13] Arnold C. Cooper, Carolyn Y. Woo, and William C. Dunkelberg, Entrepreneurs' Perceived Chances for Success, 3 *J. Bus. Venturing* 97 (1988).

when people are choosing between courses of action that will provide benefits at different times, they implicitly "discount" the value of future consumption opportunities. A person might, for example, deem the right to receive $110 one year from now as worth only $100 today. That person's "discount rate" is 10 percent.

Different people exhibit different discount rates. Those who really prefer present over future consumption have high discount rates, meaning that the future consumption opportunity must be a lot better than the current one in order for the person to forego current consumption. Others, by contrast, have low discount rates; they needn't receive much compensation for holding off on consumption.

While economists have long understood that discount rates vary among individuals, they have generally assumed that whatever discount rate a person applies to a decision is constant over time. So, for example, a person who would be indifferent between $100 today and $110 one year from now would also be indifferent between $100 one year from now and $110 two years from now. Her 10 percent discount rate is the same for both one-year time delays. Economists refer to this as "exponential" discounting.[14]

In recent years, researchers have amassed a significant body of empirical data suggesting that this is not how people really make trade-offs across time. Evidence suggests that discount rates are not constant, but that people instead discount future rewards at a greater rate when the delay occurs sooner in time. For example, while many people would rather have $100 today than $110 tomorrow, few would prefer $100 in 30 days to $110 in 31. A one-day delay that would require little compensation if experienced a month from now would, for lots of folks, be less tolerable (and would therefore require greater compensation) if experienced today. People are said to engage in "hyperbolic" discounting if the rate at which they discount future rewards is not constant but instead rises for earlier and earlier portions of the delay period.[15] A good bit of evidence suggests that this is, in fact, how people make lots of intertemporal trade-offs.

Consider, for example, overweight people who come to believe that they need to eat better and exercise more. Gazing into the future, they decide they're

---

[14] The term exponential discounting is used because the time delay in the formula for assessing the present value of a future consumption opportunity is an exponent. A future reward is adjusted by a factor of $1/(1+k)^t$, where k is the discount rate and t is the number of years until consumption. For example, for a person with a 10 percent discount rate, receiving $110 one year in the future requires adjusting $110 by a factor of $1/(1+.10)^1$ or .9091. (To complete the math, $110 * .9091 = $100.)

[15] The term "hyperbolic discounting" is used because the formula for the factor by which a future reward must be adjusted is the same as the generalized function for a hyperbola. (Don't worry. The math is beyond our scope.)

willing to forego fattening foods to secure a healthier body. When they compare next month's desserts to next year's better body, they apply a low discount rate, which leads them to ascribe greater value to the better body than to the joy from next month's desserts. But when dessert time rolls around *tonight*, the discount rate they apply to a future better body shoots up so that consuming dessert tonight seems like the value-maximizing option. After they blow it, they may start thinking again about future consumption trade-offs – say, enjoying next month's holiday parties versus feeling good in a swimsuit next summer – and jump back on the diet. But then another immediate consumption opportunity arises, and the value of looking fit next summer suddenly seems awfully small. Sound familiar? If a person engages in hyperbolic discounting of this sort, then even when her reasoning abilities enable her to ascertain the course of action that will bring her the greatest happiness (given her preferences), she may find herself lacking the willpower to stay on course.

Non-Standard Preferences

In addition to assuming that people possess the cognitive and volitional abilities to identify and follow the course of action that maximizes their welfare in light of their preferences, the rational choice model assumes that people's preferences – the degree to which they value one thing over another – are independent of the context in which choices are presented (or, to use some jargon, are "exogenous" rather than "endogenous"). Behavioralists dispute that assumption. They point to evidence suggesting that institutional arrangements, particularly the allocation of property rights and other entitlements, help determine the value people attach to various outcomes.

Most notably, behavioralists claim that people exhibit an "endowment effect" under which the value they ascribe to a thing – a piece of property, a service, a legal right – depends in part on whether or not they own it. Most of the evidence for this effect has been experimental. In dozens of experiments, the average minimum sale price that would be charged by a group of people who have been given an item (the average "willingness-to-accept" or "WTA") exceeds the average maximum purchase price that a similarly situated group of people who have not been given the item would pay for it (the average "willingness-to-pay" or "WTP"). Both measures should reflect the subjective valuation a person ascribes to the thing at issue: WTA is the minimum amount an owner would have to be paid to part with the thing; WTP is the maximum amount a non-owner would be willing to give up to get it. If owners' WTA for a thing routinely exceeds non-owners' WTP for the exact same thing, behavioralists contend, then the mere fact of ownership must enhance the subjective value attributed to the thing.

In a typical experiment, half the students in a class were given coffee mugs bearing their school's insignia, and the others were directed to examine their neighbors' mugs so that all students would have a good idea of the mugs' quality. Mug owners were then invited to sell, and non-owners to buy, the mugs that had been distributed. Specifically, each student was asked to state his or her reservation price – i.e., the student's subjective valuation of the mug – by answering the question, "At each of the following prices, indicate whether you would be willing to (give up your mug/buy a mug)?" On average, those who had been given mugs demanded roughly twice as much to sell them (WTA) as non-owners were willing to pay to acquire them (WTP).[16]

In a similar experiment, half the students in a class were given coffee mugs (for some reason, the standard item for these sorts of experiments) and the other half received big chocolate bars that cost roughly the same amount as the mugs. In tests conducted before the experiment, students were as likely to pick one of the items as the other. After they owned one of the items and were given an opportunity to trade it for the other, however, very few made the trade. Only one in ten switched from the item they were given.[17] The suggestion is that owning the items they were distributed caused students to value those items more than they otherwise would.

There is evidence suggesting that the apparent endowment effect may be a function of experimental design. For example, after economists Charles Plott and Kathryn Zeiler conducted standard coffee mug experiments and observed the usual result (WTA > WTP), they repeated the experiments using best practices for experimental design, and the apparent endowment effect disappeared.[18] Although the work by Plott and Zeiler has generated its own controversy,[19] it does call into question the stronger claims about the

[16] Daniel Kahneman, Jack L. Knetsch, and Richard H. Thaler, Anomalies: The Endowment Effect, Loss Aversion, and Status Quo Bias, 5 *J. Econ. Perspecs.* 193 (1991).

[17] Richard H. Thaler and Cass R. Sunstein, *Nudge: Improving Decisions About Health, Wealth, and Happiness* 34 (New Haven, Connecticut: Yale University Press, 2008).

[18] Charles R. Plott and Kathryn Zeiler, The Willingness to Pay – Willingness to Accept Gap, the "Endowment Effect," Subject Misconceptions, and Experimental Procedures for Eliciting Valuations, 95 *Am. Econ. Rev.* 530 (2005); Charles R. Plott and Kathryn Zeiler, Exchange Asymmetries Incorrectly Interpreted as Evidence of Endowment Effect Theory and Prospect Theory?, 97 *Am. Econ. Rev.* 1449 (2007).

[19] See Andrea Isoni, et al., The Willingness to Pay – Willingness to Accept Gap, the "Endowment Effect," Subject Misconceptions, and Experimental Procedures for Eliciting Valuations: Comment, 101 *Am. Econ. Rev.* 991 (2011); Charles R. Plott and Kathryn Zeiler, The Willingness to Pay – Willingness to Accept Gap, the "Endowment Effect," Subject

endowment effect. Most behavioral legal scholars, however, deem the evidence settled: Endowing a person with a thing causes him or her to value it more.[20]

Closely related to the endowment effect is a tendency behavioralists refer to as "loss aversion." In their "prospect theory" of human behavior, Kahneman and Tversky asserted that people tend to evaluate outcomes not in isolation but relative to an initial reference point, and they noted empirical evidence that people weigh losses from a reference point more heavily than correlative gains.[21] (Consistent with the endowment effect, if a person has to give up something she owns, she is hurt more than she is pleased if she initially gains that same thing.)

Again, much of the evidence for loss aversion is experimental. In a typical experiment, subjects were asked to imagine a coin toss in which they will win some amount of money (x dollars) if the coin lands on heads but will have to pay $100 if it lands on tails. When asked how large x must be in order for them to participate in the coin toss, most subjects responded with a number near 200. The implication is that people hate losses so much that they'll give up opportunities worth up to twice the amount of the losses in order to avoid them.[22]

The endowment effect and loss aversion, behavioralists assert, give rise to two other predictable quirks. One is a "status quo bias." If people tend to attach extra value to their initial set of entitlements, and if the losses they experience from changing things weigh heavier than the gains they experience from change, they will tend to leave things as they are. In addition, say the behavioralists, people are subject to "framing effects." Since people perceive losses as weighing more than correlative gains, whether an opportunity is framed as a gain or a loss matters.

Misconceptions, and Experimental Procedures for Eliciting Valuations: Reply, 101 *Am. Econ Rev.* 1012 (2011).

[20] In the five years following the publication of the Plott and Zeiler studies in the high-profile *American Economic Review*, fewer than 10 percent of legal publications referring to the endowment effect bothered to cite Plott and Zeiler's work. Joshua D. Wright and Douglas H. Ginsburg, Behavioral Law and Economics: Its Origins, Fatal Flaws, and Implications for Liberty, 106 *Northwestern U. L. Rev.* 1033, 1047 (2012).

[21] Daniel Kahneman and Amos Tversky, Prospect Theory: An Analysis of Decision Under Risk, 47 *Econometrica* 263, 277–79 (1979); Amos Tversky and Daniel Kahneman, Loss Aversion in Riskless Choice: A Reference-Dependent Model, 106 *Q. J. Econ.* 1039, 1041–42 (1991).

[22] In refusing to engage in the coin toss if the payment for heads is, say, $180, a subject is effectively saying that a 50 percent chance of losing $100 (expected value = negative $50) hurts him more than a 50 percent chance of winning $180 (expected value = $90) benefits him. In other words, the subject is sacrificing an expected gain of $40 [(0.5)(−$100) + (0.5)($180)] to avoid incurring a risk of loss.

Consider, for instance, two statements that convey the same information about the risks of a surgical procedure:

Statement A: "Of 100 patients who have this operation, 90 are alive after 5 years."

Statement B: "Of 100 patients who have this operation, 10 are dead after 5 years."

In numerous experiments, people presented with Statement A, which focuses on gains, are much more likely to select the procedure than are people presented with Statement B, which emphasizes losses.[23] Indeed, even experts may be subject to framing effects. Doctors deciding whether to recommend a procedure are more likely to do so if they are told "90 of 100 are alive" after some period of time rather than "10 of 100 are dead."[24]

To the extent they really exist, the endowment effect, loss aversion, status quo biases, and framing effects imply that people's preferences – and the outcomes that follow from them – are largely constructed by government policy. How government allocates entitlements influences people's preferences for those entitlements (endowment effect). People often won't give up what they've got in order to get something that they would have perceived as better had it been initially allocated to them (loss aversion/status quo bias). And people's decisions about what outcomes to pursue may turn on whether those outcomes are presented as potential gains or losses (framing effects).

If the rational choice model's *homo economicus* is Superman, behavioralism's prototypical human is Ralph Hinkley, the hapless protagonist of the early 1980s television show, *The Greatest American Hero* (Google it). Hinkley was often confused. He relied on hunches. He had remarkable powers, but he couldn't control them. He was more confident than he should have been, given his limitations. He was reluctant to disrupt the status quo. And he made lots of blunders. The same goes for us humans, behavioralists say. As a result, we routinely fail to maximize our welfare, and we suffer regret. The question is, what, if anything, the government should do about that.

AVAILABLE REMEDIES AND THEIR IMPLEMENTATION DIFFICULTIES AND SIDE EFFECTS

As usual, the available remedies for addressing the disease with which we are concerned vary in their restrictiveness. At the most restrictive end of the spectrum is a hard paternalist approach under which government planners

---

[23] Thaler and Sunstein, supra note 17, at 36.   [24] Ibid.

simply override individuals' choices when the planners have reason to believe that people wouldn't have chosen as they did but for their cognitive or volitional frailties. Such paternalism is typically implemented through commands and bans. Examples include laws requiring people to wear seatbelts or motorcycle helmets (commands) and legal prohibitions on gambling, sexual transactions between consenting adults, trans fats, and drugs whose consumption doesn't threaten harm to others (bans).[25]

At the opposite end of the spectrum from hard paternalism is a libertarian approach under which the government does nothing about people's cognitive and volitional limitations and simply lets them make their mistakes. Political philosopher John Stuart Mill famously promoted this anti-paternalist approach, writing that

> the only purpose for which power can be rightfully exercised over any member of a civilized community, against his will, is to prevent harm to others. His own good, either physical or moral, is not a sufficient warrant. He cannot rightfully be compelled to do or forbear because it will be better for him to do so, because it will make him happier, because, in the opinion of others, to do so would be wise, or even right.[26]

Although Mill penned those words more than 150 years ago, his sentiments still largely hold sway in capitalist societies. Respecting individual freedom but demanding personal responsibility is by far the most common approach to decisions that don't threaten significant harm to others, *even when* those decisions are likely to be impaired by people's cognitive and volitional frailties.

Consider, for example, people's career choices. Planning and preparing for one's career involves making a host of predictions (where heuristics and biases play a role) and may demand a great deal of volitional fortitude (which hyperbolic discounting may impair). Thus, as behavioralists would predict, people regularly make poor career decisions and suffer loss and regret as a result. In a capitalist society like ours, though, it's unheard of for government

---

[25] Many public policies have a paternalistic flavor but aren't fully paternalistic because a substantial part of their justification is to protect third parties. Drug laws that prohibit the use of substances, such as methamphetamine, that both harm users and lead them to take actions that impose risks on others would fall into this category. So would laws requiring people to participate in social insurance programs such as Social Security. A primary justification for such laws is to avoid putting other people in the position of having to care for elderly individuals who have insufficient savings at the end of their working lives. The ban on marijuana, the use of which occasions few adverse third-party effects, probably wouldn't fall into this category. It looks like pure paternalism.

[26] J.S. Mill, On Liberty (1859), published in John Gray, ed., *John Stuart Mill: On Liberty and Other Essays* (Oxford: Oxford University Press 1991).

officials to coerce people – or even to cajole them – into one career over another. The same goes for the rest of life's major decisions, many of which may be less than optimal because of people's various human frailties. We typically leave those decisions to people themselves, knowing full well that they will often screw up.

There are sound reasons for this. Hard paternalism involves at least three major difficulties that, in most contexts, would collectively impose costs exceeding the welfare losses and regret that stem from people's various cognitive and volitional frailties.

First, hard paternalism entails a significant knowledge problem. Government planners have no way of knowing how much pleasure regulatees derive from banned activities (such as marijuana use) or how much displeasure they experience when they must comply with an affirmative command (such as having to wear a motorcycle helmet). Because the goal of paternalism is to leave people better off than they would have been had they made their own decisions, planners need to be able to compare the welfare effects of deciding on one's own versus following the government's order. With some decisions – whether to wear a motorcycle helmet, perhaps – planners may have good reasons for believing their preferred course of action would almost always leave people better off than an alternative decision. But with many paternalistic policies and proposals – forcing saving or limiting borrowing, for example – government planners are really just guessing about welfare effects. And planners are humans. That means, according to behavioralists, that they're likely to be overly confident about their welfare calculations. The combination of required guessing and overconfidence is sure to generate gobs of errors on the part of the planners who have taken it upon themselves to override individuals' choices.

Public choice concerns are also significant for hard paternalist policies. Because such paternalism involves the government's coercing people to take one action over another, private interests line up to ensure that whatever course of action gets mandated is one that benefits them. Query, for example, what police unions, pharmaceutical companies, private prison corporations, alcohol and beer producers, and prison guard unions have in common. On first glance, not much. Yet, these have been the top five contributors to campaigns opposing the liberalization of marijuana laws. What the seemingly dissimilar groups have in common is that each benefits from the paternalistic policy of banning marijuana possession. Producers of prescription drugs and alcoholic beverages know they'll lose sales if people are allowed to "take the edge off" with marijuana. Prison companies and police and prison guard unions know that loosening marijuana rules will reduce the number of criminals out there, cutting into their business. All the groups spend considerable resources lobbying for the outcome that will benefit them: a paternalistic ban on the possession of a substance whose consumption appears to entail no significant third-party effects.

A third difficulty with paternalism as a remedy for cognitive and volitional frailties is that it tends to reduce *self*-protection. Just as insurance, by protecting people from the downside of risk-taking, may lead people to take inefficient risks, paternalist policies that protect people from (what the planners believe to be) "mistakes" may lead people to work less hard to overcome their cognitive and volitional limitations. As Professors Jonathan Klick and Gregory Mitchell have observed, taking people's choices away from them "reduces the incentive to search for information, carefully evaluate decision options, or develop good decision-making strategies."[27] Paternalist responses to people's systematic irrationalities may thus create a sort of "cognitive hazard" akin to the moral hazard that results from insurance. And that possibility exacerbates paternalism's knowledge problem, for planners endeavoring to enhance individual welfare need to know the degree to which their external constraints on individual decision-making will reduce choosers' self-protective efforts.

The choice between hard paternalist and libertarian approaches to individuals' cognitive and volitional limitations, then, requires balancing the welfare losses and regret that result from leaving people alone against the administrative costs of a paternalist approach plus any losses resulting from the knowledge problem, public choice concerns, and a reduction in regulatees' efforts to avoid poor decisions. Except in the narrow set of circumstances in which (1) planners are truly confident that they know what is better for people, (2) the power being exercised over regulatees is of little benefit to special interests and is thus unlikely to invite political manipulation, and (3) there is little concern about squelching regulatees' learning (say, because the decision being controlled is not one people tend to make many times), a libertarian approach is probably superior to a paternalistic one.

But there may be some middle ground between the hard paternalist and libertarian responses to people's cognitive and volitional limitations. In recent years, prominent regulatory theorists have advanced what they call a "libertarian paternalist" approach to addressing human frailties.[28] These scholars have observed that there is quite a bit of territory between

---

[27] Jonathan Klick and Gregory Mitchell, Government Regulation of Irrationality: Moral and Cognitive Hazards, 90 *Minn. L. Rev.* 1620, 1636 (2006).

[28] See, e.g., Cass R. Sunstein and Richard Thaler, Libertarian Paternalism Is Not an Oxymoron, 70 *U. Chi. L. Rev.* 1159 (2003); Thaler & Sunstein, supra note 17.

paternalism's commands and bans and libertarianism's hands-off approach. Within that territory, they say, lies an approach under which planners design "choice architecture" that steers people toward ends that are best for them (as they themselves would judge were they operating free of cognitive and volitional limitations), while simultaneously protecting people's freedom of choice by allowing them to opt out of specified arrangements should they choose to do so. The approach is paternalistic in that its purported goal is to help people do what is best for them, not to prevent harm to others. It is libertarian, proponents contend, in that it ultimately leaves people free to choose.

An oft-cited example of a libertarian paternalist approach is automatic enrollment in employer-sponsored retirement savings programs. Such programs – 401(k)s and the like – have traditionally operated on an "opt-in" basis, meaning that the employee must affirmatively sign up for the program and set a savings rate. Behavioralism predicts that the status quo bias and people's tendency to engage in hyperbolic discounting will tend to prevent employees from taking these steps, even when they would really prefer to save more. Thus, say libertarian paternalists, the rule should be revised so that if an employee does nothing, she is automatically enrolled at a moderate savings rate but can freely opt out by notifying her employer of her desire to do so. Altering the choice architecture from an opt-in to an opt-out default rule, libertarian paternalists assert, harnesses the status quo bias to "nudge" employees in the direction that is (by employees' own considered lights) good for them. But, because participation at the standard savings rate is merely a default rule, any employee who prefers another course of action may freely take it.

Many times, libertarian paternalists say, government planners simply can't avoid nudging people one way or the other. Consider a public school cafeteria. We know from experience that people tend to load up on items at the beginning of a cafeteria line and consume less of the items placed at the end. That means that how school officials arrange food selections in the cafeteria line will inevitably influence what students consume. If students would be better off eating more fruits and vegetables and fewer fattening sweets, school official should relegate desserts to the end of the line and place them far out of reach. Students who really want desserts may still choose them, but mindless selectors would be nudged toward healthful choices. And imposing some nudge is unavoidable.

There seems to be little downside to employers' automatically enrolling their employees in 401(k) programs and school officials' arranging buffet items to encourage healthful choices, especially since employers must have some default rule about savings plan enrollment and buffets must be ordered somehow. But not all policies characterized as libertarian paternalist are so clearly benign. Like all remedies for private ordering defects, libertarian paternalist policies fall along a spectrum of restrictiveness. The more restrictive policies may be more troubling than these prototypical examples.

To see why this is so, first consider the range of policies characterized as libertarian paternalist. Richard Thaler and Cass Sunstein, co-authors of the libertarian paternalist manifesto *Nudge: Improving Decisions About Health, Wealth, and Happiness,* identify the following types of policies as libertarian paternalist:

1. A *private party (or a government entity acting as a market participant) voluntarily encourages particular decisions by its contracting partners.* The two prototypical libertarian paternalist policies described above fit within this category. When a private employer automatically enrolls his employees in a 401(k) plan, he purportedly helps them overcome the status quo bias that may prevent them from making decisions that would leave them better off. If the employer offers workers the opportunity to commit today to automatically increasing savings rates when they receive future raises, a policy Thaler has promoted through his "Save More Tomorrow" plan, the employer helps mitigate employees' hyperbolic discounting.[29] When a private restaurateur or the manager of a government-sponsored cafeteria arranges menu items to emphasize healthful options, she invokes framing effects to encourage good nutrition. We'll call these "private nudges," since the party doing the nudging is either a private concern or a government entity acting as a market participant and thus facing market discipline.

2. *Government engages in messaging guided by behavioral insights.* Building on behavioralists' claims that people tend to be unduly influenced by both affective messages (i.e., those that engage feelings) and a desire to conform to the group they're in, libertarian paternalists have called on government officials to employ strategic messaging to help people make choices that are good for them.[30] Government anti-smoking campaigns, for example, often depict heart-wrenching pictures and accounts of death and dying. In many countries, cigarette packaging must bear graphic

---

[29] See Richard H. Thaler and Shlomo Benartzi, Save More Tomorrow™: Using Behavioral Economics to Increase Employee Saving, 112 *J. Pol. Econ.* S164 (2004).

[30] As an example of behaviorally informed governmental messaging, Thaler and Sunstein point to the affective and norms-based messaging campaigns some local governments have used to reduce residents' energy consumption. See Thaler and Sunstein, supra note 17, at 68–69. As the authors acknowledge, such campaigns are not true instances of libertarian paternalism because the goal is not to get people to do what's best *for them personally* but instead to reduce the externalities stemming from energy consumption.

images of cancerous lungs. These are efforts to exploit visceral emotional responses – Kahneman's reflexive, system one thinking – to enhance the efficacy of messages promoting healthful behavior. Other strategic messaging harnesses social norms to encourage people to make healthful decisions. At the state university where I teach, for example, the school's "Most of Us" campaign has blanketed campus with posters and distributed t-shirts detailing the high percentages of students who engage in responsible alcohol use (e.g., "Seven out of Ten Mizzou students consume three or fewer drinks on a Saturday night."). As one official explained, "[I]f students perceive something to be the norm, they tend to alter their behavior to fit that norm, even if it isn't reality. ... So if students think heavy drinking is normal they'll drink more. If they think responsible drinking is normal, they'll drink more responsibly."[31]

3. *Government requires private parties to disclose salient facts in simple, standardized formats.* Many consumer contracts, especially those involving financing agreements, are complicated. The seller (or lender) has opportunities to make money along multiple dimensions – upfront fees, interest charges, late payment penalties, etc. Because people are boundedly rational, they may have difficulty discerning the real price of competing contracts, and they may choose poorly. Libertarian paternalists have thus proposed that sellers and lenders utilizing complex pricing schemes be required to present price information in simple, standardized formats that will facilitate comparison shopping. Thaler and Sunstein assert that mandating standardized, simplified disclosure of contract terms is "a species of libertarian paternalism":[32] paternalistic because it is aimed at helping people make good decisions; libertarian because it doesn't restrict pricing terms outright, and it enhances people's ability to choose what they really want. (The authors gloss over the fact that the government is coercing sellers and lenders into presenting certain information in certain formats. One wonders if they would characterize the federal securities laws as libertarian.)

4. *Government imposes default provisions in private contracts.* Default provisions – contract terms that apply unless affirmatively displaced – are a key component of libertarian paternalists' choice architecture. Such provisions may act upon both the endowment effect and the status quo bias.

---

[31] Statement of Michael Haines, Social Norms Research Center Director, posted on *Tigers Take Charge*, University of Missouri, Wellness Resource Center (available at https://wellness.missouri.edu/mostofus/).
[32] Thaler and Sunstein, supra note 17, at 93.

If a default provision endows a contracting party with some right or entitlement, then the entitled person, who at least momentarily "owns" the right, may value the entitlement more than she otherwise would and may demand more to give it up. If the government imposes default provisions that are good for people, then the status quo bias may assure that those salutary defaults are rarely overridden.

Libertarian paternalists have thus recommended that the law read employee-friendly default terms – guaranteed vacation time, provisions allowing termination only for cause, etc. – into employment contracts. They have also recommended that the law not just *allow* automatic enrollment in employer-sponsored savings plans – the sort of private nudge discussed in category one – but that it *mandate* that employers automatically enroll their employees. (As Sunstein and Thaler put it, "the law might ... require employers to provide automatic enrollment and allow employees to opt out."[33]) Proponents claim that government imposition of default terms is simultaneously paternalistic and libertarian because it helps people make good decisions (paternalistic) while giving them the freedom to opt out (libertarian). Again, though, proponents seem to be ignoring the fact that someone is being coerced by the government: The employer is banned from offering a job without certain terms and is commanded to enroll employees in a savings plan.

5.   *Government imposes default provisions in private contracts and erects procedural hurdles to opting out of those provisions.* Libertarian paternalists maintain that default provisions protect freedom, while nudging people in particular directions, because they allow people who prefer terms other than those specified to opt out. But libertarian paternalists don't require that opting out be costless or even cheap. Instead, they have specifically endorsed the government's creation of procedural hurdles that raise the costs of altering the default.

Sunstein and Thaler, for example, cite the waiver provision of the federal Age Discrimination in Employment Act (ADEA) as a rule that "embod[ies] libertarian paternalism."[34] The ADEA endows employees with a statutory right not to be terminated on the basis of age, but it allows employers and employees to opt out of the arrangement.[35] As a practical matter, opting out usually involves an agreement under which the employer pays the terminated employee some amount of money (or provides some other consideration) in exchange for the employee's

[33]   Sunstein and Thaler, supra note 28, at 1176.   [34]   Ibid. at 1186.
[35]   29 U.S.C. § 626(f)(1).

agreement not to assert his ADEA rights. The ADEA specifies, though, that such a waiver will not be valid unless (1) it specifically refers "to rights or claims arising under" the ADEA; (2) the employee is advised in writing to consult with an attorney before executing the agreement; (3) the employee is given "at least 21 days within which to consider the agreement"; and (4) the agreement provides for a period of at least seven days in which the employee may revoke it.[36] Thus, the ADEA may allow *really determined* parties to opt out of the default provision (no termination on the basis of age), but it makes doing so pretty difficult.

6. *Government imposes default provisions in private contracts and dictates the substantive terms of permissible opt-out arrangements.* Libertarian paternalism, proponents say, is broad enough to include government-imposed default terms that can be waived only by agreements whose provisions are dictated by the government and cannot be altered by the parties. Sunstein and Thaler, for example, characterize as libertarian paternalist the Fair Labor Standards Act (FLSA), which effectively reads a maximum hours provision into private employment contracts but allows waiver of the provision if, but only if, workers are paid time-and-a-half for extra hours worked.[37] The authors also cite as an example of libertarian paternalism the Model Employment Termination Act (META), which imposes an "only-for-cause" termination provision into employment agreements but allows its waiver if, but only if, the parties agree that any not-for-cause termination will entitle the terminated employee to a specified severance payment (one month's salary for every year of employment).[38] While Sunstein and Thaler concede that these substantive limitations on waiver render FLSA and META "less libertarian than [they] might be," the authors still characterize the laws as libertarian paternalist because "freedom of choice is nonetheless respected."[39]

But is it, really? Aren't employers and employees flat out forbidden to choose agreements calling for long hours and no overtime or for at-will employment with no severance pay following a not-for-cause termination? When it comes to coerciveness, these policies hardly resemble the choice-respecting nudges used by a public school official who configures the school's cafeteria line to encourage healthy eating.

7. *Government bans or commands certain behavior or imposes mandatory (not default) contract terms.* Default rules are a prominent feature of libertarian paternalist choice architecture because they permit opting-out by people who prefer a different outcome. But, as evidenced by the

---

[36] Ibid. [37] Sunstein and Thaler, supra note 28, at 1187. [38] Ibid. [39] Ibid.

purportedly libertarian paternalist policies within categories 5 and 6, libertarian paternalists have little problem with the government's imposing costs on those who would opt out. It's a short step to conclude that even commands and bans – the tools of hard paternalism – may sometimes count as libertarian paternalism. As Sunstein and Thaler have observed,

> Almost all of the time, even the non-libertarian paternalist will allow choosers, at some cost, to reject the proposed course of action. Those who are required to wear motorcycle helmets can decide to risk the relevant penalty, and to pay it if need be. Employers and employees might agree to sub-minimum wage work and risk the penalties if they are caught. In this particular sense, penalties are always prices.[40]

In allowing the policies in categories 5 and 6 to count as libertarian paternalist, then, proponents leave open the possibility that the approach may include some outright commands (e.g., wear a motorcycle helmet) and bans (e.g., no wages below $x/hour), at least where the penalty for violation is a monetary fine rather than physical confinement.

As shown by the foregoing discussion (summarized graphically in Figure 9.1), so-called libertarian paternalism extends substantially beyond the subtle suggestions of the cafeteria manager. Policies characterized as libertarian paternalist range from gentle encouragements to inflexible, threat-backed commands. Calling such policies "nudges" seems a sly bit of marketing; a few are, but most aren't. A nudge becomes a shove when the government – the institution in society with a monopoly on the legitimate use of force – threatens to harm someone if he or she doesn't follow the government's orders.

In the above list of libertarian paternalist policy proposals, that point (represented by the vertical "coercion" line in Figure 9.1) comes between categories two and three. With private nudges and behaviorally informed government messaging, no threat of force is made against anyone. People may be cajoled, but they're not coerced. From the third category on, though, the government effectively says, "Do this, or else you may be punished." The government threatens to punish people who don't provide the right information in the right format (category 3), or who make offers that don't include certain default terms (category 4), or who offer the specified terms but allow them to be excluded without either jumping through the proper hoops (category 5) or replacing them with specified alternative terms (category 6), or

[40]   Ibid. at 1189–90.

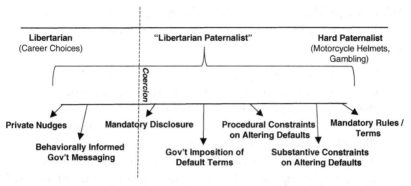

FIGURE 9.1 Options for Addressing Cognitive Limitations and Behavioral Quirks

who engage in certain behaviors or strike deals that the government deems too risky (category 7). In categories 3 through 7, *some* person's choice may be respected in the very narrow sense that he or she may, at some cost, be able to avoid the ultimate outcome government planners are seeking to promote. But make no mistake: *Somebody* is being threatened with force, not in order to protect third-parties but for the purpose of ensuring what planners believe to be a "good" outcome for a party to the contract. There's nothing libertarian about that.

Of course, to say that the policies in categories 3 through 7 are not libertarian is not to say that they're bad, only that they're misnamed. But the fact that the policies involve coercion is important in assessing their downsides, for it is the use of government coercion that generates paternalism's most significant side effects. Public choice concerns typically arise when special interests seek private benefits from government's coercive power; absent coercion, public choice concerns tend to be minor. The knowledge problem is most significant when the government coerces all participants in an industry into following some common policy. When private entities choose their own policies tailored to their specific context (as with private nudges), mistakes are less far-reaching and are subject to market discipline. Ill-informed government messaging is always subject to correction by private entities. Thus, public choice concerns and the knowledge problem do not appear to be damning side effects of non-coercive libertarian paternalist policies like the private nudges and behaviorally informed government messaging in categories 1 and 2.

Matters change when libertarian paternalism involves government coercion. When the government forces a private actor to do something in order to ensure that someone's decisions line up with his or her true preferences, the knowledge problem becomes quite significant.[41] To ensure that their schemes actually leave the intended targets better off, government planners must, at a minimum:

1. *Identify people's "true" preferences.* Libertarian paternalism purports to help people make choices that reflect their real preferences – i.e., the choices they would make were they not subject to cognitive and volitional limitations. A major source of those limitations, though, is people's allegedly *inconsistent* preferences. The purported endowment effect, for example, is based on the claim that the amount a person is willing to pay to acquire something is less than the minimum amount he would demand to sell it if he owned it (i.e., WTA > WTP). In other words, a person's preferences for the very same thing are inconsistent as entitlement to the thing (a matter irrelevant to its fundamental worth) varies. With hyperbolic discounting, people purportedly have different preferences for present versus future consumption depending on when the delay occurs (preferences for the present are stronger for near-term delays). If libertarian paternalism is to achieve the objective cited by Thaler and Sunstein – "influence choices in a way that will make choosers better off, *as judged by themselves*"[42] – then planners must have some way of determining which of people's conflicting preferences is the "real" one. It seems arbitrary to assume that WTA, rather than WTP, reflects the degree to which a person truly values an amenity. When it comes to discount rates, the matter is even more complicated because evidence suggests that people don't apply only two discount rates (a larger one for near-term delays and a smaller one for delays in the future); instead, people apply a broad range of discount rates, depending on how soon the delay occurs.[43] How is a planner to say which rate reflects a person's true preferences?

2. *Determine the extent of each cognitive or volitional defect.* As we saw above, nudges differ in their strength. The nudge resulting from a freely alterable default rule, for example, is gentler than that from a default rule that can be waived only by jumping through costly procedural hoops (as with the ADEA). To ensure that their choice architecture doesn't over-correct

---

[41]   The discussion here draws heavily upon Mario J. Rizzo and Douglas Glen Whitman, The Knowledge Problem of New Paternalism, 2009 *BYU L. Rev.* 905 (cataloguing and describing informational requirements of libertarian paternalism).

[42]   Thaler and Sunstein, supra note 17, at 5 (emphasis in original).

[43]   See, e.g., George Ainslie, *Breakdown of Will* 28–35 (Cambridge, UK: Cambridge University Press, 2001); Richard H. Thaler, Some Empirical Evidence on Dynamic Inconsistency, 8 *Econ. Letters* 201, 201–07 (1981).

people's biases by imposing nudges that are too strong, government planners must know not only what people's various biases are, but also how powerful each is. A nudge that is too strong or weak in light of the bias it aims to correct may end up hurting people by preventing them from doing what they "really" want to do.

3. *Assess the net effect of conflicting quirks.* The various heuristics, biases, and quirks identified by behavioralists often push in opposite directions.[44] When that occurs, a government planner attempting to negate the effect of the biases (so that people end up choosing in line with their real preferences) will have to figure out the degree to which the various biases offset each other. Consider retirement savings decisions. Libertarian paternalists have emphasized that people's tendency to engage in hyperbolic discounting may lead them to save too little. At the same time, people's optimism bias may lead them to overestimate how long they'll live and how active they'll be during retirement. If their optimism bias generates unrealistic expectations of a long retirement full of travel and other expensive activities, they may oversave. To craft choice architecture that will encourage people to save as they would if they didn't face cognitive and volitional limitations, government planners need some means of determining which behavioral quirk trumps and by how much.

4. *Predict how the prescribed policies will affect targets' self-protection.* As we saw in considering the side effects of hard paternalism, policies that purport to protect people from making poor decisions tend to reduce people's incentive to work hard at decisionmaking. Indeed, such a perverse outcome may have occurred with one of libertarian paternalism's poster children: automatic enrollment in retirement savings plans. Empirical evidence shows that firms that have implemented automatic enrollment have seen more employees participating in savings programs, but the amount participants are saving has fallen. Employees tend not to adjust the default savings rate, which is set below the level many chose when they had to opt-in to the savings programs.[45] Employers could, of course, just increase the default savings rate, but doing so could create problems for reasons we'll

---

[44] See Joachim I. Krueger and David C. Funder, Towards a Balanced Social Psychology: Causes, Consequences, and Cures for the Problem-Seeking Approach to Social Behavior and Cognition, 27 *Behav. & Brain Sci.* 313, 317 tbl.1 (2004) (identifying a "partial list" of 42 biases, many conflicting or contradictory, that have been recognized in the psychology literature since 1985).

[45] See, e.g., James J. Choi, David Laibson, Brigitte Madrian, and Andrew Metrick, *For Better or For Worse: Default Effects and 401(k) Savings Behavior* 2 (Pension Research Council, Working Paper No. 2002–02, 2002); Ryan Bubb and Richard H. Pildes, How Behavioral Economics

discuss next. For present purposes, the important thing to see is that paternalism is a substitute for self-protection, so when planners start taking care of things for people, people may cut back on caring for themselves. A government planner implementing a libertarian paternalist policy in an effort to leave people better off needs to know how the policy is going to impair targets' self-protective efforts.

5. *Account for heterogeneity on all these matters.* For each of the foregoing questions – What are people's true preferences? How great are their cognitive and volitional defects? How do their conflicting quirks interact? How might their self-protective efforts be affected by a nudge? – there are likely to be different answers for different people. For example, recent college graduates with young children and school debt will have different preferences for saving than will middle-aged folks nearing retirement (which is why just raising the default savings rate isn't a good solution to the problem discussed in the previous paragraph). The information needed by planners is also likely to differ across contexts. For example, the magnitude of the status quo bias might be great in one context but insignificant in another. Or, on the question of how conflicting quirks interact, hyperbolic discounting might swamp the optimism bias in one context, but vice-versa in another. The tremendous diversity among the people whose preferences libertarian paternalists are seeking to maximize and the contexts in which those people operate make it very difficult to construct generally applicable choice architecture.

In addition to this daunting knowledge problem, coercive libertarian paternalism entails significant public choice concerns. For one thing, incorporating government coercion into the scheme attracts special interests seeking to have such coercion exercised in their favor. Investment professionals, who benefit from higher participation rates in employer savings schemes, may push for government rules mandating automatic enrollment in 401(k)s; lawyers, for rules like the ADEA provision allowing opt-outs only if the employee has been directed to consult an attorney. Bringing in government coercion always invites private entities to lobby for coercion that serves their interests. And their lobbying often results in coercion that reduces overall welfare, especially when the coercion produces concentrated benefits while imposing diffuse costs.

Opening the door to coercive libertarian paternalism may also facilitate bureaucratic turf-expansion. In theory, libertarian paternalism should often

---

Trims Its Sails and Why, 127 *Harv. L. Rev.* 1593, 1618–25 (2014). See also Anne Tergesen, 401(k) Law Suppresses Saving for Retirement, *Wall St. J.* (July 7, 2011).

counsel reductions in government control; many mandates, for example, could be replaced by nudges. Yet, one almost never sees a move in this direction. That should come as no surprise. The individuals charged with implementing regulatory regimes personally benefit when government exercises more control but lose out when it exerts less. They will beat the libertarian paternalist drum when doing so may expand their authority, while ignoring libertarian paternalist ideas that would call for their power to be reduced.

Consider, for example, how the US EPA afforded asymmetric treatment to libertarian paternalist insights in its recent efforts to regulate vehicle fuel efficiency. Energy efficient automobiles and other consumer products offer people an opportunity to reduce their costs in the long run. Empirical evidence shows, though, that people apply a higher discount rate to those future cost savings than they typically apply in other market transactions. Behavioralists have asserted that this "energy-efficiency gap" – a purportedly irrational inconsistency in discount rates – is driven by various heuristics and biases, such as the salience bias.

Embracing libertarian paternalism, EPA decided the energy-efficiency gap warranted a nudge. In July 2011, the agency finalized its Motor Vehicle Fuel Economy Label Rule, which mandates that new cars bear a label disclosing an overall miles per gallon (mpg) rating, separate city and highway mpg ratings, gallons consumed per 100 miles, the driving range for a tank of gas, fuel costs in five years versus the average new vehicle, annual fuel costs, fuel economy and greenhouse gas ratings, and a smog rating.[46] The goal of the rule was to reduce the energy-efficiency gap by making fuel cost-savings salient and facilitating comparison shopping.

Five months after issuing its labeling rule, EPA joined the US Department of Transportation (DOT) in proposing new FES for passenger cars and light trucks. In their required cost–benefit analyses of the proposed rules, both agencies highlighted how the new standards would ameliorate consumer irrationality. Under DOT's analysis, 85 percent of the total benefit created by the standards would stem from addressing consumer irrationality; EPA put the figure at 87 percent. But for their salutary effect on consumer irrationality, the new rules would not have been cost-justified under either agency's cost–benefit review.[47]

---

[46] Revisions and Additions to Motor Vehicle Fuel Economy Label Final Rule, 76 Fed. Reg. 39, 478 (July 6, 2011).

[47] See Ted Gayer and W. Kip Viscusi, Overriding Consumer Preferences with Energy Regulations, 43 *J. Regul. Econ.* 248, 251–52 (2013).

Strikingly, EPA's regulatory analysis of the FES never even acknowledged the existence of its new labeling rule, a nudge aimed at addressing the very irrationalities that purportedly warranted the FES. The agency essentially assumed the labeling rule would have zero effect on consumer irrationality. When the insights of libertarian paternalism had been cited to *enhance* agency authority, EPA embraced them. When they threatened to reduce (or prevent a further enhancement of) such authority, they were ignored.[48] Given bureaucracies' tendency to expand their turf, this sort of ratchet effect is likely to be common at agencies charged with implementing coercive libertarian paternalist policies.

A third public choice concern arises because the government officials charged with implementing libertarian paternalist schemes are themselves human and thus subject to the very biases they are seeking to alleviate. (I call this a public choice concern because a key insight of public choice is that people don't magically shed their natures when they enter the public sphere; government officials remain self-interest maximizers and are subject to whatever cognitive and volitional defects afflict humans generally.) This is a point rarely acknowledged by proponents of libertarian paternalism. Indeed, one study found that, of the behavioral economics articles proposing some sort of paternalist policy response to people's cognitive limitations, 95.5 percent contained no analysis of the cognitive abilities of the policymakers themselves.[49] That's a problem because, as Sunstein has frankly acknowledged, "For every bias identified for individuals, there is an accompanying bias in the public sphere."[50]

---

[48] See W. Kip Viscusi and Ted Gayer, Behavioral Public Choice: The Behavioral Paradox of Government Policy, 38 *Harv. J. L. & Pub. Pol'y* 973 (2015). As Viscusi and Gayer observe, the agencies' failure to reference EPA's recent labeling rule

> goes to the heart of the fuel economy standard analysis, as most of the benefits needed to justify the regulation relate to consumer choice failures targeted by the new labeling rule. The EPA analysis of the fuel economy mandate should address the effectiveness of the label rule and the degree to which it ameliorates the need for an additional mandate. It is not necessarily inconsistent to have both a labeling rule and a fuel economy mandate, but any assessment of the desirability of a fuel economy [standard] should take into account the impact of the labeling regulation ... If the label rule is completely worthless and generates no benefits for consumer choice, then the EPA was remiss in issuing the regulation, and the Office of Management and Budget, the watchdog over all major new federal regulations, was remiss in permitting the agency to move forward with a rule that other EPA assessments implicitly treat as worthless. Ibid., at 986–87.

[49] Niclas Berggren, Time for Behavioral Political Economy? An Analysis of Articles in Behavioral Economics, 25 *Rev. of Austrian Econ.* 199 (2012).

[50] Cass R. Sunstein, *Why Nudge? The Politics of Libertarian Paternalism* 102 (New Haven, Connecticut: Yale University Press, 2012).

Consider an area of particular interest to libertarian paternalists: saving for retirement. Proponents of libertarian paternalist schemes aimed at increasing saving routinely contend that people tend to undersave for retirement. The actual evidence, however, suggests otherwise.[51] According to a 2006 study, most people save plenty for retirement; undersaving is a problem for only about 15 percent of American households.[52] Moreover, undersavers tend to miss their desired level of savings by only a small amount (a median deficiency of $5,260).[53] The study concluded that, "[a]lthough some households are approaching retirement with significant wealth deficits, the data ... suggest that ... households overwhelmingly are well prepared for retirement."[54] In fact, the authors noted, the "most striking aspect ... is the degree to which people are saving too much" – i.e., more than they would reasonably need for retirement.[55] Empirical evidence also shows that more Americans experience an increase rather than a decrease in annualized household wealth during their retirement,[56] and that the percentage of elderly Americans living in poverty is lower than the percentage of working-age adults below the poverty line.[57] None of this is to say that everyone is saving enough. But the evidence does call into question the claims libertarian paternalists assert in favor of coercive nudges toward greater retirement saving.

So why do libertarian paternalists contend so confidently that people tend to undersave? It's hard to say. Surely part of the reason is that people, when surveyed, often say they'd like to save more. But economists have long understood that such statements should be taken with a grain of salt. People routinely say they prefer a course of action – exercising more, eating better, consuming less alcohol – when they're not confronted with the cost of pursuing that course of action. People's *revealed* preferences – what they actually do when they must bear the costs of their choices – are a far better guide to their valuation of things than are their answers to survey questions presented in contexts in which costs are obscured. Sophisticated proponents of libertarian paternalism understand this, and yet they continue to make assertions like "People tend to undersave." How come?

---

[51] See generally Todd J. Zywicki, Do Americans Really Save Too Little and Should We Nudge Them to Save More? The Ethics of Nudging Retirement Savings, 14 Geo. J. L. & Pub. Pol'y. 877 (2016).

[52] John Karl Scholz, Ananth Seshadri, and Surachai Khitatrakun, Are Americans Saving "Optimally" for Retirement?, 114 J. Pol. Econ. 607, 626 (2006).

[53] Ibid. at 627.   [54] Ibid.   [55] Ibid. at 628.

[56] David A. Love, Michael J. Palumbo, and Paul A. Smith, The Trajectory of Wealth in Retirement, 93 J. Pub. Econ. 191 (Feb. 2009).

[57] US Census Bureau, Poverty: 2014 Highlights (2014), available at www2.census.gov/programs-surveys/demo/tables/p60/252/pov_table3.pdf.

Perhaps it is because libertarian paternalists themselves are subject to cognitive biases. "Motivated reasoning" – defined as "the unconscious tendency of individuals to fit their processing of information to conclusions that suit some end or goal"[58] – may play a role here. After all, routine undersaving helps make the case for the policies libertarian paternalists support. In addition, the salience bias, availability heuristic, and tendency toward excessive self-confidence may influence libertarian paternalists' thinking. Instances of undersaving are more salient than are instance of oversaving. We notice poor old people struggling to get along, but we never really see the loss experienced by someone who foregoes a valuable consumption opportunity – a much-needed vacation, for example – so that she can sock away more for retirement. This implies that instances of undersaving are more available to us than are instances of oversaving, which means (according to the availability heuristic) that we'll overestimate the incidence of undersaving. And, of course, we think we're children of Lake Wobegon: our probability judgments are better than average.

This is all speculation, of course. No one can say for certain why libertarian paternalists routinely conclude, contrary to the available empirical evidence, that Americans systematically undersave. The important point for our purposes is that mistakes are inevitable in a system that empowers people beset by cognitive and volitional limitations to use government force to protect others from their own cognitive and volitional limitations.

Libertarian paternalists are to be congratulated for identifying middle-ground solutions to private ordering defects and for endorsing a form of marginal cost–benefit analysis that compares regulatory proposals to their closest alternatives. The central claim of this book is that policymakers should always think of a regulatory spectrum, acknowledge that every point on the spectrum will have some upsides and some downsides, and select the point that seems most likely to maximize welfare. The libertarian paternalist project is consistent with that approach.

But libertarian paternalism is no panacea. While non-coercive libertarian paternalist policies seem benign and would probably enhance overall welfare, things get trickier when coercion enters the picture. At that point, regulators should recognize the potential downsides of proposed policies – particularly the knowledge problem and public choice concerns – and take care to ensure that those downsides do not exceed the welfare losses from letting people make their mistakes and (hopefully) learn from them.

---

[58] Dan Kahan, What Is Motivated Reasoning and How Does It Work?, *Science & Religion Today* (May 4, 2011) (available at www.scienceandreligiontoday.com/2011/05/04/what-is-motivated-reasoning-and-how-does-it-work/).

LESSONS FOR POLICYMAKERS

Behavioral economists have produced an impressive body of evidence suggesting that people predictably err in making decisions. It hardly follows, though, that a government comprised of, well, people can improve upon this unfortunate situation. In deciding whether and how to remedy people's predictable irrationalities and volitional limitations, policymakers should always balance the benefit of correcting people's mistakes against the costs resulting from regulator error, special interest manipulation of "protective" government efforts, and a reduction in people's incentives to engage in self-protection.

Under such balancing, hard paternalism's bans and commands rarely appear to be optimal. They should be used only when (1) policymakers are confident that they "know better" than the regulatees who want to pursue another course of action, (2) the power being exercised over those regulatees provides little benefit to other private interests (and thus invites little political manipulation), and (3) there are few learning benefits from having regulatees make mistakes (e.g., because people have few occasions to make the decision at issue, or because mistakes are so grave that a regulatee who chooses poorly doesn't get another chance). These prerequisites may be satisfied for, say, paternalistic motorcycle helmet mandates; for the paternalistic ban on marijuana use, they are not.

So-called libertarian paternalism, which ranges from non-coercive private nudges to bans and commands with relatively small penalties (i.e., low "prices" for violations), is a bit of a mixed bag. Libertarian paternalist approaches that do not involve coercion – e.g., private nudges and strategic governmental messaging – appear to offer a significant upside with little downside. Crossing the coercion line, however, invokes the knowledge problem and public choice concerns. Before implementing a coercive libertarian paternalist initiative, policymakers should carefully consider whether the downsides of intervention (regulator mistakes, special interest manipulation, and a reduction in self-protective efforts) will outweigh the upside of helping people avoid mistakes. In the end, a laissez-faire approach will often be optimal.

Conclusion

Closing Thoughts on Open Questions

We have now considered the primary ways that private ordering – people left to their own devices, constrained only by the common law – may systematically fail to extract the greatest possible value from available resources. We've also examined the various remedies policymakers may use to treat each of the well-known defects in private ordering. And we've seen that none of those remedies offers a perfect outcome; each will entail (1) losses from the remedy's side effects and/or its failure to completely eliminate the defect at issue (error costs) and (2) costs of administration (decision costs).

Equipped with an understanding of what costs are likely when a particular remedy is employed to address a particular defect in private ordering (the focus of the last six chapters), policymakers who are seeking to maximize social welfare will be in a position to select the remedy that seems likely to minimize the sum of error and decision costs. In many cases, the optimal remedy will be to do nothing and simply allow space for privately ordered solutions to any problems that emerge.

Most situations warranting a regulatory fix will reduce to one or a combination of the defects we have examined. That is not to suggest, however, that we have considered every systematic private ordering defect; as social institutions evolve and technology develops, we may witness new situations in which private ordering, time and again, fails to put resources to their highest and best ends. Nor should we presume that we have fully catalogued the potential remedies, identified all the pros and cons of each, or set forth a foolproof plan for selecting the optimal regulatory response. A central theme of this book is that Hayek's knowledge problem – the fact that no central planner can possess and process all the information needed to allocate resources so as to unlock their greatest possible value – applies to regulation, which is ultimately a set of centralized decisions about resource allocation. The very knowledge problem besetting regulators' decisions about what others should do similarly afflicts pointy-headed academics' efforts to set forth ex ante rules about what regulators should do. Context-specific information to which only the "regulator on the spot" is privy may call for occasional departures from the regulatory plan proposed here.

Nevertheless, embracing the principles set forth in this book will generally lead to regulatory approaches that enhance overall social welfare. Adherence to the principles would certainly represent an improvement over the regulatory status quo, in which policymakers regularly leap from identification of a symptom to implementation of a remedy. With the recent net neutrality rules discussed in Chapter 7, for example, policymakers bypassed altogether the sort of analysis this book recommends. Rather than methodically identifying adverse symptoms, asking why they were occurring, sketching out the full range of available remedies, analyzing the pros and cons of each, and selecting the approach likely to create the greatest value overall, the FCC majority just opted for a politically expedient power grab. The result is a set of heavy-handed rules that FCC chief economist Tim Brennan candidly described as "an economics-free zone." (Brennan also denied any involvement with the rules, joking soon after they were adopted that "[n]othing the FCC says necessarily reflects the views of Tim Brennan or his staff.")[1]

We can do better. This book has explained how.

Before we close, it is worth noting two matters, both central to the question of "how to regulate," that this book has not addressed. One is the issue of how existing regulatory institutions should be reformed to encourage the sort of analysis this book recommends. This is a crucial issue, but it is a bit off point for our purposes here. Before one can reform institutional structures and processes to encourage good regulation, one must have a sense of what good regulation consists of. That is this book's subject. Because the number of people involved in making policy – legislators, regulators, judges, lawyers, members of the media, teachers and students of law and policy, voters – swamps the number of people who set the formal rules about how policy is to be made, the subject addressed here should hold greater interest to more readers. It is ironic, then, that there seem to be more books out there about reforming regulatory institutions than about the substantive decisions regulators should make within the existing system. For these reasons – and because a chief way to achieve regulatory reform is to reform regulators – this book has focused on substance, not process.

My hope is that subsequent work, perhaps by readers of this book, will take up the question of how existing institutions should be altered to encourage the

---

[1] L. Gordon Crovitz, "Economics-Free" Obamanet, *Wall St. J.* (Jan. 31, 2016).

analysis this book counsels. One promising suggestion along those lines is the proposal by Robert Hahn and Cass Sunstein to expand the regulatory review requirements applicable to executive branch agencies to the so-called independent agencies.[2]

A longstanding executive order – first promulgated by President Reagan in 1981 and then tweaked by President Clinton in 1993 and again by President Obama in 2011[3] – mandates that regulatory agencies within the executive branch of the federal government engage in pre-regulation analysis akin to that recommended here. The order, which applies to regulations expected to impose annual costs of at least $100 million, requires that each subject agency:

- "identify the problem that it intends to address (including, where applicable, the failures of private markets or public institutions that warrant new agency action) as well as the significance of that problem";
- "identify and assess alternative forms of regulation";
- "[i]n deciding whether and how to regulate ... assess all costs and benefits of available regulatory alternatives, including the alternative of not regulating";
- "in choosing among alternative regulatory approaches ... select those approaches that maximize net benefits (including potential economic, environmental, public health and safety, and other advantages; distributive impacts; and equity)"; and
- "design its regulations in the most cost-effective manner to achieve the regulatory objective."[4]

Sound familiar? This looks an awful lot like, "identify the symptom, diagnose the disease, catalogue available remedies, assess the implementation difficulties and side effects of each, and pick the approach that offers the greatest net benefit."

While the substance of this executive order is spot-on, its reach is limited. The order doesn't apply to regulations by "independent regulatory agencies" – i.e., those that are not under the direct control of the President because their

---

[2] Robert W. Hahn and Cass R. Sunstein, A New Executive Order for Improving Federal Regulation – Deeper and Wider Cost-Benefit Analysis, 150 *U. Pa. L. Rev.* 1489 (2002).

[3] Executive Order 12291, 46 Fed. Reg. 13193 (Feb. 17, 1981); Executive Order 12866, Regulatory Planning and Review, 58 Fed. Reg. 51735 (Sept. 30, 1993); Executive Order 13563, Improving Regulation and Regulatory Review, 76 Fed. Reg. 3821 (Jan. 18, 2011).

[4] These mandates are all taken from the currently prevailing version of the primary executive order, Executive Order 12866, 58 Fed. Reg. 51735 (Sept. 30, 1993). The mandated review is largely coordinated by the Office of Information and Regulatory Affairs (OIRA) within the Office of Management and Budget (OMB).

members are not removable at will.[5] Such agencies include many of the most significant sources of regulations, including the Federal Communications Commission (FCC), the Federal Trade Commission (FTC), the Securities and Exchange Commission (SEC), the National Labor Relations Board (NLRB), the Commodity Futures Trading Commission (CFTC), the Consumer Product Safety Commission (CPSC), and the Consumer Financial Protection Bureau (CFPB). Subjecting the rules of those independent agencies to the regulatory review required of executive branch agencies would move our regulatory system a long way in the direction this book counsels. While there is some legal uncertainty as to whether the President has the authority to expand the executive order to cover independent agencies, the better view is that he or she does.[6] (And, of course, Congress could always grant such authority if it were found lacking.)

That's enough about our open question on institutional reforms. The other important regulatory issue that this book has left unaddressed is harder. The question is, how should regulators trade off efficiency (i.e., welfare gains) against equity (i.e., a "fair" distribution of welfare)?

From the outset, we skirted that issue by defining regulation for purposes of this book as threat-backed governmental commands *aimed at enhancing overall social welfare* by correcting wealth-destroying defects in private ordering. While we have occasionally considered the distributive effects of particular regulatory approaches (as when we discussed the regressive nature of Pigouvian taxes), the analysis in this book has generally assumed that the objective of regulatory interventions is to make society as a whole as wealthy as possible.

A number of considerations called for adopting this narrow definition of regulation for purposes of this book. First, the narrow definition allowed us to give a fairly exhaustive answer to an important question: How should one regulate if one's goal is to maximize welfare? Had we thrown additional goals into the mix, the discussion would have become unwieldy. Moreover, almost everyone agrees that enhancing welfare is *an* important objective of a regulatory regime and that, all else being equal, more wealth is better than less. Even if one ultimately decides that the best approach is not the one that maximizes welfare, that decision should be made with open eyes; regulators should know what approach would generate the greatest welfare and should have some sense of the wealth they're sacrificing by selecting an alternative regulatory regime. Finally, regulation is frequently a clumsy tool for achieving

---

[5]   Executive Order 12866 § 3(b) (exempting "independent regulatory agencies" from mandate).
[6]   See Hahn and Sunstein, supra note 2, at 1534.

distributional objectives. Often, the better approach is to regulate so as to maximize social welfare and then just engage in direct redistribution to achieve an outcome that is deemed to be equitable. It was appropriate, then, to focus the consideration here on how to regulate *so as to achieve the greatest welfare possible*.

We may now concede, however, that much of what is commonly called "regulation" outside the context of this book does not – and is not intended to – enhance aggregate welfare. Regulation in the broader sense is routinely driven by distributional concerns and often calls for people to take actions that reduce overall surplus in the name of distributing wealth more evenly. Is this book suggesting that such regulation is categorically improper?

Not at all. There are sound reasons for concluding that governmental directives should sometimes sacrifice a measure of wealth in favor of greater equity. For one thing, the view that every threat-backed governmental command should maximize aggregate welfare runs up against the same sorts of "hard cases" that bedevil the ethical theory of act utilitarianism (i.e., the view that an act is moral insofar as it creates the greatest happiness for the greatest number of people). Critics of act utilitarianism hypothesize situations in which the utility-maximizing action seems definitely wrong. What if, for example, an isolated community is so full of sadists that happiness will be maximized by torturing an abandoned baby? Act utilitarianism's answer to that question – that the moral act would be to torture the baby – conflicts with most people's considered moral judgments.

Similarly, the view that every regulation should maximize aggregate welfare generates some discomfiting prescriptions. Suppose, for example, that there are ten people in a community whose chief regulator is deciding between two policies. All the residents are equally deserving of any surplus created by the policy selected. Policy A would create value of $100,000 that would flow in equal portions to the residents ($10,000 each). Policy B would create value of $100,001, with $2 of that value flowing to one unlucky resident and the remaining $99,999 flowing in equal portions to the other nine ($11,111 each). A regulatory approach aimed solely at aggregate wealth maximization would counsel Policy B over Policy A. Most people's considered moral judgments, however, would call for implementing Policy A.

Apparent (but not real) departures from welfare-maximization for the purpose of achieving greater equity might be justified on even utilitarian grounds. If people have a "taste" for equity – that is, if they experience happiness from knowing that the benefits of public policies are being evenly distributed among members of society – then what appears to be a less efficient but more equitable policy may, in fact, be welfare-maximizing. In the hypothetical from the last paragraph, for example, Policy A (value = $100,000) would trump Policy B (value = $100,001) if residents collectively experienced value of more than $1 from knowing that the surplus was evenly distributed.

A good bit of evidence suggests that people do attach a positive value to more equal outcomes. Much of that evidence is anecdotal. Throughout the recent public discussion of income inequality, for example, many people have asserted that they would be willing to accept a slightly lower standard of living in exchange for a more even distribution of income. Such statements are subject to the usual caveats about stated versus revealed preferences, but their prevalence suggests that a taste for equity is widespread.

So do the results of a number of social science experiments. In the most famous of these, the "Ultimatum Game," one person, the "offeror," is directed to propose some division of an asset (usually some amount of money) between himself and another, the "offeree." If the offeree accepts the offeror's proposed allocation, the property will be divided accordingly. If the offeree rejects, however, neither party will get anything. The parties operate anonymously: The offeror, not knowing with whom she will be matched, proposes an amount to allocate to the offeree, and the offeree, not knowing who his offeror is, states the minimum amount he must be offered in order to take the deal.

If the players are acting like rational, self-interest maximizers, the expected outcome is for the offeror to propose to give the offeree the minimum amount possible (say, $1 out of $10 if the thing being split is a pile of ten one dollar bills). The offeree, in turn, should accept whatever he's offered, for the alternative is to walk away empty-handed.

When the game is actually played, that's not what tends to happen. Instead, offerors offer to give offerees some amount closer to half the pie (say, $4 out of $10), and offerees tend to refuse offers that are relatively low – even though their refusal means they get nothing. While there has been much debate over what's going on here, a leading theory is that there's something about humans that makes them willing to give up wealth in order to honor some sense of fairness. Offerees do just that, and offerors, expecting such action from offerees, adjust their behavior accordingly.

It seems humans aren't alone in exhibiting a willingness to sacrifice wealth for fairness. Research by primatologists Sarah Brosnan and Frans de Waal found that female capuchin monkeys do the same.[7] Brosnan and de Waal trained pairs of monkeys to give human handlers small granite rocks. In exchange for her rock, a monkey would receive a reward: a cucumber

---

[7] Sarah F. Brosnan and Frans B. M. de Waal, Monkeys Reject Unequal Pay, 425 *Nature* 297 (Sept. 18, 2003).

slice. This was apparently a good deal for the monkeys, who were almost always willing to play along – at least so long as they were treated equally. After a while, the researchers began giving one of the moneys in each pair a yummy grape instead of a cucumber slice. At that point, many of the non-favored monkeys refused to participate in the routine, choosing to forego a sweet deal (a cucumber slice for very little work) rather than sanction an unfairness. The situation only worsened when the primatologists began giving grapes to some monkeys without receiving their pebbles in exchange. Such unthinkable unfairness was enough to drive a full 80 percent of the non-favored monkeys out of the game – even though their non-participation meant no more easy cucumbers! Those monkeys, it seems, were willing to sacrifice wealth in order to make a statement about fairness.

It may be, then, that we humans and our ancestors are hard-wired, or at least conditioned, to favor equitable outcomes *and* to be willing to sacrifice some wealth to attain them. If that's the case, our regulatory regime should allow for approaches that may not appear to maximize aggregate welfare but do seem to produce more equitable outcomes. And if that is so, then policymakers should have some sense of how to trade off equity against efficiency.

So why did this book leave that question untouched? In addition to the reasons set forth above (i.e., the discussion would have been too unwieldy; policymakers still need to know what approaches maximize welfare; there are better ways to ensure equity than through regulation), there is the simple fact that your author has no idea what the answer is. At this point, all he can say is that regulators should recognize that such a trade-off exists and, if they choose to make it, they should do so with eyes wide open.

Perhaps a reader of this book will someday set forth a plausible approach to deciding when and to what extent efficiency should be sacrificed for equity (suggested title: *How to Redistribute: A Guide for Policymakers*). In the meantime, we may content ourselves with the knowledge that we have made a valiant effort to figure out how to regulate so as to create as much welfare as possible.

Index